ECONOMICS

Published 2002 by Grolier Educational
Sherman Turnpike
Danbury, Connecticut 06816

© 2002 Brown Partworks Limited

Library of Congress Cataloging-in-Publication Data

Pro/con
   p. cm
 Includes bibliographical references and index.
  Contents: v. 1. The individual and society – v. 2. Government – v. 3. Economics – v.
4. Environment – v. 5. Science – v. 6. Media.
  ISBN 0-7172-5638-3 (set : alk. paper) – ISBN 0-7172-5639-1 (vol. 1 : alk. paper) –
ISBN 0-7172-5640-5 (vol. 2 : alk. paper) – ISBN 0-7172-5641-3 (vol. 3 : alk. paper) –
ISBN 0-7172-5642-1 (vol. 4 : alk. paper) – ISBN 0-7172-5643-X (vol. 5 : alk. paper) –
ISBN 0-7172-5644-8 (vol. 6 : alk. paper)
  1. Social problems. I. Grolier Educational (Firm)

HN17.5 P756 2002
361.1–dc21

                                                                    2001053234

Printed and bound in Singapore

SET ISBN 0-7172-5638-3
VOLUME ISBN 0-7172-5641-3

For Brown Partworks Limited
Project Editors: Aruna Vasudevan, Fiona Plowman
Editors: Sally McFall, Dawn Titmus, Matt Turner,
Chris Marshall, Ben Way
Consultant Editors: Jane Lanigan and Timothy M. Shaw, Professor of
Commonwealth Governance & Development & Director, Institute
of Commonwealth Studies, School of Advanced Study,
University of London
Designer: Sarah Williams
Picture Researcher: Clare Newman
Set Index: Kay Ollerenshaw

Managing Editor: Tim Cooke
Design Manager: Lynne Ross
Production Manager: Matt Weyland

GENERAL PREFACE

"All that is necessary for evil to triumph is for good men to do nothing."
—Edmund Burke, 18th-century British political philosopher

Decisions

Life is full of choices and decisions. Some are more important than others. Some affect only your daily life—the route you take to school, for example, or what you prefer to eat for supper—while others are more abstract and concern questions of right and wrong rather than practicality. That does not mean that your choice of presidential candidate or your views on abortion are necessarily more important than your answers to purely personal questions. But it is likely that those wider questions are more complex and subtle and that you therefore will need to know more information about the subject before you can try to answer them. They are also likely to be questions about which you might have to justify your views to other people. In order to do that, you need to be able to make informed decisions, be able to analyze every fact at your disposal, and evaluate them in an unbiased manner.

What is *Pro/Con*?

Pro/Con is a collection of debates that presents conflicting views on some of the more complex and general issues facing Americans today. By bringing together extracts from a wide range of sources—mainstream newspapers and magazines, books, famous speeches, legal judgments, religious tracts, government surveys—the set reflects current informed attitudes toward dilemmas that range from the best way to feed the world's growing population to gay rights, and from the connection between political freedom and capitalism to the fate of Napster.

The people whose arguments make up the set are all acknowledged experts in their fields, and that makes the vast differences in their points of view even more remarkable. The arguments are presented in the form of debates for and against various propositions, such as "Does Global Warming Threaten Humankind?" or "Should the Media Be Subject to Censorship?" This question format reflects the way in which ideas often occur in daily life: in the classroom, on TV shows, in business meetings, or even in state or federal politics.

The contents

The subjects of the six volumes of the set—*Individual and Society, Government, Economics*, the *Environment, Science*, and *Media*—are issues on which it is preferable that people's opinions are based on information rather than simply on personal bias.

Special boxes throughout *Pro/Con* comment on the debates as you are reading them, pointing out facts or analyzing arguments to help you think about what is being said.

Introductions and summaries also provide background information that might help you reach your own conclusions. There are also comments and tips about how to structure an argument that you can apply on an everyday basis to any debate or conversation, learning how to present your point of view as effectively and persuasively as possible.

VOLUME PREFACE
Economics

Why economics?

Economics is relevant to almost every aspect of life today, from how much money you have in your pocket and how much tax you pay, to the poverty of certain nations and causes of international conflict. In the new millennium a number of ongoing and interrelated trends are taking place across different economies worldwide. These trends constitute the backdrop to the following *Pro/Con* debates, which largely focus on the U.S. economy but refer to the broader global context as well.

What are the trends?

First, the international economy is becoming more completely global than ever before. That is partly due to the end of the Cold War and the rapid, if uneven, incorporation of the former "socialist" states into the capitalist system during the 1990s. The increasingly global nature of the world economy can be seen in the near-universal reach of corporations, logistics, brands, and franchises.

Second, from the 1980s onward economic analysis and policy have been dominated by the assumption that the "free market" is crucial to the efficient functioning of economies, while government intervention—in the form of provision of welfare services,

the operation of public utilities, and various other forms of economic regulation—should be scaled back to an absolute minimum if nations are to prosper and grow. However, this has been criticized by a number of well-known economists and analysts.

Third, for around 15 years—up until the mid-1990s—Asian economies experienced unprecedented rates of economic growth, which was followed by a series of intense "crises" in the second half of the 1990s. Suddenly neither the Japanese model nor the miracles of the so-called "tiger economies" in Asia seemed quite so attractive in investment terms. Meanwhile, other emerging markets, like the Soviet Union, suffered a series of crises near the turn of the century. Although international organizations, such as the International Monetary Fund, were able to step in to bolster crisis-hit nations, some commentators believe that the world economy cannot absorb many more such shocks without becoming seriously destabilized.

Economics provides interesting resources to examine some of these issues and also areas of more traditional economic debate. The editors hope that you will find the book a useful tool when debating some of the most crucial economic issues facing the world today.

HOW TO USE THIS BOOK

Each volume of *Pro/Con* is divided into sections, each of which has an introduction that examines its theme. Within each section are a series of debates that present arguments for and against a proposition, such as whether or not the death penalty should be abolished. An introduction to each debate puts it into its wider context, and a summary and key map (see below) highlight the main points of the debate clearly and concisely. Each debate has marginal boxes that focus on particular points, give tips on how to present an argument, or help question the writer's case. The summaries to the debates have supplementary material to help you do further research.

Boxes and other materials provide additional background information. There are also special materials on how to improve your debating and writing skills. At the end of each book is a glossary that provides brief explanations of key words in the volume. The index covers all six books, so it will help you trace topics throughout the set.

background information
Frequent text boxes provide background information on important concepts and key individuals or events.

summary boxes
Summary boxes are useful reminders of both sides of the argument.

further information
Further Reading lists for each debate direct you to related books, articles, and websites so you can do your own research.

other articles in the *Pro/Con* series
See Also boxes list related debates throughout the Pro/Con series.

marginal boxes
Margin boxes highlight key points in the argument, give extra information, or help you question the author's meaning.

key map
Key maps provide a graphic representation of the central points of the debate.

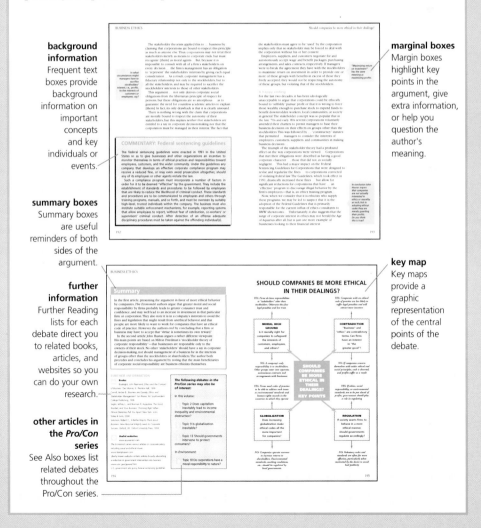

CONTENTS

7

PART 1
ECONOMIC SYSTEMS

The form of economic organization with which people in westernized countries are most familiar is capitalism. This system, based on the private ownership of property and the generation of private wealth through investment, has dominated much of the world for over 200 years. At its heart lies the notion of a free market, as expressed by the Scottish economist Adam Smith in the 18th century. The most efficient form of economic organization, Smith argued in 1776 in *An Enquiry into the Nature and Causes of the Wealth of Nations*, was one in which supply—the amount of goods or services available—and demand—how many people wanted those goods or services—set prices, wages, and what products an economy or a country produced. Any external intervention, such as government regulation, would only make an economy less efficient.

Though dominant, capitalism is not unchallenged as a form of economic organization. People have long objected to the extremes of wealth and poverty it creates, and the economic, social, and political inequality that results. While economists argue that capitalism is inefficient, others assert that it is immoral because it is unfair.

The main alternative to a capitalist economic system to emerge in the 20th century was communism. The communist system was based on a strong 19th-century tradition of socialism, which was itself a reaction to the inequities and harsh living conditions brought about by the industrialization and urbanization that followed the Industrial Revolution.

Advocates of socialism argued that factories and businesses should be removed from private ownership to create a classless society. Ownership would pass to the state, to community groups, or workers' associations. Communism, as formulated by Karl Marx and Friederich Engels in the mid-19th century, argued that a classless state could only be achieved by the violent overthrow of capitalism.

During the 20th century revolutions established communism in a number of countries, particularly the Soviet Union and China. They and their satellite states ran planned economies in which the state set production targets, established wages and prices, and organized the workforce. Although the system reduced some of the visible extremes of wealth and poverty associated with capitalism, it introduced new inequality and corruption, and often proved inefficient. The countries of the former Soviet Union and its allies largely abandoned planned economies after 1989; China increasingly encourages private entrepreneurship.

A third economic system combines elements of the free market and the planned economy. So-called mixed economies leave the majority of businesses in private hands, though often subject to regulation, but make the state responsible for key sectors, such as transportation or energy provision, and for the provision of services such as health and education. Most developed economies today are mixed economies.

Topic 1 asks whether capitalism is the best form of economic arrangement. Robert Bearce argues that it is, leading to better products, improved services, increased production, and higher

our time are human inequality and environmental destruction." The reduction of such "costs," he argues, can be better achieved by state intervention. By contrast, Madsen Pirie reflects a consensus at the start of the 21st century that economic growth is "respectable." He asserts that the free market will lead to a narrowing of the gap between rich and poor nations.

Topic 3 Does Privatization Always Benefit Consumers? studies what happens when economies transfer assets from state ownership to the free market. Capitalist thought argues

> *"The market came with the dawn of civilization and is not an invention of capitalism.... If it leads to improving the well-being of the people there is no contradiction with socialism."*
>
> —MIKHAIL GORBACHEV, PRESIDENT OF THE SOVIET UNION, 1990–1991

standards of living. By contrast, *New Internationalist* argues that traditional capitalism has many costs that are traditionally overlooked, such as its impact on the environment. Capitalism alone cannot deal with noneconomic factors that are vital to people's social and "economic" lives.

Capitalism's costs?

The next topics focus on issues arising from the contemporary capitalist marketplace: consumer rights, environmental impacts, and income inequalities. Topic 2 asks *Does Capitalism Inevitably Lead to Income Inequality and Environmental Destruction?* David Ransom argues that "the two overarching political issues of

that such a transfer leads to increased efficiency, more competition, and greater choice for customers. But do such benefits always occur?

The 20th century was dominated by the contrast between capitalist and communist economic systems. *Topic 4 Will IT and the Internet Create a "New Economy"?* discusses the possibility of a new type of system reliant on knowledge rather than goods and spurred by new communications technologies. Jonathan Rauch argues that IT can transform traditional industries. The article from *The Economist*, however, reports the collapse of many new economy firms early in 2001, when the value of IT shares crashed around the world.

Topic 1
IS THE FREE MARKET THE BEST FORM OF ECONOMIC ORGANIZATION?

YES
"FREE ENTERPRISE—FOR ALL"
THE FREEMAN, VOL. 34, NO. 5, MAY 1984
ROBERT BEARCE

NO
"THE ECONOMIST'S BLIND EYE"
NEW INTERNATIONALIST, ISSUE 232, JUNE 1992
WOLFGANG SACHS

INTRODUCTION

At the start of the 21st century the two largest economies in the world, the United States and Japan, were free-market economies. That is to say, their economy was based largely on the private ownership of business and a minimum of state regulation of production and consumption. In both countries the private sector provided about 70 percent of total output, or Gross Domestic Product (GDP), while the public (government-funded) sector provided the remainder.

Supporters and critics of the free market are essentially supporters and critics of capitalism itself. In a capitalist system the principle means of production, distribution, and exchange lie in private (individual or corporate) hands and are competitively operated for profit. Personal gain can be made through the investment of capital and labor, and people have the right to own land or property. The notion of capitalism is rooted in free enterprise,

which advocates nonintervention by governments and free trade among nations. The system is regulated by supply and demand, which means that although people make decisions based on their individual welfare, the results benefit society as a whole. This connection was explained in the 18th century by the economist Adam Smith (1723–1790), who first formulated the concept of the free market: "Every individual is continually exerting himself to find out the most advantageous employment for whatever capital he can command. It is his own advantage, indeed, and not that of the society, which he has to view. But the study of his own advantage naturally, or rather necessarily, leads him to prefer that employment which is most advantageous to the society."

Advocates of the system assert that free enterprise is a natural and voluntary result of the efforts and interaction of millions of individuals sharing their wisdom and abilities for personal good and gain. People can buy and sell goods for their own economic gain, but they also supply goods according to demand, thus creating an efficient system. Individuals are rewarded for their labors and their abilities depending on what effort they are willing to make.

Despite the apparent success of the free market in countries such as the United States, however, there are strong arguments in favor of systems that incorporate a greater or lesser degree of government regulation. There are two main bases for criticism, moral and economic. Many critics argue that free enterprise results in an unfair society. They assert that the unregulated pursuit of profit disadvantages the poor, the sick, and minority groups. The economic argument against the free market is that it is not as efficient as Smith proposed. Supply often does not, in reality, meet demand. Entrepreneurs realize that by restricting the supply of certain goods, demand will exceed availability, and the goods thus become sought-after "luxury goods." The businessman or businesswoman can charge higher prices for these goods.

Some critics of the free market propose a more egalitarian economic system, such as socialism or communism, in which everyone would be treated equally, and goods would be distributed on a fair basis. Most modern economies, however, are mixed economies, which combine a large free-market sector with some state ownership of businesses, or nationalization, and a certain degree of government intervention—such as minimum wage laws, working conditions regulation, or the provision of pension and health insurance plans.

There is a political dimension to the debate in addition to its economic foundations. The free-market, capitalist system is closely associated in the minds of many observers with the freedom of political expression and democratic forms of government. Planned economies have largely been implemented by authoritarian governments. The suppression of economic activity, these critics argue, is a suppression of fundamental political and personal freedoms.

The following two articles lay out arguments for and against the free-market system. Robert Bearce argues that capitalism allows people to act and work as they please and be rewarded for it. Wolfgang Sachs conversely argues that free enterprise has brought a pervasive and negative presence to the world and that some traditional systems of economic organization are more humane and spiritual.

FREE ENTERPRISE—FOR ALL
Robert Bearce

"Capitalism stinks!" That is the conclusion reached not long ago by the authors of a textbook on economics. The book further stated that our social problems can be solved only when American capitalism is destroyed.

Hostility toward free enterprise (capitalism) has not decreased over the years. There are many "public opinion molders" today who believe free enterprise has failed. They say inflation is caused by greedy businessmen and industrialists. Corporations are making "excessive" profits. Free enterprise and our economic system are ignoring the elderly, minorities, the handicapped, and poor.

The author begins by listing the main points that he intends to disprove and argue against.

These charges are false....They attack free enterprise as it relates to profits, competition, "Big Business," and corporations. Somehow, these aspects of capitalism are evil—"a threat to the consumer...."

What is free enterprise?

Let's face the facts. First, what we know as capitalism ... isn't a system at all. Free enterprise is not a humanly devised plan for economic activity. Instead, it is the natural, voluntary collaboration of millions of individuals sharing their respective abilities, wisdom, energy, skills, and creativity for personal good and the general welfare of everyone.

Bearce introduces capitalism (free enterprise) as the most natural of economic systems. In what ways do you think capitalism is "natural" while socialism is not?

Free enterprise is industry, agriculture, finance, and commerce. Most important, it involves all of us—teachers, mechanics, nurses, clerks, students, corporation presidents, housewives, and store managers. Capitalism is millions of individuals cooperating freely to provide products and services for one another. We buy, sell, work, and produce, and thus manage our own economic lives as we choose.

Basically, there are three main principles to free enterprise:
- We are free to think, choose, and act as we best see fit, not harming others in doing so.
- We are rewarded for our labors in proportion to our individual abilities and ... effort we are willing to put forth.
- We have a right to private ownership of property....

Those individuals who foolishly think that "capitalism stinks" refuse to accept the truth about free enterprise. No other economic system—socialism, fascism, communism, or the welfare state—can ensure individual freedom and promote the general material welfare as capitalism has done. Free enterprise has succeeded because we have intelligently answered four important economic questions having to do with our daily lives:

- What goods should be produced? In what quantities?
- What services will be ... [provided], when, and where?
- Who will produce the goods and perform the services?
- How will the goods and services be distributed? In other words, who gets what?

Free enterprise says that free individuals—not government agencies [and] boards—should answer the four questions....
All of us are consumers, and free enterprise permits a sensitive market ... to respond to our needs and wants. The "free market" is an accurate description of capitalism. Services and goods are produced freely in response to popular demand. Production and services are determined by what people want and how much they are willing to pay.... This is cooperation and voluntary exchange in the free market. It is true economic freedom ... and good economics.

The author outlines the four key questions that any economic system needs to address if it is to function effectively and be able to allocate limited resources to meet people's needs and wants.

"Agriculture, manufacture, commerce, and navigation—the four pillars of our prosperity—are the most thriving when left most free to individual enterprise."
—THOMAS JEFFERSON, THIRD U.S. PRESIDENT

The success of the free market depends upon ... competition. Competition opens the way for new ideas and superior productivity. Companies work hard to please the consumer who is always looking for better, less expensive products.... Competition is generated by millions of consumers who have economic freedom to express their likes and their dislikes....

The author introduces the idea of competition. In what way do you think competition is the cornerstone of a free market or capitalist economic system?

Fruits of competition
Free market competition leads to new products, better products, superior services, increased production, more jobs, higher wages, and ultimately a higher standard of living for

everyone.... [Competition] brings out the best in business as well as in individuals....This spirit of competition can exist, though, only when we are permitted to keep the fruits of our labor—the "fruits" being personal income or profits....

The importance of profit

Why do some people think that competition and making a profit are immoral?

Like competition, profits are looked upon as being a bit immoral.... Is it immoral for an individual to use his abilities and energies in constructive work as long as he does not infringe upon the freedom of other individuals to do the same? Is it wrong for one business to compete with a rival company in an attempt to provide an improved service or better product?

Certainly not, and both the wage earner and wage-payer deserve paycheck and profit, respectively.... Just as the free market rewards the employee with a paycheck in return for hard work and personal effort, so free enterprise gives a just return to the hard-working company. The company's profit is proof that it has met its responsibility or goal of fulfilling the needs of individuals.

Bearce addresses the perception that corporations make excessive profits. Have you heard of cases in which you think the profits made are obscene?

But don't some big businesses and corporations make excessive profits? No, even though their earnings might amount to billions, these industries do not reap "excessive" or "obscene" profits.... Profits are the key to prosperity, and we should be thankful they reach into billions of dollars....

How profits are used

Just what happens to a company's total profits...? Are they squandered by corporate bosses? No, [they are] divided between funds for reinvestment and funds to pay shareholders who have stock in the company. These shareholders are just ordinary, average people from all walks of life—professors, farmers, small businessmen, factory workers, and retired people. They have labored over the years, saved their money, and freely invested in the work of the corporation.

Besides paying dividends to shareholders, profits are used to improve and expand production. Profits are reinvested, providing business with needed capital. Capital ... is put to work replacing worn-out equipment, constructing new plants, and otherwise building up a more efficient, productive enterprise. This capital reinvestment creates more jobs, higher wages, better working conditions, and more prosperity—prosperity that benefits all of us....

Profits provide the fuel that keeps our economy going and growing. They are both the means and motivation for material progress. Profits stimulate the release of human energy—an energy more vital to free enterprise than petroleum, natural gas, or nuclear energy....

The tyranny of socialism

Under ... socialism, the government owns and/or controls the means of production. All areas of the economy are in the hands of the government—commerce, agriculture, industry, health care, housing, and others. Under the welfare state, the government owns and/or controls the results of production. Money is taken from the producers in society and given to the non- or low-producers....

As the government adopts more and more welfare-state programs, the incentive to work is dampened. This applies to both the wage earners and non-producers in the citizenry. Businessmen and hard-working taxpayers ask themselves why they should continue exerting themselves when the government will tax away their income for the benefit of others. Industrious individuals see little reason to work hard, save, invest, and expand economic activity....

The welfare state also destroys the incentive of the low-producer to strive harder. A business that is failing because it cannot or will not meet consumer demand simply calls upon the government to subsidize its losses. Instead of exercising more energy, ingenuity, hard work, and responsibility to achieve success, the business relies upon the federal government for help. Likewise, individuals will reject responsibility for their own lives when the government is ready to give them food, housing, and medical care.

Is the author's comparison between welfare and socialism a valid one? Do you think people's incentive to work and to take responsibility for their lives is really "dampened" by welfare programs?

Conclusion

Through free market economics, we have enjoyed the good life of freedom and material well being.... For too long, Americans have been uninformed and misinformed about free market economics and the nature of government power. We have been led to believe that business has caused our economic troubles and that action by the federal government is the solution. These mistaken beliefs must be corrected. Government is the problem, not the market.

Bearce sees government intervention as the main source of economic problems. By comparison, what does he see as the main benefits of the free market?

THE ECONOMIST'S BLIND EYE
Wolfgang Sachs

NO

Indian leader
Mahatma Gandhi
(1869–1948) was a
lawyer who fought
for Indian
independence
through
nonviolent
protest and civil
disobedience.
Jawaharlal Nehru
(1889–1964)
became India's
first prime
minister when
independence was
achieved in 1947.

"Should India ever resolve to imitate England, it will be the ruin of the nation." In 1909 … Gandhi formulated the conviction upon which he then, over a period of 40 years, fought for the independence of India. Although he won the fight, the cause was lost; no sooner was independence achieved than his principle fell into oblivion.

Gandhi wanted to drive the British out of the country in order to allow India to become more Indian; Nehru, on the other hand, saw independence as the opportunity to make India more Western….

A more spiritual path

Gandhi was not won over to technical civilization … because he saw in it a culture which knew no more sublime end than that of minimizing bodily effort and maximizing physical well-being. He could only shrug his shoulders at such an obsession with gaining comfort; as if a good life could be built on that! Didn't India's tradition, undisturbed for thousands of years, have more substantial things to offer?

Gandhi insisted on a society which, in accordance with Hindu tradition, gave priority to a spiritual way of life…. In his eyes, India was committed to an idea of the good and proper life that contradicted the ideals prevalent in England during the age of automation. For this reason, a wholesale imitation of the West was simply out of the question….

Nehru disagreed. He saw no alternative but to introduce the young nation to the achievements of the West as soon as possible and take the road towards an economic civilization…. He found Gandhi "completely unreal" in his vision. Though he intended to avoid the excesses of capitalism, he still viewed Indian society primarily as an economy, that is, as a society defining itself in terms of its performance in providing goods.

*What "excesses of
capitalism" might
the author be
referring to here?*

From an economic viewpoint … people are seen as living in a situation of scarcity, since they always have less than they desire. The most noble task of politics is, therefore, to create the conditions for material wealth; and this in turn requires the reorganization of society from a host of locally based subsistence communities into a nationwide economy.

Nehru thus fostered precisely that Western self-delusion that was also at the core of the development idea—that the essential reality of a society consists in nothing else than its functional achievements.... From this viewpoint, the economy overshadows every other reality—the laws of economy dominate society and not the rules of society (dominate) the economy....

When production is not god

Observing a group of Maya Indians who work their fields in the mountains around Quiche in Guatemala, and seeing the barren ground, the primitive tools, and the scanty yield, one might easily come to the conclusion that nothing in the world is more important to them than increasing productivity. Remedies could swiftly be found—better crop rotation, improved seeds, small machines, privatization, and anything else ... business management might recommend.

All this is not necessarily wrong but the economic viewpoint is notoriously color blind—it recognizes the cost-yield relation with extreme clarity, but is hardly able to perceive other dimensions of reality. For example, economists have difficulty in recognizing that the land bestows identity upon the Indians since it represents the bridge to their ancestors. Likewise economists often fail to note the central

The "cost yield relation" is the same as productivity. It refers to the ratio of inputs (usually land, labor, and capital) compared to output of a good or service.

For this Mayan family, shown at the end of a day's farming, the land is part of their identity.

importance of collective forms of labor, in which the village community finds visible expression. The outlook of the Maya is incompatible with that of the economists.

Economic efficiency not the only criteria

To put this in the form of a paradox—not everything that looks like an economic activity is necessarily a part of economics. Indeed, economics offers only one of many ways of looking at goods-oriented activities.... In every society things are produced, distributed, and consumed; but only in modern Westernized societies are prices and products, conditions of ownership and work, predominantly shaped by the laws of economic efficiency....

> *"Economic efficiency" is an economic situation in which no one can be made better off without somebody else being made worse off.*

The Bemba in Zambia, for example, see a good harvest or a successful hunting expedition as a gift from their ancestors—they court the ancestors' favor in the hope of higher production. Then there are the cycles of cultivation practised by farmers in Maharashtra, which neatly fit into the yearly round of weddings, festivals, and pilgrimages. New methods of cultivation can soon disrupt this social calendar.

In societies that are not built on the compulsion to amass material wealth, economic activity is also not geared to slick, zippy output. Rather, economic activities like choosing an occupation, cultivating the land, or exchanging goods, are understood as ways of enacting that particular social drama in which the members of the community happen to see themselves as the actors. That drama's story largely defines what belongs to whom, who produces what, and how it is exchanged. The "economy" is closely bound up with life but it does not stamp its rules and rhythms on the rest of society. Only in the West does the economy dictate the drama and everyone's role in it....

> *What do you think the author means by everyone's role being dictated by the economy? Do you think he is correct?*

An invention of the West

Adam Smith was the first thinker who, when using the term "market," no longer envisaged a locally determinable outlet for goods, but that society-wide space throughout which all prices intercommunicate. This innovation was no accident, but mirrored a new social reality: an economy of national scope. Before then ... one could hardly find trade between different regions of the same country.

> *Adam Smith (1723–1790) was a Scottish economist and philosopher famous for his book The Wealth of Nations.*

Of course from time immemorial there has been trade ... but this was trade with distant countries.... History knows markets in all shapes and sizes, but they were local and temporary places of exchange between towns and the surrounding countryside.

In Adam Smith's century, however, the nation-state drew a web of trade relations over the whole of society and established the domestic market. Like today's developing countries, the young states of that time pushed hard to make economic principles prevail everywhere, be it only to finance their own existence. That was the birth of the national economy....And Smith became the theoretician of a society governed by the rules of the market.

The author is comparing the developing countries of today with countries that were industrializing during Adam Smith's time.

Alternatives to the economy?

The transformation of society into a political economy was … only achieved after a prolonged struggle demanding many sacrifices. After all, people were not shaped by a commercial ethos—… the merchant was not yet an entrepreneur, land was not saleable, competition was frowned upon, usury disreputable, and those who worked for wages lived on the fringes of society. As a result, the progress of capitalism was punctuated by bitter disputes about whether and to what extent land and forest, grain and money, and workers themselves, could be treated as commodities.

In the last decades, similar radical changes have taken place in large parts of the Third World as economic ideology has tightened its grip. Traditions of sufficiency have been pushed aside, local exchange relations dissolved, collective forms of ownership broken up, and subsistence economies wiped out. For a long time the guiding light of international development policy was to create societies of paid workers and consumers everywhere. Experts scrutinized countries to identify "obstacles to development" which were hampering the free mobility of "production factors." No cost was too high and few sacrifices were too great in the quest to turn societies into smoothly-running political economies.

The author gives examples of the changes that have taken place in the Third World. How has the spread of "free market" ideology resulted in such changes?

Without any doubt, miracles were thus wrought.... However, it is becoming ever clearer that a disaster is in the offing. At the very moment the economy has finally achieved worldwide dominion, social disruptions, and environmental destruction have become rampant. The domination of the economy is showing its menacing side.... In fact the economy, during its rise to the top, has stamped out alternatives to itself....

How is it possible to reinvent (economies) that allow people to live gracefully without making them prisoners of the pernicious drive to accumulate? Maybe there will be more creative power in the Third World to meet this challenge because … many people there still remember a way of life in which economic performance was not paramount.

The author is talking about free market economies when he talks about "the economy." What alternatives do you think have been "stamped out"?

Summary

In his article Robert Bearce argues that the free market is the best and most natural form of economic system because it allows people freedom of thought and the right to choose and act as they see fit, and rewards them for their labors according to their abilities. Such a system also allows people the right to own property. Furthermore, since free-market or capitalist systems depend on competition, they lead to better products and services, wider consumer choice, increased production, and ultimately, a higher standard of living for everyone. Bearce states that by contrast, socialism is tyrannical and actually dampens the incentive to work as wage earners question why they should work hard when their money is being used to fund nonearning groups and people who are less productive.

In the "no" article from the *New Internationalist*, on the other hand, Wolfgang Sachs argues that the economy should not be the dominating force in society. He gives examples of traditional societies in which economics and amassing money are not the be all and end-all of life. At the same time, it is argued that as capitalism becomes more and more important, "social disruptions and environmental destruction have become rampant."

The key map on the opposite page sums up the main points to the argument.

FURTHER INFORMATION:

Books:
Gardner, Stephen H., *Comparative Economic Systems*. Fort Worth, TX: Dryden Press, 1997.
Lindblom, Charles E., *The Market System: What It Is, How It Works, and What to Make of It*. New Haven, CT: Yale University Press, 2001.

Articles:
Kilcullen, R.J., "Free Enterprise and Its Critics." Macquarie University, Open Learning, Australia.

Useful websites:
www.economist.com/
The Economist magazine contains articles on a wide range of economic issues.
www.oneworld.org/ni/
New Internationalist magazine addresses international topics, particularly those relevant to developing countries.

IS THE FREE MARKET THE BEST FORM OF ECONOMIC ORGANIZATION?

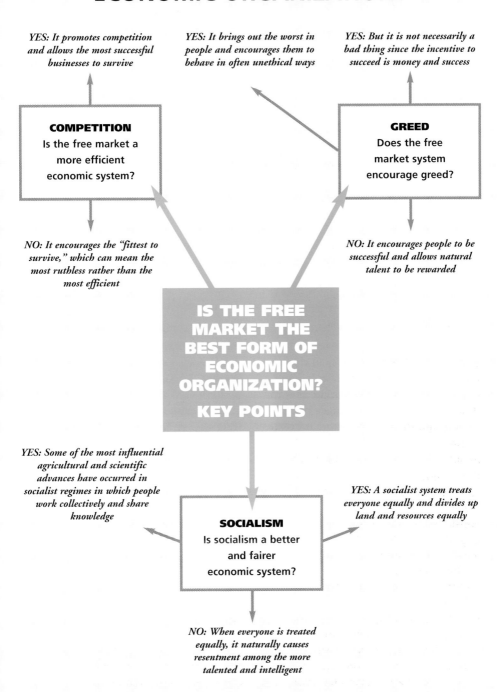

YES: It promotes competition and allows the most successful businesses to survive

YES: It brings out the worst in people and encourages them to behave in often unethical ways

YES: But it is not necessarily a bad thing since the incentive to succeed is money and success

COMPETITION
Is the free market a more efficient economic system?

GREED
Does the free market system encourage greed?

NO: It encourages the "fittest to survive," which can mean the most ruthless rather than the most efficient

NO: It encourages people to be successful and allows natural talent to be rewarded

IS THE FREE MARKET THE BEST FORM OF ECONOMIC ORGANIZATION?

KEY POINTS

YES: Some of the most influential agricultural and scientific advances have occurred in socialist regimes in which people work collectively and share knowledge

YES: A socialist system treats everyone equally and divides up land and resources equally

SOCIALISM
Is socialism a better and fairer economic system?

NO: When everyone is treated equally, it naturally causes resentment among the more talented and intelligent

Topic 2

DOES CAPITALISM INEVITABLY LEAD TO INCOME INEQUALITY AND ENVIRONMENTAL DESTRUCTION?

YES

"RED AND GREEN: ECO-SOCIALISM COMES OF AGE"
NEW INTERNATIONALIST, ISSUE 307, NOVEMBER 1998
DAVID RANSOM

NO

"THE VIRTUE OF WEALTH"
THE ECONOMIST, THE WORLD IN 2001, 2000
MADSEN PIRIE

INTRODUCTION

In some circles capitalism is a dirty word. It is linked inexorably in the minds of many critics with greed and exploitation. Such critics argue that the drive to create profit damages both society and the natural world. It creates victims in the shape of the poor and exploited, whose labor actually creates the wealth of the successful capitalists; and it damages the environment by placing profit above other considerations. Critics argue that the ongoing destruction of the world's rain forest or proposals to drill for oil in as yet untouched parts of the natural world are examples of capitalism's inability to look beyond simple monetary profit. These feelings lay in part behind anticapitalist protests that occurred in major cities in America and Europe at the start of the 21st century.

Not everyone believed that capitalism was inevitably a negative system, however. During the latter part of the 20th century successful capitalism seemed a widely acceptable face of modern U.S. society. In many ways the U.S. system contrasted positively with the planned economies of communist states such as the former Soviet Union and China. Those economies were associated with corruption, economic shortages, inefficient production, and lack of consumer choice, among other things. After the downfall of the Soviet Union in 1989 Russia and its allies virtually all abandoned planned economics in favor of a greater or lesser degree of capitalism.

Neither of the major U.S. political parties proposes fundamental changes to the capitalist, mainly free-market economy. That does not mean, however, that Americans are unaware of criticisms of the system. While some people, particularly in the business community, argue in favor of reducing economic regulation, others seek ways to modify the system that retain a traditional capitalist framework but avoids its worst excesses.

America's tradition of individualism—the pursuit of individual profit and advantage—has always been balanced by a tradition of mutualism. Mutualism advocates cooperative action to try to lessen capitalism's negative social effects, such as the unequal distribution of wealth. Labor unions, community groups, and savings associations bring people together to increase their economic power. In the United States, as in many other countries, successful capitalists pay higher taxes to fund socially beneficial systems of education, welfare, and health provision. Without the rich, some economists and politicians argue, the economy would not produce enough money to pay for the poor. In this argument capitalism is the most promising solution to the problems it has itself created.

Impact on the environment has also prompted some observers to reinterpret rather than overthrow capitalism in order to seek ways to lessen the inevitability of environmental damage. Instead of judging the success of businesses on purely monetary grounds, for example, some economists argue that a true analysis of business profitability must take into account nonmonetary factors, such as environmental impact, social desirability, consumer preference, and so on.

This type of cost analysis might show drilling for oil in an unspoiled wilderness as being more expensive than drilling in areas that are already being exploited. Consumer preference for organic foodstuffs might persuade businesses to opt for more expensive methods of farming.

In the same way, some people argue, businesses cannot be judged alone. Business has global costs—in the shape of the reduction of the world's forests, or in what many people see as the exploitation of the world's poorer countries—that traditional forms of capitalism cannot take account of.

> *"We cannot remove the evils of capitalism without taking its source of power: ownership."*
> —NEIL KINNOCK, BRITISH POLITICIAN

The following articles consider whether capitalism inevitably has negative effects. In the first, "Red and Green," David Ransom cites examples of capitalism's damaging effects on society and the environment. He uses the example of the Amazon rain forest to argue that human inequality and environmental destruction are linked. He concludes that unless it is restrained, global capitalism will seek to destroy anything that opposes it.

Madsen Pirie, however, in "The Virtue of Wealth" suggests that economic growth offers a solution to problems. He points out the benefits of capitalism for society and the environment: The better off are ideally placed to be the environment's protectors. Communist countries, he states, were the world's worst polluters. He argues that inequality has fallen sharply in the past 50 years, and that economic growth in Asia has closed the world wealth gap.

RED AND GREEN
David Ransom

In January 1991 the Amazon was in a state of chaos. I had been searching for any trace of logic in the tangle of rain forest destruction, and was feeling pretty much defeated, when I arrived at the Manaus office of an American environmental scientist, Philip Fearnside.

It's a question of who is profiting [he said]. If that profit, and the costs, were evenly distributed, it wouldn't be happening. It wouldn't be worth the candle for anyone individually. The fact is that influential people are making money and poor people out in the forest are paying the price. It's all perfectly logical, from the point of view of the people who are making the money.

The word "oligarchy" refers to a form of government in which the ruling power belongs to a small number of people.

He was referring to the construction of hydroelectric dams for smelters and factories exporting aluminum cans. He had done some pretty conventional "cost-benefit" calculations, and they simply didn't add up—unless, that is, you happened to be a member of the oligarchy in Brazil, the most unequal country on earth. For a cause no greater than beer and soft drinks, the rain forest had been flooded, disease and displacement had seeped into thousands of lives, precious indigenous cultures had been trashed. Because nothing much to the disadvantage of the Brazilian oligarchy has happened since, it comes as no great surprise to me that the destruction of the Amazon rain forest has continued apace....

Without any doubt, the two overarching political issues of our time are human inequality and environmental destruction, the consequences of which may be starkly visible in places like the Amazon but apply almost everywhere....

Do you find this a surprising connection for the author to make?

It is ... increasingly clear that inequality and destruction are directly linked. Indeed, it would be very much harder to demonstrate that they are not linked, given that they are both happening at the same time. They are also interacting in complex ways that accelerate their growth alarmingly.

This is because global consumer capitalism, unless it is restrained, grows faster and faster. Anything not devoted exclusively to the service of its immediate interests it seeks to destroy. The destruction is compounded because it must either grow or blow: it cannot contain itself. It is self-destructive, too, shot through with contradictions that make it blow precisely because it grows, like some force-fed hothouse vegetable.

"Creative destruction"

One such contradiction is that it feeds by inflating profits, deflating wages, and thus increasing inequality. This precipitates a crisis—because the labor we sell can't buy all the things it makes—that ultimately undermines its imperative to grow, producing an almighty bang of the kind that is ringing in so many ears at this very moment. Successful capitalists have a name for this—"creative destruction" ...

The idea that people's wages do not allow them to buy all the things that they make was first put forward by Karl Marx (1818–1883), the founder of communism.

Because socialism knows how this works, it has lost none of its explanatory power. But socialists have a few problems of their own.... Not the least of these is that they are said to be dead, replaced by smooth but insubstantial Third Way figures who speak in tongues about "social justice" and "equality of opportunity," the perfect expression of which is a lottery. Nor does it help very much that Karl Marx has been resurrected in the salons of orthodoxy, on the strict understanding that although he may have been right about capitalism he was wrong about communism. See, for example, John Cassidy, "The Return of Karl Marx," *The New Yorker*, October 20 and 27, 1997.

For a discussion about the ideas of Karl Marx and the countries that followed socialist and communist economic policies, see The Rise and Fall of Communism, pages 34–35, in this volume.

Socialists' biggest difficulty, however, is that they've been very much better on the redistribution of wealth than its redefinition. They longed simply to get their hands on the levers of the capitalist wealth machine, rather than redesign it. They should have listened to ecologists sooner. There is, as it turns out, no great theoretical problem with adding a Green contradiction to a Red analysis of capitalism, because there are environmental limits to capitalist growth. But it entails accepting also that there can be no prospect whatever of creating a distinctively "socialist" economy that does not respond to ecological imperatives as well. The most interesting, though dense, discussion of this point can be found in the U.S. magazine *Capitalism, Nature, Socialism*, and especially the work of James O'Connor.

Lifeworld

Radical philosophers like André Gorz have meanwhile been conducting an ... enquiry into the nature of wealth. They propose the existence of a "Lifeworld" that encompasses everything we aspire to as individual and social human beings.

"The economic" should rightly occupy just a small part of it, but has taken over our lives. What, after all, is the point of material wealth, if it does not enhance our well-being? How is this to be achieved if we are enslaved to the economic machine? See André Gorz, *Capitalism, Socialism, Ecology* (1994)....

Gorz is ... uncertain whether capitalism is capable of being transformed by gradually pushing back the boundaries of "the economic," and in particular by reclaiming more free time from work, as he recommends.... But he is quite clear that equality, ecology, and the well-being of humanity as a whole can only be advanced if capitalism is transformed ...

In July 2001 The Washington Post ran an article about the difficulties workers in the United States face about deciding whether to take a vacation. It reported that taking a vacation is often seen as a sign of weakness.

Socialism is based on an enormous insight [says Wolfgang Sachs].... Technical progress provides us with a floor under which nobody has to fall. Scarcity can be removed. The hope of socialism is that all people can lead a dignified life. Environmentalism adds another dimension. It says there is not just a lower limit, there is also an upper limit. There is a threshold beyond which there can be no more justice or democracy because progress, or wealth creation, takes a form in which not everybody can participate. There is a ceiling. If you go beyond it, wealth creation becomes oligarchic in nature.

New world disorder

Forget all rhetoric to the contrary—without a powerful state, capitalism would have foundered a long time ago. Leave aside, if you will, the state's role in securing private property, containing unrest, bailing out private banks, financing unemployment, devising new forms of Armageddon, fighting extremely profitable wars, and creating "favorable conditions" generally so that corporations, the rich, and the powerful can be free to pay no taxes and plunge us into renewed catastrophe. Consider just this: according to the United Nations, in the early 1990s the state subsidized environmentally damaging industrial activities—energy, water, roads, agriculture—worldwide to the tune of at least $710 billion every year (Human Development Report, 1998, UNDP). To put this into perspective, $710 billion is 14 times what is required to eradicate absolute poverty.

In August 2001 President George W. Bush's energy bill, which backs oil and gas drilling in Alaska's Arctic National Wildlife Refuge, was passed by the House of Representatives. What were the arguments for and against this bill?

So the state is an active player in the new world disorder. If we are serious about change then it simply doesn't make sense to leave it to its own devices. We can argue about what the state should be doing. We can even propose that in an ideal world it would cease to exist. We can suggest that since global consumer capitalism is so good at looking after its own interests then the proper job of democratic government is to look after ours. But, to get from here to there, popular democracy must prevail.

We are led to believe, of course, that it already does. Why, this is the age of democracy, is it not? Latin America is so much better now, with all those blood-soaked generals confined to barracks! Pity poor Africa—but salute Nelson Mandela! Papa Doc, Mobutu, Marcos, Suharto—all gone! And the Berlin Wall!

Papa Doc, Mobutu, Marcos, and Suharto were all ousted leaders of repressive regimes.

Market economies like gravity

A few months ago a little cameo was played out in Moscow. Bill Clinton, in town for a last tango with Boris Yeltsin, likened "market economies" to the force of gravity: this, mark you, amid the ruins of "bandit" capitalism in Russia. One of the laws of gravity, Clinton should properly have added, is that what goes up must come down. Shortly afterward, the legendary speculator George Soros—who is credited with precipitating the latest Russian collapse—forewarned us that "the global capitalist system … is coming apart at the seams" (*Guardian*, September 16, 1998).

"Maori march on Wellington to oppose the Multilateral Agreement on Investment.… Thousands of Argentinian teachers go on hunger strike against World Bank-imposed education cuts.… Indian farmers protest against the World Trade Organization and the takeover of their agriculture by transnational corporations.… Citizens around Europe pull up genetically modified crops.… Around 300,000 protest against globalization in Seoul.… The G8 summit in Birmingham is ringed by 70,000 Jubilee 2000 demonstrators calling for Third World debt to be scrapped.…" The litany could go on, and had Katharine Ainger not given me this list as an introduction to her article I would not have known a fair bit of it myself, even though it is my job to keep pace with events.

Ransom is referring to a list given to him by Katharine Ainger who produced an article in the same issue of New Internationalist from which this extract is taken. To read Ainger's article see www.oneworld.org/ni/index4.html.

A Left Green politics

These are the forces of creative construction, the harbingers of a Green Left politics that might eventually achieve what neither Reds nor Greens can do on their own. Whether we are called "social movements" or "civil society," whether we think of ourselves as trade unionists or eco-warriors, whether we are impelled by class division or by the rape of nature, with capitalism at the crossroads once again we should not underestimate our own strength nor fail in our responsibility to work together.

THE VIRTUE OF WEALTH
Madsen Pirie

NO

The coming year will mark the return to respectability of economic growth. It has endured several decades of abuse and has been charged with everything from destroying individual cultures to despoiling the planet. Assorted demonstrations against international capitalism and the World Trade Organization have all had themes in common: they were antiprogress, and specifically antigrowth. Yet economic growth is a legitimate target for humanity to pursue. It is good in and of itself, and a solution to many of mankind's abiding problems.

The environment and natural resources

We were told, notably by the *Club of Rome Report* in 1972, that economic growth would lead us to use up scarce metals and minerals, depleting limited resources that "belong to future generations." In fact nearly all of these resources are more plentiful now (measured by price) than they were then.

It has also become apparent that wealthier countries are better able to protect the environment. It turned out to be the poorer countries of the socialist bloc that polluted most. The richer, capitalist, counties were able to afford the introduction of emission controls and water purity standards, and to enact measures to control the disposal of toxic waste. It is the poorer countries of the developing world that can least afford the often expensive techniques that accompany cleaner and safer production. Those that become rich should be able to produce their energy and their manufactured goods in less damaging ways.

The cities of the rich countries will, on the whole, be far less polluted in 2001 than they were in 1901. The shift away from coal has brought huge improvements in air quality. Rivers and water are cleaner. If cities are noisier today, they smell less. As economic growth lifts countries out of poverty, they, too, will be able to afford the luxury of cleaner air and water.

Emulating California

As for the destruction of "individual cultures," the poorer countries have made it clear that they prefer not to remain as theme parks of picturesque poverty for rich tourists to enjoy

The author is saying that the price of certain resources has dropped since 1972, and he is using this measure to judge them to be more plentiful.

In 2001 President Bush refused to sign the Kyoto protocol, which aims to reduce greenhouse gas emissions. The United States is the world's biggest producer of these gases.

from their luxury hotels. Given the choice, they prefer to be wealthy, even if it means becoming like other wealthy countries. Put at its most politically incorrect: the whole world wants to be like California.

The most persistent charge against growth is that it is widening the gap between countries and even within countries. The claim is that in both cases the rich are growing richer and the poor are falling further behind. This uses relative poverty as the measure, rather than the absolute command of resources that matters for people at subsistence level. But even on this measure, the charge will not stick in 2001.

What do you think the author means by the terms "relative poverty" and "absolute command of resources"?

The poor set the pace

The Gini coefficients, which measure the degree of inequality in income distribution, show a sharp fall world inequality in the past half-century. Economic growth in Asia has spectacularly closed the world wealth gap. Paul Ormerod, an economist, points out, "The economic success of East Asia has liberated millions of people from lives of unremitting drudgery and toil, and has sharply reduced world income inequality."

By 2001 many Asian economies, particularly that of Japan, had gone into recession.

The upward path of economic growth has spread to China, and now India. This will destroy the argument of those who have valued India for its chaotic, overpopulated poverty, where spiritual values prevailed over profits. India will be one of the world's fastest-growing economies in 2001, which will do more for the street poor of Calcutta than a generation of aid. Most South American countries are following the same road. The prospect is for further reductions in the inequalities of world income between countries. Much of Africa is still mired in poverty, but it is becoming exceptional, rather than a typical case.

Inequality within countries

Do you agree with the author's assertion that economic growth does not create more inequality?

The idea that growth exacerbates inequalities in income distribution within countries is also wrong. The equality of the poorer countries is an equality of deprivation. Even the much-touted inequalities in the United States and the United Kingdom over the past two decades are exaggerated. Wealth distribution in Britain is almost exactly the same as in France. And the inequality in America today is not different from the level France had in the mid-1970s.

The moral argument against growth

There is a moral argument against growth but it, too, is proving specious. It is that growth directs us excessively towards material things such as consumer goods, at the

Part of Singapore's huge Funan IT Mall. Dramatic economic growth in East Asia and farther afield has led to a big fall in world inequality of wealth.

expense of self-fulfillment and high moral or cultural goals. The counter-attack now gaining ground is that it is subsistence which causes material preoccupation. If you are not getting enough to eat, it has to preoccupy your thoughts and activities. It is wealth, generated by growth, which brings choice and culture. It enables people to choose leisure time, if they wish, to devote to charitable and voluntary work, or to self-education. It is wealth which enables people to be generous. In other words, growth and wealth bring the necessary space and opportunity for moral advancement.

Growth has been sneered at for 30 years, mostly by those who enjoy its benefits. Many problems have been laid at its door during that time. In the early years of this [21st] century it will be seen, however, as the prime tool for advancing the lot of mankind.

Summary

David Ransom uses the example of the Amazon and the chaos that capitalism has wrought there to underline its unfair effects. In his view the Amazon is being destroyed and its people's culture trashed—all to create more money from soft drinks and beer for a small minority. He believes that these practices are being carried out on a global scale. Capitalism has become unrestrained, is growing too fast, and seeks to destroy in order to make profits. He sees the future struggle against capitalism lying in the hands of ecosocialists—those who adhere to the successful parts of socialism while embracing the ideas of ecologists. This is the Red (socialism) and Green (environmentalism) of his argument. He points out that capitalism needs to be transformed in order to accept the importance of humanity's well-being. He concludes that it is the Green Left of politics, through anticapitalist demonstrations, that will change the face of capitalism for the better.

The opposing view is taken by Madsen Pirie, who believes that capitalism is due a resurgence in respectability after years of abuse. He believes that the abuse came from a spirit of antiprogress which is in direct opposition to economic growth. He points out that wealthier countries are better able to protect the environment and that poorer countries who embrace capitalism will be able themselves to produce and manufacture in less damaging ways. Economic growth helps countries attain a better standard of living, and in the last hundred years rich countries have become less polluted. Speaking of effects on individual cultures, he points out that given the choice, these cultures would prefer to be wealthy rather than poor and take advantage of all the benefits entailed. Economic growth has actually reduced the world income inequality, he says, as more countries grow economically, especially in East Asia. He lists the benefits that wealth can bring and suggests that those who attack growth are usually the ones who most enjoy its benefits.

FURTHER INFORMATION:

Books:

Edmunds, John C., and Karen Maccaro, *The Wealthy World: The Growth and Implications of Global Prosperity.* New York: John Wiley & Sons, 2000.
Seligson, Michael A., and John T. Passe-Smith, *Development and Underdevelopment: The Political Economy of Global Inequality.* Boulder, CO: Lynne Rienner Publishers, 1998.

Useful websites:

www.cepr.net
The Center for Economic and Policy Research website includes economics articles and information.

The following debates in the Pro/Con series may also be of interest:

In this volume:

Topic 1 Is the free market the best form of economic organization?

Topic 8 Should wealth redistribution be part of government policy?

DOES CAPITALISM INEVITABLY LEAD TO INCOME INEQUALITY AND ENVIRONMENTAL DESTRUCTION?

YES: Global consumer capitalism has created a scarcity of natural nonrenewable resources, such as oil

YES: In the 1990s the state subsidized $170 billion worth of environmentally damaging industrial activities

YES: The world is full of examples in which capitalism has caused environmental destruction

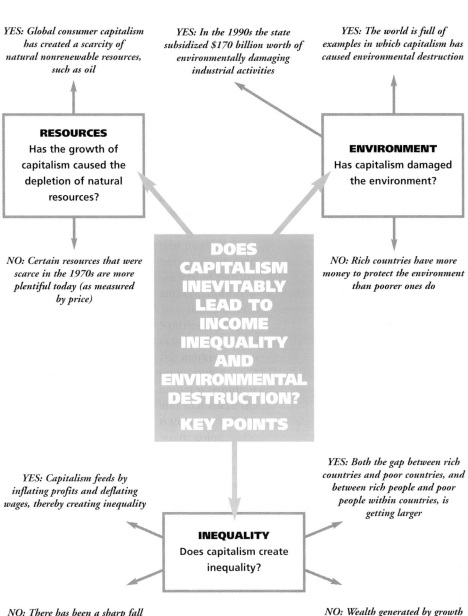

RESOURCES
Has the growth of capitalism caused the depletion of natural resources?

ENVIRONMENT
Has capitalism damaged the environment?

DOES CAPITALISM INEVITABLY LEAD TO INCOME INEQUALITY AND ENVIRONMENTAL DESTRUCTION?

KEY POINTS

NO: Certain resources that were scarce in the 1970s are more plentiful today (as measured by price)

NO: Rich countries have more money to protect the environment than poorer ones do

YES: Capitalism feeds by inflating profits and deflating wages, thereby creating inequality

YES: Both the gap between rich countries and poor countries, and between rich people and poor people within countries, is getting larger

INEQUALITY
Does capitalism create inequality?

NO: There has been a sharp fall in inequality in the last 50 years. Economic growth in Asia has closed the world wealth gap.

NO: Wealth generated by growth brings choice and culture. Growth is the prime tool for advancing the lot of humanity.

THE RISE AND FALL OF COMMUNISM

Communism is a system of political and economic organization based on the writings of Karl Marx in which property is owned by the state, and all citizens share in its common wealth. The system became synonymous from 1917 to 1989 with the former Soviet Union. Although communism collapsed in the Soviet Union and much of Eastern Europe in 1989, China, Cuba, and North Korea remain as testament to communism's survival in various forms.

1848 The German intellectual Karl Marx and his partner Friedrich Engels publish *The Communist Manifesto*, outlining their idea that the workers would overthrow the state to produce a communist society.

1917 The Russian Revolution overthrows the Russian Empire and brings to power a Bolshevik (communist) government led by Vladimir Lenin (1870–1924). In the following years Lenin establishes the Soviet Union (USSR).

1919 American Communist Party founded.

1924 Joseph Stalin (1879–1953) becomes leader of the USSR following Lenin's death.

1930s Stalin institutes central planning of the Soviet economy and collective agriculture, beginning a period of rapid industrialization but also harsh repressive measures under which millions of citizens die.

1936 The show trials begin, in which many important members of the Russian Communist Party are put on public trial, denounced as counter-revolutionaries, and executed. The purges spread through Russian society over the next few years until most people there are living in terror.

1945 Civil war breaks out in China between nationalist and communist armies. After the loss of some 12 million lives the Communist Party of Mao Zedong is victorious.

1945 At the end of World War II Stalin occupies eastern Germany and forms an alliance with Albania and Yugoslavia, which have established communist regimes. In the Far East, meanwhile, the Soviet sphere now includes former Chinese territory, including Mongolia, northern Korea, and other areas.

1945 to 1949 Communist governments are established in Bulgaria, Hungary, Romania, Poland, and—following a Soviet-supported coup—Czechoslovakia. The Soviet-supported East and the American-supported West begin the "Cold War," a long ideological battle between communism and capitalism.

October 1, 1949 The Chinese People's Republic is established. Mao's government seizes land from private individuals and redistributes it among the peasants, executing landowners. Virtually all economic activities fall under government control.

1953 Stalin dies.

1956 A popular uprising breaks out in Hungary, where the communist leader, Imre Nagy, is forced from office. The revolt is harshly suppressed by the Soviet-supported communists.

1958 Mao launches the country's second five-year plan, the "Great Leap Forward." It proves to be an economic disaster, resulting in famine, disease, and the deaths of an estimated 20 million people.

January 1, 1959 Cuban dictator Fulgencio Batista is overthrown by revolutionary forces led by a young lawyer, Fidel Castro. In the face of U.S. opposition to his Marxist policies, Castro turns to the Soviet Union for support.

1961 The communist government of East Germany builds the Berlin Wall to try to prevent citizens fleeing to the West. The wall becomes a symbol of the division between capitalist West and communist East.

1962 Soviet attempts to supply arms to Castro lead to the Cuban Missile Crisis, a tense standoff between the U.S. and the USSR.

1966 Mao launches the Cultural Revolution, an attempt to reinvigorate Chinese Communism. Enthusiastic young communists denounce, punish, and execute former communist leaders until their violence forces Mao to abandon his policy.

1968 The communist government in Czechoslovakia introduces major reforms collectively known as the "Prague Spring." Soviet and other Eastern European troops invade and suppress the reform group led by Alexander Dubçek.

1960s to 1980s The communist governments in Hungary, Poland, Czechoslovakia, and Yugoslavia take gradual steps to introduce economic liberalization, improving consumer choice, and manufacturing goods for export.

1976 Mao Zedong dies.

1981 Deng Xiaoping, the Chinese leader, institutes economic reforms, including

reducing government controls, abolishing the commune system, and permitting private ownership of land.

1986 Mikhail Gorbachev is elected leader of the Soviet Union and begins reform based on the ideas of glasnost ("openness") and perestroika ("reconstruction").

1989 The Berlin Wall falls, followed by the communist governments of many Eastern European countries. Bulgaria, Czechoslovakia, East Germany, Hungary, Poland, and Romania begin moving away from planned economies and toward market-based systems.

March 1990 East Germans vote for the reunification of Germany and a western-style political and economic system. The reunification takes place on October 3.

December 1991 The Soviet Union is formally disbanded, the consequence of increasing unrest, nationalism, and severe economic problems. Independence is restored to the republics. Attempts to institute market reforms, including privatization plans, throw the economies into disarray.

1990 to 1996 The 21 former Soviet republics register economic contractions between -26 percent (Georgia) and -3.5 percent (Uzbekistan). Russia itself records an annual negative growth rate of 9 percent.

1997 As other East Asian countries face economic setbacks, China goes on expanding. Economic modernization continues, ensuring gradual growth. Russia, now the world's 12th largest economy, joins the "Group of Seven" (G7), henceforth the G8.

1999 China joins World Trade Organization.

2000 Vladimir Putin replaces Boris Yeltsin as president in Russia.

Topic 3

DOES PRIVATIZATION ALWAYS BENEFIT CONSUMERS?

YES
"PRIVATIZATION AND AMERICAN BUSINESS"
THE FREEMAN, VOL. 26, NO.10, OCTOBER 1997
LAWRENCE W. REED

NO
"THE PIRATE PRIVATEERS"
NEW INTERNATIONALIST, ISSUE 259, SEPTEMBER 1994
DANI SANDBERG

INTRODUCTION

Privatization refers to the transfer of enterprises run by the state into private ownership. It is the opposite of nationalization, in which private enterprises are subsequently acquired and run by the government. In the 20th century, particularly after World War II (1939-1945), many westernized economies carried out nationalization programs. Contemporary economic thought stressed the importance that the state be in charge of essential services, such as water or electricity, or those such as transportation, in which private enterprise was unlikely to meet public needs because of the high costs of building infrastructure—for example, a rail network.

From the 1980s, however, increasing costs and the renewed popularity of free-market economic theories, which argue for a reduction in government involvement in the economy, have seen moves in many nations to privatize nationalized industries. In the United

States, for example, many prisons were sold to private firms, and many local government services, such as garbage collection, were auctioned to private contractors. In the United Kingdom the Conservative government sold off two-thirds of state-owned concerns between 1979 and 1997, making over $100 billion (£67 billion), including the rail network, gas, electricity, and the coal and steel industries.

One of the major arguments in favor of privatization is that it leads to benefits for consumers such as lower prices and an increase in choice and quality. Public utilities and industries, critics argue, do not face competition—they are often monopolies—and, because they are underwritten by taxpayers' money, have no commercial pressure to improve efficiency. In countries such as Britain, France, and Italy nationalized industry became a byword for poor products, absenteeism, labor unrest, and poor management.

The answer to such problems, as advocated by classical free-market economics, was to open these sectors of the economy to competition by privatizing businesses. Competition would encourage improved products, product choice, and lower prices as firms tried to increase their share of a finite market. Internal efficiency would result from improved management and a more motivated workforce. There would also be political advantages as governments benefited from the price of the sale and gave up subsidizing inefficient industry.

Supporters of privatization can point to numerous successful sell-offs in which consumers now have more choice, and prices have dropped overall. In other cases, however, such as the British water industry, postprivatization companies faced little more competition than previously. They are still effectively monopolies.

In other cases governments sold firms cheaply that went on to make huge profits. That causes resentment from voters and charges of "selling off the family silver." Supporters of privatization argue that pricing firms cheaply is the only way to encourage for-profit companies to take on responsibility for unattractive businesses. Governments also often impose regulations on privatized businesses, including a limit on possible profits.

One of the causes of most criticism of privatization is wrapped up in the central contradiction between public service on one hand and profit maximization on the other. It is that privatized firms do not operate in the public interest, but in their own, or rather their shareholders,' interests. An example critics often cite is the sell-off of the British rail industry.

The nationalized company British Rail was privatized in 1994, the share issue raising some $7.5 billion. In an effort to introduce increased competition, the government sold off the company in pieces, while offering massive subsidies to encourage bidders. One of these companies, Railtrack, became responsible for running infrastructure— the track, signaling, and so on. Three other companies bought the trains, which they leased to about 20 train-operating companies that were charged with actually running train services.

Critics allege that the breakup made the railways more dangerous than before. The need to avoid paying fines to the train operators pressured Railtrack into not closing tracks for repairs. The consequence, as those critics see it, was the fatal train derailment on October 17, 2000, at Hatfield, near London, in which four people died when a worn rail broke as a passenger express passed over it. The previous year a crash blamed on poorly maintained signals killed 31 people in a London suburb. While some observers blame such crashes on the structure introduced by privatization, some trace their causes back to the underinvestment and inefficiency of the nationalized rail service.

The following two articles put the case for and against the benefits of privatization. Lawrence W. Reed argues that the superiority of private industry is almost unquestioned and reflects a profound human need for competition and incentives. Dani Sandberg, on the other hand, sees privatization as benefiting only profiteers among the international establishment. Sandberg cites examples from Latin America and Africa to show how consumers bear the cost of privatization.

PRIVATIZATION AND AMERICAN BUSINESS
Lawrence W. Reed

YES

"Privatization," in its broadest sense, is the transfer of assets or services from the tax-supported and politicized public sector to the entrepreneurial initiative and competitive markets of the private sector. The superiority of the latter is now approaching the status of undisputed conventional wisdom—the private sector exacts a toll from the inefficient for their poor performance, compels the service provider or asset owner to concern him- or herself with the wishes of customers, and spurs a dynamic, never-ending pursuit of excellence—all without any of the political baggage that haunts the public sector....

In an interdependent world getting smaller through the speed of transportation and communications, no community of people can compete successfully without ridding itself of costly public enterprises and liberating the entrepreneurial spirit. Recognition of that fact is at the root of today's dramatic privatization revolution—from Moscow to Manila to my hometown of Midland, Michigan.

Human nature

The theory is simple, but grounded in profound truths about the nature of humans and their response to incentives and disincentives. Tie up the performance of a task with red tape, bureaucracy, and politics within a system that is guaranteed to exist regardless of outcome, and the result is usually mediocrity at great expense. Infuse competition, accountability, and the fear of losing valued customers ... and mediocrity becomes the exception, excellence the rule....

When it is handled properly and with care, privatization harnesses the powerful market forces of competition, accountability, and incentive. It means that government officials don't have to be hemmed in by an indifferent bureaucracy; instead, they can take advantage of the best available buys. State and local governments have routinely experienced cost savings of 10 to 40 percent through privatization, often with significant improvements in the way an asset is managed or a service is delivered. When

In what way does the private sector "exact a toll" for inefficiency and force the producer of a product or service to be more concerned with the "wishes of customers"? Why might this not be the case in the public sector?

Why are public or state (nationalized) enterprises "guaranteed to exist regardless of outcome"? Why might this result in "mediocrity at great expense"?

assets and services are left entirely in private hands from the very start, and the government "middleman" is eliminated, even greater efficiencies are possible.

Contracting out and commercialization

The most common form of privatization—contracting out to private firms—has become more than just a trend. With decades of experience, it has become something of a science at the local level in America. We now know what it takes to make this work, including: open, competitive bidding for contracts that are subject to periodic renewal; careful writing of the contract terms to incorporate clear language and appropriate safeguards; and effective monitoring … to ensure the contract is being carried out as expected.

Commercialization is another form of privatization. That happens when a unit of government simply says, "We are no longer going to perform this work with our own workforce. We are not going to contract it out either. We are … going to get out of this business altogether. The customers we used to serve can take care of the job themselves by contracting with the private provider of their individual choice."

Commercialization is how cities across America have pulled out of the garbage collection business. The citizens themselves choose one of several private, competitive firms that specialize in picking up and properly disposing of garbage. There are no middlemen, no taxes, no interminable city council meetings that must be endured if you wish to register a complaint. You hire the service and if you are not happy, you fire it and hire a different one. This form of privatization tends to enhance citizens' liberties and spare their pocketbooks if it is done right. Other forms of privatization include:

- the outright gift or sale by government of a physical asset (a piece of equipment or a building, [say]) to a private entity;
- the issue of "vouchers" that can be redeemed in the marketplace instead of direct public provision of a service, giving recipients choices where they had none before;
- the sale of stock in a newly privatized company that was formerly state-owned;
- the end of subsidies and the red tape and onerous regulations that inevitably accompany them, which then liberates the industry to produce "for the market" rather than for the government.

Each of these forms, of course, has its pros and cons. But let there be no mistake about this fact: Privatization in its various forms has now become nothing less than a revolution….

"Contracting out" is when the government employs an outside firm to carry out some specific task previously performed by government employees—for example, road sweeping or cleaning in a public hospital.

Can you think of any potential problems people might encounter with their garbage being collected and disposed of in this manner?

This is the form of privatization that the Thatcher government in the United Kingdom was known for during the 1980s.

A group of prison inmates start boot camp. Prison management is one of the roles of state governments most frequently privatized.

Critics argued that stocks of public housing were reduced to such an extent by this policy that there was no longer enough cheap housing available for those who really needed it. Should governments have a duty to provide low-rent housing for poorer citizens?

Global privatization

Former British Prime Minister Margaret Thatcher taught us much about how to privatize. During her tenure, she sold off seven major commercial airports … in a careful, studied, and public way that maximized popular support. More than two million citizens bought 1.4 billion shares of stock in the airport privatization effort.

Moreover, Thatcher sold a million units of public housing by offering them to tenants at prices that were well below market value. The tenants who previously complained about the indifference of distant, bureaucratic management became the new management. With pride of ownership working its wonders, whole neighborhoods were subsequently transformed—broken windows were replaced, torn screen doors were repaired.… And the British treasury was relieved of the burden of throwing huge subsidies down the rat hole of public housing. The British experience with privatization bears testimony to a time-honored principle of human action: what you own, you take care of; what nobody or "everybody" owns falls into disrepair.

Many state-owned companies were privatized under Thatcher—the huge and ubiquitous British Telecom being the foremost example.… In the space of ? decade, Margaret Thatcher sold off $40 billion in state enterprises. The number of British households owning stock rose from 2 million to 12 million. And about three-quarters of a million government employees were transferred from public to private payrolls. Once the post-war "sick man of Europe," Britain came to life.

In a few places around the world, privatization is occurring because the enlightened leaders in power are motivated by free market ideas....

In most places, however, privatization is occurring for more pragmatic reasons. Countries, states, provinces, and communities have hit the "tax wall," meaning they have no more room to raise taxes. Doing so would either violate some constitutional or statutory limit, or send people and businesses packing. In other cases, government simply has not kept pace with technology and productivity advances and must rely upon private enterprise to put its unique expertise to work. So hard-pressed politicians are forced to exercise the best or only option they have—privatization.

Privatization in the United States

Let us bring this closer to home and focus now on the United States exclusively. At the federal level, little has been privatized but much could be....

At the state level, there is much more dynamic activity. States are privatizing utilities, prison management, data processing, foster care, and a long list of other items....

It is, however, at the local level of government—counties and cities and schools—where the privatization revolution is having the greatest impact. You name it, just about any asset or service that a local government owns or provides has been privatized somewhere, in some manner. That includes fire protection, police protection, waste-water treatment, street lighting, tree trimming, snow removal, parking structures, railroads, hospitals, jails, and even cemeteries....

All citizens who value freedom, and the free markets that give life to that freedom, should be encouraged by the privatization revolution. A better ... public sector is much more than a "good government" issue. It is a moral imperative and it leaves us better served, freer, more responsible.

Can you think of any services in your area, either at the state or local level, that have been transferred from government to private ownership? Do you think this transfer has improved the service or made it worse? In what way have things improved or deteriorated?

THE PIRATE PRIVATEERS
Dani Sandberg

Development GAP is the Development Group for Alternative Policies, an organization looking to demonstrate alternatives to prevailing policies and programs in the developing world.

A tidal wave has been rolling over the boundaries of the state and crushing the influence of democracy almost everywhere….The result has been what Doug Hellinger of Development GAP in Washington calls the "greatest ever transfer of public wealth into private hands."

The wave first formed in Chile after the military coup in 1973, which created a democracy-free "green-field site" ideal for practical experiments. It spread to the United Kingdom under Margaret Thatcher and the United States under Ronald Reagan, to Aotearoa/New Zealand, over the Iron Curtain to Eastern Europe and the territory of the former Soviet Union, then on to the Third World. It flattened the remnants of "public enterprise" and further enriched a tiny, already wealthy international establishment.

By 1992 more than 80 countries … had "privatized" some 6,800 previously state-owned enterprises (SOEs). The majority were not, however, in the rich industrial countries that were promoting privatization and buying most of the assets, but in Eastern Europe and the developing world. In Africa there have been 373 privatizations, compared to just 170 in the rich industrial countries that belong to the Organization for Economic Co-operation and Development (OECD).

Natural monopolies

Many public enterprises are what is known as "natural monopolies." This means that technical factors— for example, the necessity of a large and expensive infrastructure such as telephone cables or water pipes— prevent the efficient existence of more than one producer.

Many of the SOEs were, in effect, monopoly suppliers of essential public services like water, electricity, or telephones. Painful experience has proved that if such services are run by private monopolies they are so unrestrained in their search for profit that they cannot be tolerated in democratic societies. Private monopolies also break the rules of competition in a "free market." So for most of this century conventional wisdom was that essential public services must either be run by the state or operated under stringent democratic supervision.

Undervalued

But since the mid-1970s people have somehow been convinced, or simply informed, that if public monopolies are flogged off to form private ones everyone will be better off.

Some are. But fabulous earnings by many of the newly-private monopolies were predictably balanced by sharply rising charges to "customers."

The profiteering process had begun even earlier with the undervaluation of the public assets that were sold off. In the United Kingdom British Telecom was undervalued by at least $5 billion and in Argentina the state telephone company ENTEL by some $4 billion, or four times its selling price. This was a pattern repeated over and over again. Taken together, such undervaluations amounted to a massive subsidy to private profit by public donation.

In the United Kingdom as in Chile a gloss of "popular capitalism" was briefly put on public sales, encouraging share ownership among the general public. Because of the undervaluations there were some gains when small, first-time buyers sold their shares, as most of them very quickly did. The bulk of shares ended up in the hands of the financial establishment. "Popular capitalism" quickly vanished from the vocabulary of privatization.

One of the arguments for privatization is that it improves efficiency and drives down prices. Why might prices actually increase in this case?

Benefits to the rich and powerful

In Mexico an already-extreme concentration of wealth and power was intensified by the process of privatization. A group of some 35 businessmen who already controlled nearly a quarter of Mexico's Gross National Product (GNP) took a leading part in virtually all the privatizations of public utilities—they were the only people who had the money. Here, as elsewhere in Latin America, shares in the new private monopolies sponsored the growth of stock markets where massive speculative profits could be made—again by those who had the money to start with.

In Chile between 1975 and 1979 most of the local banks were sold for a song to the handful of families that already dominated Chile's finance and industry. So disastrous were the results for Chile's financial "stability" that a program of renationalization had to be hurriedly cobbled together. During the second round of privatizations that began in 1985 by far the largest chunk of stock in ENDASA, the electricity utility, was made available to members of the armed forces.

Large "speculative profits" are often made on the sale of state-owned enterprises because the initial share price is usually much lower than the true value of the stock. Once the company is floated on the stock exchange, the share price increases, allowing profits to be made by shareowners.

Debt for assets

In the 1990s a new and particularly lucrative variation on this theme has emerged. What are called "debt-for-equity swaps" exchange Third World debt for national assets, particularly in Latin America, and especially where state-owned commercial assets can be linked to world markets. Because debtor

Do you think this sort of arrangement is fair—for developing or less developed countries to pay their way out of debt by selling off national assets to foreign companies or banks? Or for countries to gain access to currency by selling off access to local natural resources to private firms?

governments are in a relatively weak position and international banks … in a much stronger one, complex currency deals invariably produce knock-down sales of state assets to foreigners. Something very similar has been going on in Eastern Europe and the territories of the former Soviet Union. Access to Russia's huge natural resources has been gained in bargain-basement deals. In 1990 the Gorbachev Government gave De Beers, who monopolize the world diamond market, an exclusive five-year concession on all Soviet diamond production in exchange for $1 billion in desperately-needed foreign currency. The most conservative estimate put the real value of Russian diamond production during this period at five times this amount.

Manufacturing industry in Africa required a high degree of government involvement to establish. Now these industries are being privatized. In Togo, for example, the World Bank … supervised the sale for $9.3 million of two textile mills to a group of U.S.-South Korean investors in 1985. Just one of the mills had cost the state $50 million five years earlier. The Government also gave the new owners a guarantee that no competitors would be tolerated.

Agents of private business

Governments began to act like the agents of private interest, transferring liability for bad debts or failed money-grabbing exercises onto populations. In Uruguay during the 1980s huge debts incurred by the *frigoríficos*, the meat-packing factories owned by the country's élite, were simply "taken over" by the military government on the grounds that this was a "strategic" industry. Assets were handed over for peanuts while liabilities were dumped on the people.

In what way would this takeover have benefited the owners of the meat-packing factories in Uruguay? Why do you think the government forced the takeover?

Of course not all governments are democratic and SOEs are not necessarily run in the public interest. SOEs, just as much as private monopolies, can indeed be inefficient and operate in the interests of corrupt governments and local élites. When it came to the crunch, few people were willing or able to defend them against the pirate privateers.

Privatization in New Zealand

Just how completely this process became conventional political wisdom can be glimpsed from Aotearoa/New Zealand, where it was a Labour Government that came to power in 1984 and promised to free the country from the grip of an interventionist "welfare" state. Within 10 years Aotearoa was being hailed by the OECD, the World Bank, and credit-rating agencies as a model for reform worldwide.

Labour's Finance Minister, Roger Douglas, devised "Rogernomics," Aotearoa's more extreme version of "Reaganomics." He, together with other key players in the new order, went on to set up consultancies that collected $102.5 million in fees during the asset-sales program. Consultants from Aotearoa are estimated to have earned between $70 and $100 million from international business during 1992 alone.

The relationship between both Labour and—after 1990—conservative National Governments and big business began to cause simmering unease. The National Party's Wellington division urged, during a funding drive directed at business in 1992, that "those who benefit directly from the policies of the Government must be encouraged to support the return of the Government by their donations."

This process will have to stop when there is nothing left to privatize. Perhaps we shall then be persuaded to buy shares in governments rather than vote for them. What we are left with in the meantime, however, is a return to the nightmare of private monopolies running essential public services. This creates a democratic vacuum with ever-sharper divisions between rich and poor. The question that needs answering urgently now is how this vacuum is to be filled.

General Augusto Pinochet (right) of Chile with President Jorge Videla of Argentina. Privatization began in Chile after Pinochet's military coup in 1973.

What does this quote imply about the nature of the relationship between the government and big business in New Zealand at the time? What are the implications for democracy?

Summary

Lawrence W. Reed argues that the superiority of private enterprise over the public sector is virtually undisputed. It has brought governments savings of up to 40 percent. This efficiency, he argues, comes because the free market is the natural form of economic organization for humans, who are spurred on by incentives, competition, and accountability. He describes some of the main forms of privatization—contracting out and commercialization—before describing Britain's experience with another form of privatization in which stock was sold off in previously state-owned enterprises. Reed argues that the impulse behind privatization is not motivated entirely by idealism but by pragmatism. Governments can no longer afford to pay for inefficient nationalized industries; privatization is the only alternative.

Dani Sandberg concentrates less on the efficiency of privatization and more on its political consequences. She describes the process as the transfer of public wealth into private hands. The financial establishment buys stock cheaply but then has the chance to make massive profits by raising costs to consumers. These new monopolies, she argues, are so greedy for profit that they become antidemocratic. Citing the results of privatization in Latin America, Africa, and New Zealand, Sandberg argues that governments consistently undervalue businesses and sell them for less than they are worth. This leaves the country's citizens having to pay more to cover the difference, while the privatized company is free to make profits enabled by the state.

FURTHER INFORMATION:

Books:

Farazmand, Ali (Editor), *Privatization or Public Enterprise Reform?: International Case Studies with Implications for Public Management*. Westport, CT: Greenwood Publishing Group, 2000.

Savas, Edmund S., *Privatization and Public-Private Partnerships*. New York: Chatham House, 2000.

Sclar, Elliot D., and Richard C. Leone, *You Don't Always Get What You Pay for: The Economics of Privatization*. New York: Cornell University Press, 2000.

Useful websites:

www.oneworld.org/ni
The New Internationalist is a communications organization based in Oxford, England, that reports on issues of world poverty and inequality.
www.whirledbank.org/development/private.html
"Privatization and the World Bank" examines how countries are being forced to sell off public industries.

The following debates in the Pro/Con series may also be of interest:

In this volume:
Topic 1 Is the free market the best form of economic organization?

Topic 5 Does government intervention do more harm than good?

Topic 12 Should rich countries cancel "Third World debt"?

Topic 14 Should companies be more ethical in their dealings?

DOES PRIVATIZATION ALWAYS BENEFIT CONSUMERS?

YES: Nationalized businesses often have no competition, and because they are funded by government, there is no incentive to improve efficiency

YES: Privatized companies fight each other for customers, so they have to improve efficiency and cut prices

NATIONALIZATION
Are nationalized businesses inefficient?

COMPETITION
Does privatization always increase competition?

NO: Nationalization is the most efficient way to guarantee certain public goods, particularly if the industry is a "natural monopoly"

NO: Many privatized companies are "natural monopolies." It is difficult to introduce any competition into these situations without compromising efficiency.

DOES PRIVATIZATION ALWAYS BENEFIT CONSUMERS? KEY POINTS

YES: By removing industries from government control, privatization saves them money that can be cut from taxes

YES: Privatized companies put profit before anything else, including safety and customer care

GOVERNMENT
Does privatization mean that consumers pay less tax?

SAFETY
Does privatization mean lower safety standards?

NO: Governments often undervalue the industries they sell off, so consumers end up subsidizing private businesses through their taxes

NO: Competition means that any company that was unsafe would lose its customers, so privatized firms have to ensure that their services are safe

Topic 4

WILL IT AND THE INTERNET CREATE A "NEW ECONOMY"?

YES

"THE NEW OLD ECONOMY: OIL, COMPUTERS, AND THE REINVENTION OF THE EARTH"
THE ATLANTIC ONLINE, JANUARY 2001
JONATHAN RAUCH

NO

"IS THERE LIFE IN E-COMMERCE?"
THE ECONOMIST, FEBRUARY 1, 2001

INTRODUCTION

The huge growth in computer technology in the last decade of the 20th century was heralded at the time as marking not only the emergence of a whole new business sector but also a whole new way of doing business. At the forefront of this revolutionary change would be the World Wide Web and the Internet. The development of e—or electronic—commerce would enable sellers and customers to come together without the need for expensive stores; markets would become global; smaller firms would be able to compete with larger. There would be problems—new opportunities for credit-card fraud, for example—but technology would create a vast opportunity for business.

For much of the 1990s this vision seemed to be taking shape. Around the world entrepreneurs launched new companies—dubbed "dot coms" after the suffix that was commonly part of their web address—to take advantage of the new opportunities. Some, such as the bookseller Amazon, took advantage of the fact that e-stores did not have to hold physical stock to offer "the world's biggest selection," millions of books that it could order direct from publishers' warehouses. Lastminute.com used the Net to put suppliers with stock to shift—tour operators, car dealerships, and so on—in touch with consumers seeking bargains. Let'sbuyit.com allowed consumers who wanted to buy the same product to band together in order to generate bulk discounts from the manufacturer. Other typical electronic businesses promoted themselves purely on the grounds of convenience: Banking, grocery shopping, and searches for second-hand books or records became possible without leaving the house.

In the late 1990s new technology shares boomed on stock markets around the world. So-called new economy companies were valued at millions, even billions, of dollars even though they held little physical stock and, even in the case of the long-established Amazon, not only failed to make profits but generated huge losses. That did not seem to deter investors, who were eager to buy into the potential rather than the actuality.

On the back of the new companies stocks rose in associated high-technology sectors such as media and telecommunications. Then, in 2000 the new technology market crashed. As investors lost their confidence, the value of dot coms fell rapidly. Many went out of business. Even the more established companies in the sector—Cisco, Intel, Microsoft, Nortel, Oracle, Vodafone—began to issue warnings of falling sales and profits.

"[A new economy] is ... more often declared than defined, but if there is one fundamental change at its heart, it must be the move from an economy based on the production of physical goods to an economy based on the production of knowledge."

—LAWRENCE H. SUMMERS, TREASURY SECRETARY

But did the dot com crash represent the end of the vision of a new economy? Or was it simply a sign of the natural cycle of growth and contraction that characterized the "old economy"? Some observers see it as a necessary antidote to the unbridled optimism of the 1990s and as part of an essential clearing out of weaker companies from a maturing sector.

In the first of the following articles Jonathan Rauch argues that despite the crash, the Internet has not so much created a new type of economy as brought about an evolution of the old. He identifies a difference between an economy based on the manufacture and trade of products, and the emerging knowledge or information economy. The latter, he argues, is characterized by what people know rather than what they make. This development is fundamentally linked to the communication and organizational power of computer technology. The evolutionary process he describes has produced what he identifies as "the new old economy."

The author of *The Economist* article, on the other hand, argues that the e-economy is much the same as the old economy. He condemns analysts who unreasonably boosted the Internet as marking the birth of a new economy. The fantastic expectations this launched were never really reflected in the real value of many dot com companies. He goes on to discuss the rapid rise and fall of the dot com companies, suggesting that those that survived the recent Silicon Valley collapse were very much part of the old economy. In his opinion, the big players—such as Yahoo!, Amazon, and eBay—have not survived because they are virtual companies on the cutting edge of the new economy. On the contrary, they have prospered, relatively speaking, because they run businesses along extremely similar lines to those in the old economy and have managed to trade and maintain growth as a result of this strategy.

THE NEW OLD ECONOMY
Jonathan Rauch

"Knowledge, not petroleum, is becoming the critical resource in the oil business"—Jonathan Rauch

The author writes a firsthand account of how technology is transforming the old economy.

> Jonathan Rauch uses a firsthand account of drilling for oil to illustrate how this "old economy" industry has been improved by "new economy" technology.

This was not a good day. The drillers had hoped to reach their objective that morning, but something downhole had chewed up two mud motors in succession, and now a seal just above the blowout preventer had sprung a leak. On the drill floor seven roustabouts and the driller were using wrenches and sledgehammers to loosen heavy bolts on the diverter housing. I had no trouble seeing how a roustabout might lose a fingertip.

It was a bright, hot afternoon, and the derrick offered no shade; the men on the drill floor were soaked with sweat and spattered with drilling mud. I was standing off to one side, in shade behind the driller's cage, not lifting a finger, and I felt a stream of sweat under my hard hat become a small river behind my right ear. Just about then I heard myself thinking, "Silicon Valley this ain't."

Yet, in some respects, this is like Silicon Valley. The Pompano crews were drilling a well named Margarita, and Margarita was a computer's brainchild. Geologists could not have found this prospect with the computer technology available even four or five years ago, and drillers could not have drilled it as efficiently with the technology available then. Margarita's objective lies under salt, as does much of the oil in the Gulf of Mexico. People in the oil business have been striving to master the salt for years: Learn to see through salt—and then to drill through it quickly and accurately—and you open new reserves, potentially large ones.

> Can you think of other examples of computer technology transforming traditional "old economy" industries?

Technological improvements

"There's salt in the North Sea, there's salt off Africa, there's salt off Brazil," Doug Stauber told me as we left Pompano later that day. Stauber is one of BP's geologists, and Margarita is his project. The series of mechanical failures meant it would be at least another few days before he knew whether Margarita would succeed. But Stauber betrayed no anxiety. In general, geologists lack the natural demonstrativeness of, say, tax accountants and insurance adjusters, and Stauber's only emotional display had been when he went down to the production deck to give affectionate pats to two of his favorite wellheads— "my good wells," he called them. In his fifteen years in the oil business Stauber had worked on fifty or so wells, including many of the wells at Pompano. I ventured that Margarita must seem routine. "Oh, no," he said. "It's got all my attention."

The new old economy

In a speech last May, Treasury Secretary Lawrence H. Summers, an economist of distinction, reflected on what people are calling the new economy. The notion is "both palpable and amorphous—more often declared than defined," he said. "But if there is one fundamental change at its heart, it must be the move from an economy based on the production of physical goods to an economy based on the production and application of knowledge."

Lawrence H. Summers was sworn in as Treasury Secretary on July 2, 1999. You can find out more about his policies at www.choosetosave. org/wdc/forum/lhs-bio.htm.

The new economy, Summers said, seems to behave differently from the old industrial and agrarian models. "Consider the classic Smithian model of wheat: When prices rise, farmers produce more, consumers buy less, and equilibrium is restored at a lower level of demand." This, Summers said, is a "negative-feedback" economy—one that is bounded by near-term constraints of supply and demand. An analogy, he suggested, might be a thermostat that shuts down the furnace when a house overheats.

To find out more about Adam Smith, one of the first economic theorists, see www.utdallas. edu/~harpham/ adam.htm.

"By contrast," Summers said, "the information economy will increasingly be a positive-feedback economy." In the traditional economy new technologies and products start out expensive and rare, and only gradually become cheap and common; think of refrigeration, the automobile, and the long-distance call. In the new economy, additional capacity seems to become available so quickly and inexpensively—such as what happened with the microchip—that traditional supply constraints are almost trivial. "In such a world," Summers said, "the avalanche, rather than the thermostat, becomes the more attractive metaphor for economic policy."

More details of Summers' speech can be found at www.ustreas.gov/ press/releases/ps922 .htm.

If there is a new economy, its effect might logically be to increase the country's capacity to produce goods without running up against shortages and thereby triggering inflationary pressures. In effect, the economy's speed limits would be raised. Sure enough, the economy produced higher growth in real output per worker, as well as lower

COMMENTARY: The rise of Silicon Valley

Silicon Valley has been at the center of high-tech innovation since the 1960s, but the region really caught the public imagination in the 1990s with the rise of Internet technology and the enormous amount of wealth that it generated. The spectacular speed of business growth led many to believe that the technology sector was the start of a new kind of economic development, characterized by fast, aggressive, and innovative companies.

Unimaginable amounts of money were generated for individuals and corporations overnight. In 1999 alone, Silicon Valley was home to 12 percent of America's fastest growing 500 firms, and an average of 11 new companies were setting up every day. Countries around the world flocked to the Valley, desperate to study and re-create the phenomenon in their own towns and cities. So what went wrong?

Ultimately, it would seem that the Internet dream did not happen—people were not prepared to trade online as expected, and new technology was not embraced fast enough. Venture capitalists became wary of investing, stock value plummeted, smaller companies overspent their limited and declining funds on marketing campaigns, and businesses that failed to make good on their loans were forced into bankruptcy. Only the big companies were able to survive the turnabout in their fortunes. However, the tech sector is bullish about the boom-and-bust nature of its industry, and many observers are confident that it will once again rise from the ashes.

unemployment in the 1990s than in the 1970s or the 1980s, while keeping inflation at a substantially lower rate. That is cause for celebration, but it is also puzzling.

Economists agree that to the extent the economy has changed, "information technology"—the computer and its many offshoots—must have a good deal to do with it. In the three decades since 1970 the power of microprocessors increased by a factor of 7,000. Computing chores that took a week in the early 1970s now take a minute. According to the Federal Reserve Bank of Dallas, the cost of storing one megabit of information, or enough for a 320-page book, fell from more than $5,000 in 1975 to 17 cents in 1999. All well and good. But the computer revolution has been going on for years, whereas the economy's turbocharge came only in the second half of the 1990s. Why?

For more information about the evolution of computer power see www.islandnet. com/~kpolsson/ comphist/.

The Internet

The Internet might seem to be a reasonable answer, and no doubt it has helped. However, according to Robert E. Litan, the director of economic studies at the Brookings Institution, in Washington, D.C., the Internet is still much too small a factor in America's $10 trillion economy to account for the productivity surge. Nor, economists say (although this point is disputed), is the new economy proper—the software, hardware, and dot com sectors—large enough to have brought about more than part of the surge. Something else is at work, but what? It is not crazy to suspect what I think of as the "new old economy."

For more information about America's economy see orl.grolier.com /ea-online/wsja/text/ ch03/articles/ ec001-a.htm.

Investigating the new old economy

Although at this point no one can prove anything, a story that seems plausible to many economists and business executives goes like this: In the 1980s, old economy businesses tended to waste much of what they spent on computers and software. Companies in traditional industries would drop a PC on every desk and declare themselves computerized; they would buy spreadsheet programs and word-processing software and networking equipment that as often as not just substituted new frustrations for old ones. This began to change, however, as software and hardware grew in power, and as companies began learning how to use them not just as conveniences or crutches but to change the nature of the job.

At first the impact was too small to show up in the national economic statistics. However, each innovation enabled other innovations, none of them revolutionary but all of them combining in an accelerating cascade. By the second half of the 1990s the aggregate effect on productivity became large enough to register in the national accounts, and the line between the new economy and the old economy began to blur. That is the story of the new old economy.

Do you think that computers have revolutionized business? Have your parents or teachers noticed a "revolution" or an "evolution" during their working lives?

As stated, nothing can be proved—at least not yet. But oil is about as old as modern industries come. If John D. Rockefeller, who lived from 1839 to 1937, rose from the dead today, he would probably need to struggle to get his mind around the Internet. But if you flew him out to Pompano and let him squint up at the derrick, he would know immediately what was going on. Finding and producing oil is still about poking holes in the ground and canning what comes out, and in most people's minds it has long epitomized dirty industry and the reality of limits to growth. In a number of respects, however, the oil business has begun to behave more like the new economy than the old. It is in the midst of the sort of technological change that Summers compared to an avalanche; and the bang that started the avalanche came not from the oil fields but from Silicon Valley.

IS THERE LIFE IN E-COMMERCE?
The Economist

NO

Last year's American football championship, the Super Bowl, marked the peak of dot com mania, with 17 dot coms paying up to $3m each for 30-second television spots. This year's event marked its nadir. One ad for a brokerage pictured a dot com ghost town, with a faded TieClasp.com sign, abandoned PimentoLoaf.com offices and something that looked like the Pets.com sock puppet lying crumpled in the dust. "Invest wisely," warned the broker. Good advice. What does it mean?

Valuing dot coms has been a well-nigh impossible task from the beginning. Had you decided that Yahoo! could not possibly be worth $1 billion in 1997, as the market then said, you would have missed a three-year run that took it to more than 100 times that figure. But had you decided to believe the market last spring and bought Yahoo! then, you would now have lost 80 percent of your money.

Meanwhile, in the real world

Through it all, Yahoo! has grown steadily, becoming a dominant Web media company more or less according to plan. So too for eBay, the web auctioneer. Throughout the rise and fall of the dot coms, analysts have been forced to come up with increasingly other-worldly formulas to justify current prices, to say nothing of their targets. Investors have been tossed like corks in a storm.

Now comes particularly hard-to-digest news from Amazon, the biggest dot com and among the most controversial thanks to the massive losses it has incurred as it has grown. As its many critics have warned, its "get big fast" philosophy made it too big, too soon: It is closing two facilities and laying off 1,300 employees. But in the same announcement it promised to turn a profit by the end of the year.

Generating profit

Note that it was operating profit, not net profit, that Amazon was promising, so debt payments, options costs and potential losses from investments may keep the bottom line in the red for a while, even on the firm's own projections. But considering that for much of its existence it has faced doubts

Find out more about the problems associated with valuing Internet companies at www.nesd.org.uk/valuing dotcoms.html.

For more information about Amazon's business philosophy see www.ecommerce times.com/perl/story/36.html.

over whether it could sell even books, to say nothing of more complex items, at more than they cost when all the picking, packing and shipping was factored in, Amazon is answering its harshest critics. About one key thing, it was right: It does seem to have found a way to make money while continuing to grow (although not nearly as quickly as it once did). It is not going to run out of money and go bust.

Does that make its shares a good buy? As the article "Amazon, Yahoo! and eBay grow up" argues, the three big dot com leaders are, by normal measures, extraordinary businesses. They have grown quickly, built global brands in record time, and count their customers in the tens of millions. Two of the three have even made decent sums while doing so. But at the same time as they have expanded they have become less perfectly virtual and more like ordinary firms. At some point that ought to mean more ordinary valuations.

Managing business growth

Yahoo! has 3,260 employees and rises and falls with the advertising business like other big media firms. As eBay expands into products such as cars it must enter into joint ventures with bricks-and-mortar firms, splitting profits. This is even more true for Amazon, which looks more like a bricks-and-mortar company by the day. It has built warehouses around the world and staffed them with an army of temporary workers. Where four years ago it took up two floors of a building on one of the worst streets in Seattle, today it sprawls over the city, occupying a former hospital and seven other buildings. All three companies are slowing down as they get larger, moving from triple-digit growth to mere double-digits.

"Bricks-and-mortar" refers to companies that have real-world, physical premises, such as a store. Clicks-and-mortar refers to companies that have both an online presence and real-world premises.

Integrating technology into business

Amazon uses technology spectacularly well, but so does Wal-Mart. This is why analysts are increasingly thinking of it as a "best of breed retailer," something of a back-handed compliment. It is nice to be best of breed, but retailers trade at very different multiples to dot coms, even today. Wal-Mart trades at about 26 times future earnings. Apply the same multiple to Amazon (assuming operating margins of 10 percent by 2004) and it would have to increase its domestic business by 50 percent a year and its international business by nearly 100 percent a year to justify its current price. Given that it predicts its overall growth will slow to 20 to 30 percent this year, that would be a stretch.

"Best of breed" refers to a specific business—such as a chain of book stores—as being the market leader.

Cyber cafes are a common sight on streets and in shopping malls, but will they attract people who are not linked to the Internet to become involved in e-commerce?

Or do the calculation another way. Big American retailers today tend to trade at a valuation of about one times 2001 revenue. Amazon is predicting that its revenues this year will be $3.3 billion to $3.6 billion. Its market capitalisation is more than $6.5 billion. That would suggest that despite falling 85 percent from its peak, it still has a way to go.

But that is to value it exactly as a traditional retailer. Although Amazon is certainly more like one than it may have originally set out to be, there are still clear differences. Because it holds all its inventory in centralized warehouses, the firm turns it over much faster than bricks-and-mortar retailers do. With rapidly depreciating products such as consumer electronics, that is a huge advantage. Low inventory as a percentage of sales also helps it grow economically because costs tend to scale with the number of units shipped, not their value. This may allow it to make money in categories that are thought of as low-margin. Thanks to the Internet, its potential customer base continues to grow at impressive rates.

Building real-word assets

Amazon argues that its main advantage is that it can grow without paying to build new physical stores. This should give it a lasting advantage in return on capital employed. But it is notable that so far it has had to build a local warehouse for each new country it has entered. As long as its ability to serve, say, all of Europe from its German warehouse depends on forces outside its control, such as the efficiency of European transportation firms, it cannot expand as cheaply as it would like. Amazon was built on the premise that online retailing offered extraordinary advantages over the traditional model. The jury is still out on some of these, but even where they show up they look rather less amazing in the flesh.

The author points out how some new economy businesses still rest on the traditional foundation of trade—moving around physical commodities.

Blurring the line

The same is true to a lesser degree of Yahoo! and eBay. Yahoo! looks more like a media company every day, especially now that AOL-Time/Warner has redefined the genre. At its root eBay is just a marketplace. The fact that both are built on the Internet implies growth rates and efficiencies the physical world rarely see. But eventually the distinctions between the two worlds begin to blur. The dot com leaders may well be among the great companies of the future, but increasingly they will not be thought of as a class unto themselves. Nor, one suspects, will their shares.

Read more about the Time/Warner buyout by AOL at news.cnet. com/news/0-1005-200-1518888.html.

Summary

The authors tackle the debate in slightly different ways, but both draw firm conclusions. Jonathan Rauch argues that computer technology has revolutionized old economy industries, effectively creating a "new old economy." This is not to say that we now have two parallel economies—or a radically new economy—just that computers and information technology have helped evolve commerce in a fundamental and irreversible way that could not have happened without this development.

The Economist article looks at the rise and fall of Internet businesses, and criticizes the speculators who predicted that this technology was going to reinvent the world's economy. The author looks at the big players, such as Amazon, eBay, and Yahoo!, and suggests that they survived the dot com fallout because they were managed in the same way that successful old economy companies are run, not because they are pioneers in the new economy. The author argues that these businesses are going to become increasingly similar to old economy companies if they are going to profit in the future.

Despite the different opinions put forward in the articles, both acknowledge that information technology and the Internet have had a major impact on the way business is conducted today. And even if these changes are not as revolutionary as predicted, both writers see reasons to be optimistic about future changes in the global economy.

FURTHER INFORMATION:

Books:

Fingar, Peter, Ronald Aronica, and Bryan Maizlish, *The Death of "e" & the Birth of the Real New Economy: Business Models, Technologies & Strategies for the 21st Century*. Tampa, FL: Meghan-Kiffer Press, 2001.

Omae, Kenichi, *The Invisible Continent: Four Strategic Imperatives of the New Economy*. New York: HarperBusiness, 2001.

Sowell, Thomas, *Basic Economics: A Citizen's Guide to the Economy*. New York: Basic Books, 2000.

Spector, Robert, *Amazon.Com: Get Big Fast*. New York: HarperBusiness, 2001.

Useful websites:

www.ecommercetimes.com
News about e-business, technology, and current affairs.
www.amex.com
The American stock exchange online.
www.brint.com/interest.html
A new economy business portal.

www.firstmonday.dk/issues/issue2_7/goldhaber/
New economy news and analysis.
www.utdallas.edu/~harpham/adam.htm
A history of economic theorist Adam Smith's economic philosophy.
www.feedmag.com/invent/ledbetter.html
Site exploring the Internet economy.

The following debates in the Pro/Con series may also be of interest:

In this volume:
   Topic 13 Should governments intervene to protect consumers?

In *Media*:
   Topic 13 Will the Internet create a global culture?

WILL IT AND THE INTERNET CREATE A "NEW ECONOMY"?

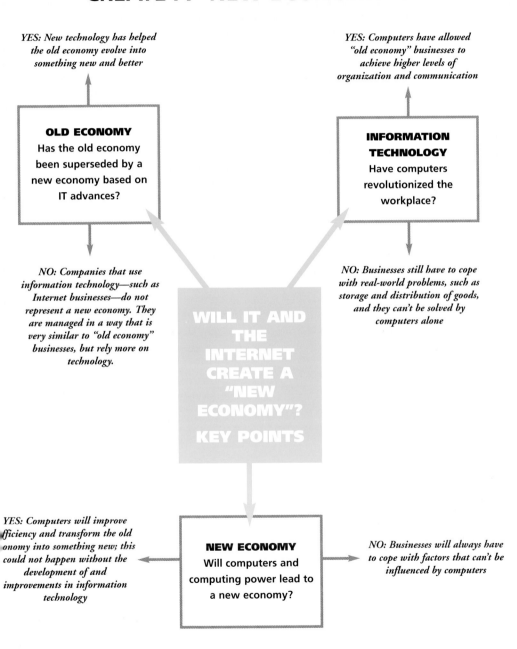

YES: New technology has helped the old economy evolve into something new and better

YES: Computers have allowed "old economy" businesses to achieve higher levels of organization and communication

OLD ECONOMY
Has the old economy been superseded by a new economy based on IT advances?

INFORMATION TECHNOLOGY
Have computers revolutionized the workplace?

NO: Companies that use information technology—such as Internet businesses—do not represent a new economy. They are managed in a way that is very similar to "old economy" businesses, but rely more on technology.

NO: Businesses still have to cope with real-world problems, such as storage and distribution of goods, and they can't be solved by computers alone

WILL IT AND THE INTERNET CREATE A "NEW ECONOMY"? KEY POINTS

YES: Computers will improve efficiency and transform the old economy into something new; this could not happen without the development of and improvements in information technology

NEW ECONOMY
Will computers and computing power lead to a new economy?

NO: Businesses will always have to cope with factors that can't be influenced by computers

ARGUMENTATION SKILLS

Argumentation is everywhere in society—in schools, courts, Congress, and in millions of essays and reports written every day. Why is argumentation important? Because it will help you develop the ability to use evidence to support an opinion through the process of reasoning. That is an invaluable skill, and one that is useful in everyday life.

Relevancy

Modern argumentation theory has its basis in Greek and Roman society, along with much philosophical, economic, mathematic, and political thought. The Greeks and Romans believed that argument was the way to define truth, allowing them to settle disputes in a reasoned and methodical way.

Argumentation allows us to examine our own and each others' ideas carefully. It enables us to weigh all the evidence, to make judgments on the nature of the material before us, and to question the methods of research and investigation, so that in the end we can come to a reasoned, objective conclusion. Argumentation allows us to treat the thoughts and views of other people with consideration and respect.

Reason, ethics, and emotion

According to Aristotle, the Greek philosopher who died in 322 B.C., a person who wants to convince someone else may appeal to the person's reason (logos), ethics (ethos), or emotion (pathos). This idea still holds true; and when writing an essay, you need to use all three to create a reasoned argument.

Reason

To win over your readers, you must intelligently present all the supporting facts and figures in a reasonable way.

- Informal reasoning requires you to link general claims with specific data.
- Inductive reasoning begins with specifics and moves to a more general conclusion. In writing, this means asking yourself if your general conclusion is valid, and if you have given your readers enough evidence to persuade them that your reasoning is sound.
- Deductive reasoning generally draws a conclusion from two or more facts.

Ethics

People must think that you are honest and have good intentions before they will believe you. If you misrepresent evidence or seek to hurt a group or individual, you will quickly alienate your audience.

Emotion

Emotional appeals must be used with restraint and discretion; otherwise they will be counterproductive, and your writing will sound exaggerated and "over the top." However, an argument that is carefully reasoned will not be hurt by a touch of pathos. Careful choice of words can add strength to a presentation.

STRUCTURING YOUR ARGUMENT

Ancient philosophers identified a number of textual elements that go to make up arguments. The various parts of an essay include: introduction, statement of the case, proposition, refutation, confirmation, digression, and conclusion.

Introduction (exordium)	Should draw your reader in. Builds common ground. Clarifies why the case is important.
Statement of case (narratio)	Gives necessary and important background information. Highlights situational context. Characterizes and defines issue in terms favorable to your viewpoint.
Proposition statement (propositio)	States your central proposition. Present it carefully. Can also set up expectations by indicating subpoints for consideration.
Refutation (refutatio)	Examines and refutes opposing arguments. Exposes bad reasoning through questioning, such as: Has all the evidence been considered?
Confirmation (confirmatio)	Develops and supports the argument with evidence, statistics, examples, and citations from experts. Argues with authority, value, and purpose. Base your appeal on reason.
Digression (digressio)	Use anecdotes (sparingly) to entertain and appeal to ethos and pathos.
Conclusion (peroration)	End with conviction. Be clear, simple, and direct.

KEY WORDS

Certain words are used to indicate the different stages of an argument. You can find examples of this type of language elsewhere in this volume.

Argument indicators:	"Should," "must," "ought," "necessarily"
Premise indicators:	"Since," "because," "for," "as," "inasmuch as," "for the reason that"
Conclusion indicators:	"Therefore," "hence," "thus," "so," "consequently"

PART 2
GOVERNMENT AND ECONOMIC POLICY

For most of the 20th century two extremes dominated the world's economies. On one hand was the free-market system of capitalist economies, in which governments intervened as little as possible in the marketplace. On the other was the planned or command economy run by communist states such as the People's Republic of China or the Soviet Union and its eastern European allies. In the second half of the century most developed nations evolved a mixed economy, combining free-market principles with a certain amount of nationalization and state welfare provision.

The conflict between the two great economic systems was effectively resolved for many observers in the years after 1989, when the collapse of the Soviet Union saw Russia and its previous allies largely embrace capitalist economic organization. The precise role of government involvement in a mixed economy is still the subject of intense political debate, however. At its heart lie two central questions: How much should government intervene in the economy, and does government intervention have any effect?

The extent of government intervention is controversial. Most states have seen rising costs for the provision of health, education, old-age pensions, and so on. Many took over state ownership of key industries such as transportation or energy production. In the 1980s, however, the governments of Ronald Reagan in the United States and Margaret Thatcher in the United Kingdom set out to "roll back" the state's role in the economy and get away from "big government." They privatized industry and sought to increase competition, efficiency, and consumer choice.

Opponents of a noninterventionist approach argued not only that government had an obligation to look after its most vulnerable citizens, but that the free market was not in fact the most efficient way to provide certain goods or services. The 1990s brought a general return to a more interventionist approach, though most governments are now wary of high levels of economic involvement.

Part of that wariness stems from political ideology, but part is also due to the fact that there seems to be little concrete evidence that government intervention achieves anything beyond relatively limited goals. Even full-scale command economies largely failed to create a more equitable society, for example, or increased living standards for their citizens. In particular, governments seem limited to seeking to ameliorate the worst effects on their citizens of recession or unemployment.

Government policy seems unable to disrupt the natural business cycle of growth and contraction that creates such problems.

Governments face new problems, however. Consumer rights, the need to protect the environment, and the phenomenon of globalization (see pages 118-129) challenge established political and economic thinking.

Topics of investigation

The topics in Part 2 discuss general and specific issues of government intervention. *Topic 5 Does Government Intervention Do More Harm Than Good?* shows the intensity of the debate. Two professional economists take virtually opposite views of the free market. Mark Skousen's assessment of health care reflects ultimate confidence in the private sector. He argues that more rather than less market freedom will benefit everyone. Robert Kuttner, on the other hand, forsees wealth distribution becoming increasingly unfair because of the erosion of the safeguards provided in a mixed economy against poverty.

Welfare state issues

Among government's range of responses to economic disparities are the provision of welfare and the imposition of a minimum wage. Two topics deal with these issues. *Topic 6 Should Welfare Be Abolished?* considers the provision of health care and social security to vulnerable citizens. It is a contentious subject. Some people believe that the existence of a welfare system encourages laziness and dependency among its beneficiaries. Others argue that the safety net it provides is the only way that society's victims have any chance to regain a better place in society. Howard Baetjer asserts that welfare should be abolished because it has not diminished poverty. An article from *The Economist* argues that welfare in the United States has virtually been abolished, and that the nonworking poor depend on government support.

Topic 7 Is the Minimum Wage Fair? considers a piece of legislation that has long been established in the United States but which other industrialized countries still resist. Requiring employers to pay a certain amount for labor lifts living standards and does not raise costs to the point that they harm businesses, argues the Economic Policy Institute. Keith Wade draws on an unlikely example—the full-employment economy of Saudi Arabia—to argue that a minimum wage takes away jobs and the self-respect of workers.

Wealth distribution

The final debate in this section asks *Should Wealth Redistribution Be Part of Government Policy?* This issue is growing in importance because, despite overall economic growth in the late 20th century, income disparities still widened in most states. In the last two decades of the 20th century statistics suggest that after inflation the average income for the poor fell and that for middle income families barely rose, while for the highest earners real income increased by over 30 percent.

Authors at the Economic Policy Institute argue that progressive taxes, in which the rich pay more, can bring more balance to this situation. Charles W. Baird, however, argues not only that the income gaps are not as large as they seem, but that "… they are both desirable and just." The poor, he concludes, have chosen to be poor.

Topic 5
DOES GOVERNMENT INTERVENTION DO MORE HARM THAN GOOD?

YES

"CORRECTION, PLEASE! THE FREE MARKET WORKS FINE, EXCEPT..."
THE FREEMAN, VOL. 44, NO. 9, SEPTEMBER 1994
MARK SKOUSEN

NO

"THE VANITY OF HUMAN MARKETS: ROBERT KUTTNER CHALLENGES THE
PREVAILING ORTHODOXY OF LAISSEZ-FAIRE ECONOMICS"
THE ATLANTIC MONTHLY, FEBRUARY 26, 1997
WEN STEPHENSON AND ROBERT KUTTNER

INTRODUCTION

The economic role of governments has long been the subject of political and economic debate. The government's role is the defining characteristic that separates planned, free market, and mixed economies. While in a planned (socialist) economy the state authorities determine prices, output, and production, in a free market these fundamental economic variables are all determined purely by market forces—that is, by the workings of supply and demand. Hence, in a planned economy the government's role is crucial in terms of what is produced and to whom that output is allocated. In a purely free market economy, on the other hand, the government's role may be limited only to the maintenance of law and order.

In reality most economies are mixed economies—neither planned nor free market, but somewhere between these two extremes. Within the mixed economy framework, however, there is an extremely variable role for government. For example, there may be a large number of state-run (public) industries, universal provision of free health care, education, and substantial welfare payments for the low-paid and the unemployed. Alternatively, the government may take a far less interventionist approach. In the United States many public institutions have been privatized, and the welfare state has been "rolled back" to such an extent that the bare minimum of benefits remain in place—Medicare (medical care, particularly for the aged), Medicaid (health care for the poor), and some welfare payments to people who agree to retraining or taking low-paid work.

The late 1990s marked at least a temporary end to the era of evangelical "neoliberalism," which opposed almost any form of government intervention in the economy. However, this noninterventionist ideology still has supporters today and certainly left a legacy of reduced state-sector provision not only in the United States, but across much of the developed world.

In the new millennium there is growing, sometimes reluctant recognition that the free-market form of capitalism advanced by Ronald Reagan and Margaret Thatcher is but one variant of state-market relations, and that European social democratic forms (often with much larger public sectors) may offer advantages in terms of less inequality and crime or an enhanced quality of life for poorer individuals.

"A government big enough to give you everything you want is a government big enough to take from you everything you have."

—GERALD R. FORD, 38TH U.S. PRESIDENT, ADDRESS TO CONGRESS, 12 AUGUST 1974

The mid-1990s article by Mark Skousen is symptomatic of the confidence placed in the market by orthodox economists and other policy analysts before the current period of revisionism. He advocates that more rather then fewer market forces are needed if quality of life and services are to be enhanced in the United States. He focuses on the political economy of health care in the United States—a highly emotional issue. Skousen is most reluctant to restrain the market, suggesting that the U.S. government is too interventionist already. He asserts

that a return to basic economics would be efficacious in all sectors of the economy:"Are medical services really that different from soap, cars, or baseball tickets?" The commitment of Mark Skousen to "market principles" such as supply and demand, non-discrimination, and accountability, seems complete, despite the problems that capitalism has faced in recent years given the complexity and diversity of the global economy and ecology. He concludes: "Imitating national health programs in Canada and Europe won't do because they violate market principles.... The solution to the so-called health care crisis is to get government out of the picture."

By contrast, Robert Kuttner suggests that modern economies need a balance between the market, the state, and civil society, in part to ensure less inequality and corruption. Being interviewed 30 months after the Skousen essay, Kuttner highlights a backlash among economists against overreliance on the market:"There's a backlash on the environment … 2,000 economists say global warming in a genuine threat and that there needs to be a world-wide regulatory scheme to deal with it or we're going to face a catastrophe. These are economists, not environmental nuts."

Kuttner expresses skepticism about the legacy of two decades of shrinking government intervention in economies and proposes a new balance between state and nonstate actors. In response to the continued faith in the market of economists such as Mark Skousen, Robert Kuttner calls for different ideas, policies, and politics:"What is the counterweight to the ideology of unfettered laissez faire? The political mobilization of ordinary people."

CORRECTION, PLEASE! THE MARKET WORKS FINE EXCEPT...
Mark Skousen

YES

> *"In health care today, fundamental principles of the marketplace do not apply. Prices are not determined by supply and demand."*
> —"America's Economic Outlaw:The U.S. Health Care System," *The New York Times*, October 26, 1993

What does the author mean by "operates with almost total disregard for ... economic principles"? Why is it that many governments provide systems such as Medicare and Medicaid, or even provide free health care, for their citizens?

I don't know why I keep picking on *The New York Times* for my column. Maybe it's because it reflects the conventional wisdom of today's policymakers, which is wrong more often than not about the basic principles of economics.

Late last year, as health care became a national issue, *The Times* ran a cover story contending that America's health care system "operates with almost total disregard for basic economic principles" and therefore deserves special treatment by government. "Prices are not determined by supply and demand or by competition among producers. Comparison shopping is impossible. Greater productivity does not lower costs."

But are medical services really that different from soap, cars, or baseball tickets? Let's go back to Economics 101 to analyze the health care debate. We shall see that, contrary to *The Times's* statement, supply and demand are working all too well in the health care industry. On the next page is a graph of supply and demand for product X.This simple graph teaches us three grand principles which, if followed, will easily explain (and resolve) the health care crisis.

Skousen wishes to demonstrate how markets for practically all goods and services, including even a special case such as health care, operate better without government intervention of any kind.

Market principle #1: supply and demand
First is the principle of supply and demand. When supply is free to adjust for changes in demand, prices move quickly toward equilibrium without creating shortages or surpluses. As demand increases, prices rise, [whereas] as supply increases, prices decline.

Why is the cost of health care rising so rapidly? Two reasons: first, increasing demand from Medicare and Medicaid, which today accounts for 65 percent of all medical expenses; second, restrictions by the American Medical

Association on the number of students admitted to medical school and limitations on what services nurses and paramedics are permitted to perform.

Market principle #2: non-discrimination

Second is the principle of non-discrimination. Note in the graph [below] that everyone tends to pay the same price for product X. No matter what your income, religious beliefs, or color of skin, you pay the same price as everyone else. Republicans and Democrats pay the same amount, Pe, for the same product. So do rich and poor, Christians and atheists, secretaries and engineers. In the free market, as customers compare prices and producers compete, price discrimination is minimized and products are universally available.

Maintaining the principle of non-discrimination in the marketplace is essential. If prices were based on income, there would be little incentive to work harder and earn more income, or for businesses to compete and shoppers to compare prices.

However, this principle is being eroded. Private insurance premiums are still the same for each participant, but an increasing share of medical costs is being borne by taxpayers based on income level. The Medicare tax is now an unlimited tax on income (2.9 percent). The Clinton health plan would make matters worse by making monthly medical insurance premiums a percentage of income, not a fixed amount.

"Price discrimination" means charging different people different prices for the same good or service. Do you think it is fair to charge rich people more than poor people for health care or education, for example?

Hillary Clinton's health care plan was proposed by the Clinton administration around the time that this article was written. It failed to be enacted into law.

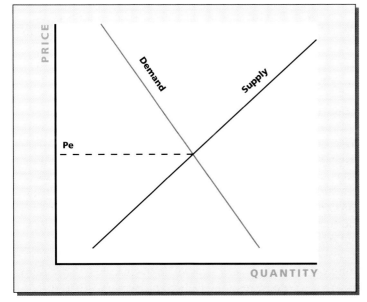

Graph showing the supply of and demand for product X.

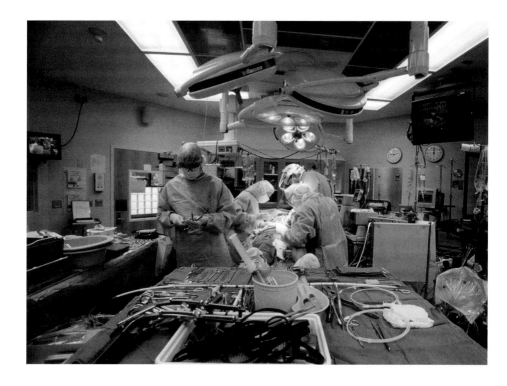

A heart bypass operation in progress. Health care in the United States is not seen as being fully accountable because people do not pay the full cost of treatment.

In addition to health care, can you think of any other goods or services for which the people who benefit do not always pay the cost, or the full cost, of what they are receiving?

Market principle #3: accountability

Third is the principle of accountability. The graph [on page 67] suggests that you, the customer, pay a specified price, Pe, for each product you buy, or for each unit of service you use. In other words, there is a direct link between beneficiaries and payers. Those who benefit from a service should pay for it. That's a cardinal principle of sound economics. If you buy one loaf of bread, you pay $1. If you buy two loaves, you pay $2.

When people don't pay for the services or products they are using, there is a tendency to overuse the benefits and less incentive to keep costs down. The connection is obvious: if you use a doctor's services, you should pay for them. If you use more, you pay more. And if you use less, you shouldn't have to pay the same amount as someone who uses more.

The principle of accountability is also disintegrating. The link between payers and beneficiaries is breaking down. In more and more cases, Medicare users are not paying the bill, taxpayers are.

Another major source of trouble is the pervasive use of employer-paid medical insurance to pay for even routine doctor visits. When employees know that someone else—the insurance company—is going to foot the bill, there is less incentive to shop around and to limit the number of visits to the doctor or the hospital's emergency room. Fortunately, the insurance companies do attempt to maintain some form of cost control on hospitals and doctor services, but the current system is less than optimal.

Who's to blame?

The author of the *Times's* article blames the market for America's health care problems, but the real cause is the government's failure to let the market operate fully. Even employer-paid medical insurance is, in a way, a government creation. High corporate taxes encourage businesses to offer a wide variety of fringe benefits, which are tax deductible to corporations and tax-free income to employees.

Contrast the health care industry with the dental industry. The dental market does not suffer from the problems facing the medical industry (spiraling costs, bureaucracy, long waits at medical facilities) largely because (1) most dental services are paid for directly by the patient, and (2) the number of dental students is not restricted. These two factors, patient accountability and expanding supply, have worked to keep the price of dental care down. Despite *The Times's* dire pronouncement, market principles do work.

How to resolve the health care problem

What should be done to improve the situation? Imitating national health programs in Canada and Europe won't do because they violate market principles. (If you want to know the weaknesses in each country's health care system, analyze each according to the three market principles). Analyzed according to these market principles, Clinton's health care plan won't work either. The cost of medical services would vary according to income, beneficiaries wouldn't pay directly for medical services, and a new federal agency would impose cost controls on drugs and other medically related services. The result would be shortages, bureaucracy, higher costs, reduced services, and less research and development.

The solution to the health care crisis is to get government out of the picture. Private insurance would be able to solve the problem … through flexible deductibles and co-payment arrangements. This would encourage competition and comparison shopping to control costs, stimulate medical advances, and encourage preventive care and exercise. The United States would then be reassured of her position as the nation with the world's best health care system.

The author is saying that government intervention, through Medicare benefits, high taxes, and so on, has distorted the health care market to the point where it can no longer work properly.

Skousen believes that everyone should take out private medical insurance. People would still have to pay a proportion of their medical bills, so maintaining a connection with the three economic principles. Do you think this is a good solution?

THE VANITY OF HUMAN MARKETS
Wen Stephenson and Robert Kuttner

NO

The author is setting the scene in terms of the economic ideology that prevailed at the time of the interview. This was a time when the first voices of dissent were being raised after some 20 years of reduced government intervention across much of the developed world.

Intervention to "temper the free market" often includes subsidized or free provision of health care and education, and the provision of unemployment and welfare payments.

… If the prevailing winds are blowing in favor of ever-expanding and freer markets, in the past few months there have been some notable gusts in other directions. The billionaire financier and philanthropist, George Soros, wrote in the February issue of *The Atlantic Monthly* that the main threat to our "open society" is no longer communism but capitalism. A … book by the journalist William Greider, *One World, Ready or Not: The Manic Logic of Global Capitalism*, warns that "Our wondrous [economic] machine … appears to be running out of control toward some sort of abyss."…

Enter Robert Kuttner, … author of *Everything For Sale: The Virtues and Limits of Markets.…* Exploring the way markets really work, he asks what are their proper boundaries and seeks "to reclaim a defensible middle ground." Kuttner recently spoke with *Atlantic* editor Wen Stephenson.

Stephenson: Central to your argument in *Everything for Sale* is a conviction that a "mixed economy"—one in which the government intervenes to temper the free market—is necessary not only for a healthy economy but also for a decent, civil society. Don't most economists … take the mixed economy for granted? Is anyone really advocating true laissez-faire economics?…

Kuttner: There has been a whole intellectual current, beginning in the 1970s, that has argued that most of what government does can be done better by the private market.… The center of gravity is much further to the right on this issue than it was twenty years ago. For example, … you've got the movement to deregulate and privatize, the feeling that when government has to intervene at all it should intervene in a market-like way. Then you've got the more extreme people who are almost absolutist libertarians. There's a book out by Charles Murray that basically says you can shut down most of the government. There's the Law and Economics movement in the law schools, which benefits from tens of millions of dollars of right wing foundation money. So there are economists and other ideologues who may not think that we can exist with no government but who do think we ought to have a "night-watchman state," where the only role of government is to protect personal security and property—and everything else you can leave up to the market....

Now, is there a backlash starting? I think there is. Let me give you some examples. First of all, the market is trying to rationalize health care through managed care. The market does that by denying people benefits to which they're entitled, by giving secret incentives to doctors who work for [Health Maintenance Organizations] HMOs, and by trying to figure out who's likely to get sick and then denying them insurance in the first place. People don't like that.

There's also a backlash against the conversion of labor markets into something that more nearly resembles a textbook model. It used to be that there was a kind of bond, a kind of implicit social compact, between the company and the individual. Today if there is somebody on the street who will do your job for 20 percent less, you're out of work unless you take the pay cut. More and more people are contingent workers—temps and part-timers. The labor market is more brutal, more like a product market. People don't like that.

There's a backlash on the environment, too. A statement out this week signed by 2,000 economists says that global warming is a genuine threat and that there needs to be a world-wide regulatory scheme to deal with it or we're going to face a catastrophe. These are economists, not environmental nuts.... The world's most astute trader of currencies, George Soros, said that he used to be worried about the communist[s] ... as the greatest threat to society, but that now he's worried about the capitalist threat....

Stephenson: In the *Atlantic* cover story you mention, George Soros makes this statement: "Wealth does accumulate in the hands of its owners, and if there is no mechanism for redistribution, the inequities can become intolerable." Do you believe that such inequities are becoming—or have already become—intolerable in the United States? How do you react to such a statement coming from someone like George Soros?

Kuttner: Clearly the division of society into more rich and more poor is the direct result of the erosion of all of the buffers that were constructed during the period when the mixed economy was thriving. We have lower rates of tax on wealthy people; we have less transfer of income to poor people; we have relatively less money going to institutions that give people what the English call social income—that is,

HMOs provide health care to members and their families within a fixed geographical area in exchange for fixed payments determined in advance.

Do you think it is fair that labor markets are increasingly flexible, like the markets for any other "product"? Or should people be treated differently to other "economic resources"?

If inequities become "intolerable" in a country, how might this become a threat to civil society?

income that you get as a citizen rather than as an employee, whether you're rich or poor. The kind of society that bolsters people against the extremes of the marketplace has been under assault for twenty years, and not surprisingly the distribution of income is more extreme than it was a generation ago. That's problem number one.

Second, in addition to the problem of income distribution there is the problem of the market's encroaching on realms that are not supposed to be marketized, like public life. You see this in the campaign-finance scandals where money thinks it can buy everything. Politics is supposed to exist in a realm different from markets, and yet in practice public office is for sale.

The third problem is the stability and efficiency of an economy that is totally marketized. I make the argument that we need to temper markets not just because of distributional extremes and not just because there are realms where markets don't properly belong, but also, and somewhat more controversially, because markets sometimes price things wrong or because markets go haywire, as in stock market crashes and depressions. You need to temper markets in order to make capitalism itself more stable and efficient....

In what economic realms might markets "not properly belong"?

Stephenson: In your estimation, is there any hope that our economy can create enough jobs on its own to move significant numbers of those currently receiving assistance from welfare to work? How does wealth redistribution fit into the picture? What, if anything, can the government do at this point, given the political realities of the moment?

For example, the Fed could cut interest rates, so making borrowing cheaper. This should have the effect of encouraging more investment in the private sector, so reducing unemployment.

Kuttner: ... First of all, the Federal Reserve can take its foot off the brake, let the economy grow faster, and let the unemployment rate in the private sector come down. Secondly, we need to recognize that a lot of people who have been on welfare are people who are difficult to make employable. Employers, not without reason, have some hesitancy in hiring former welfare recipients. People need training, people need child care. A lot of people on AFDC [Aid to Families with Dependent Children] have very disorganized lives—they have difficulty meeting the expectations of conventional jobs. It's the role of government to get these people back into the job market.

Now, on the other question—wealth redistribution—I don't think there's much support, politically, in the United States for explicit wealth redistribution, but I think there's a lot of support for implicit wealth redistribution. A very good

See Topic 8 Should wealth redistribution be part of government policy? on pages 102–113 of this volume.

example of that is Social Security. Another very good example is Medicare. If you didn't have Social Security and Medicare a lot more people would be poor. So by using the tax system you reduce poverty. But people don't think of it as redistribution. The same thing is true of public schools, and of subsidized mass transit, where you are subsidizing a service that poor people, because they don't have as much private purchasing power, would otherwise get less of.

Is taxing people who have jobs in order to pay for Social Security and Medicare for those people who do not have jobs a "good" form of government intervention?

Stephenson: Lester Thurow, reviewing William Greider's new book, *One World, Ready or Not: The Manic Logic of Global Capitalism*, in the March *Atlantic*, points to what he calls "the ideological paradox of our time." He writes, "Capitalism is myopic and cannot make the long-term social investments in education, infrastructure, and research and development that it needs for its own future survival. It needs government help to make those investments, but its own ideology won't allow it either to recognize the need for those investments or to request government help." This sounds very much like what you and others are saying right now. What, if anything, can be done to alter the prevailing ideology of unfettered laissez faire?…

In what way might capitalism be said to be destroying itself?

Kuttner: …There are a couple of ways you change minds and change policies. One is through the power of ideas and the other is through politics. What is the counterweight to the ideology of unfettered laissez faire? The political mobilization of ordinary people. It is wealthy … people, for the most part, who think that you shouldn't interfere with free markets, and it's people who are more vulnerable, who don't have the kind of security that wealth buys, who think that you need "countervailing institutions," as John Kenneth Galbraith called them. Right now there's so much cynicism about politics that ordinary people don't bother to vote. If you restore faith in the possibility of public improvement, ordinary people will start voting and you'll get a countervailing ideology that translates into new public policy.

John Kenneth Galbraith (1908–), one of the 20th century's leading economists, favored a fairly interventionist approach by governments.

Summary

The economists Skousen and Kuttner approach the issue of government intervention in the U.S. economy from very different perspectives and assumptions, leading to opposite proposals. For Skousen, who concentrates on health care provision, there is far too much government involvement in the economy. Because certain goods and services are subsidized or provided free to the low-paid and the unemployed, this results in overdemand and the inefficient use of resources. His solution is for the government to get out of the picture, leaving the provision of health care to market forces. Kuttner, by contrast, believes that the purely free-market ideology of the last two decades of the 20th century and the shrinking role of government across many traditionally state sectors have gone too far. For him governments need to devise new forms of state–private partnerships in agreed, transparent, and accountable ways to protect consumers.

FURTHER INFORMATION:

Books:

Gans, Herbert J., *The War against the Poor: The Underclass and Antipoverty Policy*. New York: Basic Books, 1996.

Shaffer, Henry G., *American Capitalism and the Changing Role of Government*. New York: Praeger Publishers, 1999.

Skocpol, Theda, Ira Katznelson, and Martin Shefter, *Social Policy in the United States*. New Jersey: Princeton University Press, 1995.

Trattner, Walter I., *From Poor Law to Welfare State: A History of Social Welfare in America*. New York: Free Press, 1999.

Useful websites:

www.theatlantic.com
The Atlantic is an online journal that publishes articles and interviews on a wide range of subjects.
www.epinet.org
The Economic Policy Institute is a nonprofit, nonpartisan think tank that seeks to broaden public debate about strategies to achieve a fair and prosperous economy in the United States.
www.libertyhaven.com
The Liberty Haven website publishes articles taken from *The Freeman*, the journal of the Foundation for Economic Education Inc., which is a broadly libertarian organization.

The following debates in the Pro/Con series may also be of interest:

In this volume:
Topic 1 Is the free market the best form of economic organization?

Topic 2 Does capitalism inevitably lead to income inequality and environmental destruction?

Topic 6 Should welfare be abolished?

Topic 7 Is the minimum wage fair?

Topic 8 Should wealth redistribution be part of government policy?

Topic 13 Should governments intervene to protect consumers?

DOES GOVERNMENT INTERVENTION DO MORE HARM THAN GOOD?

YES: A healthier, better educated population will eventually aid economic growth and development

YES: Capitalism needs government intervention to provide infrastructure, research, development, etc. But this is prevented on an ideological basis.

YES: Growing inequalities between rich and poor will eventually result in civil unrest

THE GREATER GOOD
Do free, or at least subsidized, health care and education benefit society as a whole?

CAPITALIST THREAT
Will capitalism end up destroying itself through promoting inequality and because of its non-interventionist ideology?

NO: People must be "accountable" for the benefits they receive from a good or service. People overexploit health care provision because they do not pay the full costs for its use. This is an inefficient use of resources.

NO: The markets, if left unhindered, will provide everything the economy needs to grow and prosper. The benefits of this will eventually "trickle down" to the poorer members of society.

DOES GOVERNMENT INTERVENTION DO MORE HARM THAN GOOD?
KEY POINTS

YES: Paying taxes today will probably benefit you in the future. Many women take some time off work to have children, everyone gets sick sometimes, people eventually grow old, and many will need some kind of government help.

YES: Some members of society, for example, the elderly, the sick, and single mothers, are not in a position to help themselves. The government should tax those who work so that adequate funds can be made available to these individuals.

ETHICAL CONTEXT
Is it morally right for the stronger, wealthier members of society to intervene to help the poor and the weak?

NO: Taxation of the rich to help the poor creates dependency and laziness. Tax is also a disincentive for people to work.

"REAGANOMICS"

The term "Reaganomics," named for Ronald Reagan, president of the United States from 1980 to 1988, became synonymous with the supply-side economic policies that the Reagan administration adopted. The year before Reagan entered the White House, Margaret Thatcher's Conservative government in Britain came to power and focused on similar economic policies. Such policies concentrated on reducing income taxes, promoting competition and productivity in business, and reducing government spending on social security provision and welfare.

Policies of J. M. Keynes

From the Great Depression era of the 1930s up to the late 1970s most Western governments followed a broadly Keynesian approach to economic policy making. Keynesianism arose following the publication of British economist, J. M. Keynes' book *The General Theory of Employment, Interest, and Money* in 1936. Written against a backdrop of depression and high unemployment, the work led to a general acceptance that fiscal policies—the manipulation of taxation and government spending—could be used in order to stimulate demand so as to ensure full employment without losing control of inflation. Such policies were known as "stabilization" policies. During this period it was largely accepted that markets could, and often did, fail, and that part of the government's role was to correct market failures. It was also accepted that there was a trade-off between unemployment and inflation: When unemployment increased, inflation fell, and vice versa.

The failure of Keynesianism

Following the oil crisis in the early to mid-1970s, world prices rose dramatically, and economies such as those in Europe and the United States suddenly began to experience both high rates of inflation and high unemployment. With the perceived failure of Keynesianism the free-market, classical, or laissez-faire approach to economics began to gain new popularity, particularly with the election of Margaret Thatcher's Conservative government in Britain in 1979 and Ronald Reagan's Republican administration in 1980.

Laissez-faire is a 19th-century French term meaning "let it happen" and refers to a belief in a "hands off" approach by government. Within such an approach the government's role is limited to the protection of property, maintaining a stable currency, and providing certain public goods (for example, defense and policing). Everything else—such as the problems of unemployment, inflation, and maintaining a steady economic growth rate—are left to the free markets.

In keeping with such traditional theories, Reagan and Thatcher argued that the government could not affect economic activity in the long run through boosting demand. Rather, they argued, if there was high unemployment, for example, it would eventually drive down average wage rates and lead to a reduction in labor supplies and an expansion in labor demand. Equilibrium (full employment) would eventually be restored through the operation of the market mechanism itself, so there was no need for government intervention.

Monetary policy

Another strand of this new conservatism in economic policy—a conservatism known as Reaganomics in the United States—was monetarism or supply-side economics. Proponents of such an approach believe that supply always creates demand. So, according to monetarists such as the American economist Milton Friedman, the booms and busts of the business cycle are not affected by fiscal policy but, rather, by changes in the money supply in an economy and interest rates. By controlling the amount of money in circulation and through altering interest rates (so making credit cheaper or more expensive), governments can prevent the economy overheating (booming) or falling into recession. Other supply-side economic policies adopted by Reagan focused on barriers to higher productivity. The administration argued that if government stimulated the production of goods, demand would be created, and the economy would grow.

Tax cuts and privatization

When it came to stimulating supply, Reagan's economic adviser Arthur Laffer argued that income tax rates in the United States were so high that people were working and investing less than they otherwise would. As a result, an important method of economic stimulation adopted by the administration was the reduction of income taxes. Although it was the wealthy that benefited most from this policy, it was felt that these people were more likely to invest in business, creating jobs and hence wealth elsewhere—among the more needy— later on. This is known as "trickle-down" economics. In addition, industry regulation had to be cut in order to provide incentives for businesses to boost productivity. Deregulation took place in industries such as domestic air travel and the privatization of previously state-funded (public) enterprises.

Budget deficit

However, because government revenues, at least initially, were to be reduced because of lower income taxes, the government also needed to reduce spending. Although Reagan made significant cuts in welfare, military spending nearly doubled during his years in office. Although tight monetary policy kept inflation down, recession still hit the economy. The end result was that the government continued to spend more than it received in revenues, and during Reagan's tenure in office the national debt increased from $730 billion to $2.1 trillion. The era of "Reaganomics" is today seen by most economists as a strange mixture of successes and failures—of low inflation, low taxes, and reduced government regulation, but also the deepest recession in half a century, higher levels of government spending, and a spiraling budget deficit.

Topic 6
SHOULD WELFARE BE ABOLISHED?

YES
"DOES WELFARE DIMINISH POVERTY?"
THE FREEMAN, VOL. 34, NO. 4, APRIL 1984
HOWARD BAETJER JR.

NO
"OUT OF SIGHT, OUT OF MIND"
THE ECONOMIST, MAY 18, 2000

INTRODUCTION

In every society there are groups of people who, for various reasons— whether it be their age, physical or mental disabilities, or single parenthood—find it difficult to work or to support themselves. Welfare is a formalized means by which society can support such people. In the United States welfare most commonly refers to government-funded programs that provide economic support, social services, or goods to the unemployed or underemployed. Social welfare provides a broader network of programs aimed at helping a wider range of people in society to function and live adequately. The money to support these programs comes primarily from government funds and public taxes.

The issue of welfare has always been controversial. While most developed countries have some system of welfare in place, critics argue that giving financial and social aid to people in need leads them to become dependent and lazy, and to take advantage of the system itself. Instead of being a support mechanism, welfare in this instance becomes the income for greedy people to "milk the system." Supporters of the system argue that this is far from true. In reality, the majority of people who receive aid live below the poverty line and are unable to find work because of their circumstances. Among this group are the elderly, people in care, the sick, and immigrants. A significant proportion of welfare recipients are single parents, who are unable to hold down full-time jobs because of their family commitments but cannot find adequately paid part-time work and are thus forced to accept welfare.

The basis of the modern U.S. system is rooted in the Great Depression of the 1930s. Around three-quarters of the population spent almost all of their yearly incomes on consumer goods such as food and clothing. The Social Security Act was passed in 1935 as part of Franklin D. Roosevelt's New Deal program and amended in 1939. It provided social welfare programs such as Old Age and Survivor's Insurance (OASI) for retired men and women and their families. In 1946 the Social Security Administration (SSA) was set up to oversee the provisions of the act. Several different federal agencies have overseen social security programs since 1935, including the Federal Security Agency and the Department of Health and Human Services (HHS).

In 1965 President Lyndon B. Johnson declared a war on poverty in his domestic reform program called the Great Society. He introduced Medicare, which provides medical assistance for retired people and a small percentage for the disabled. In 1995 the program cost $114.8 billion and provided for about 40 million people.

"From each according to his abilities, to each according to his needs."

—KARL MARX, FOUNDER OF MODERN SOCIALISM

Both government officials and the public have become increasingly critical of welfare programs in the last few decades, saying that they create dependency and cost too much. Since the 1960s increasing numbers of Americans have become dependent on welfare, including Aid to Families with Dependent Children (AFDC), which provided cash support to parents and children in need. Whereas in 1960 about 4 percent of children received AFDC benefits per month, in 1996 about 13 percent of all children received benefits, costing about $22 billion. There were calls for the program's reform.

In 1996 President Bill Clinton reformed the welfare system. He introduced the Personal Responsibility and Work Opportunity Reconciliation Act (PRWORA) and the Illegal Immigration Reform and Immigration Responsibility Act (IIRIRA). The AFDC was replaced by Temporary Assistance for Needy Families (TANF).

Under TANF states decide how potential recipients apply for support, and federal funds cannot be supplied to families who have been on assistance for more than five years. States supply job-training, subsidized employment, and child-care programs. Under IIRIRA almost all illegal immigrants and most legal ones who had lived and worked in the States for fewer than 10 years were denied food stamps, and states could also deny TANF, Medicaid, and other benefits. The act was heavily criticized by supporters of welfare.

The following articles agree that welfare has not diminished poverty but draw very different conclusions. In the first article Howard Baetjer Jr. argues that welfare creates inefficiency. He points to the disparity between the amount spent on welfare and the amount the poor actually receive, and argues that the money should be spent on improving employment. His case is not so much for completely abolishing welfare but for returning care of the needy to private organizations. In the second article *The Economist* agrees that the welfare system has done little to relieve U.S. poverty rates but argues for expanding the system to include more of the nonworking poor. While incentives for the poor to work have soared, it says, there are still hurdles to overcome, such as the lack of adequate public transportation and low-cost housing and the high cost of child care.

DOES WELFARE DIMINISH POVERTY?
Howard Baetjer Jr.

YES

Does government-provided poor relief decrease the amount of poverty? That it does is an assumption at the heart of our nation's very large antipoverty programs. In fact those programs were instituted for the purpose of making themselves obsolete. Shortly before passing the Social Security Act in 1935 ... Franklin Roosevelt declared to Congress, "The Federal Government must and shall quit this business of relief.... Continued dependence upon relief induces a spiritual and moral disintegration, fundamentally destructive to the national fiber...."

Does welfare ... really help solve the problem of poverty? There is good reason to believe that it does not. What is worse, there is substantial evidence that welfare impedes progress against poverty. In our country, worst of all, welfare seems to have increased poverty. What follows is a brief summary of the thinking and evidence that lead to this surprising conclusion....

Do you agree with the author's assertion that poverty is overcome only when people are self-supporting? How would you define poverty?

Three guidelines for analysis

As one considers the problem of poverty, one should keep three basic truths in mind. The first ... is ... poverty is finally overcome only when people are self-supporting.... Thus an essential objective of any antipoverty program must be to maximize self-sufficiency.

The second basic truth ... is: prosperity depends on production. Unless physical goods are produced in the first place ... there can be no prosperity for anyone.... Other things being equal, the more goods there are in the world—food, shelter, medicine, electric light, shoes, water heaters, and so on—the more there is to go around and the less poverty there will tend to be.... Thus an important means of reducing poverty is increasing production.

The third truth ... [is that] we must look beyond the immediate advantages such programs provide to welfare recipients—the food stamps, Medicaid, increased income, and the like—and see other effects of the welfare process as a whole. For example, how do welfare programs affect employment, wage rates, productivity, and prices (all of which are important to the poor)?

Let us turn to some indirect effects of welfare that we would expect to occur.

Predictable effects of welfare

A first observation is that the incentives associated with welfare tend toward unwanted results.... The benefits go to people who ... are relatively unproductive, while the funds to pay for them come, through taxation, from people who are relatively productive.... For human beings, benefits are positive incentives while taxes are negative incentives. Thus the welfare system tends to encourage unproductiveness and discourage productivity.... Accordingly welfare tends to diminish both self-sufficiency, since it leads more people to accept unemployment, and production, since the productive potential of those people is not turned into goods....

From a purely economic standpoint, we must look beyond the visible welfare benefits and compare them with other positive effects that might have occurred in the absence of welfare.... For an important example, consider that the billions of dollars that go into the welfare system are no longer available for other things—such as investment. Many dollars spent on welfare would otherwise have been invested in new tools, new buildings, and the like. This investment would have had concurrent positive effects of creating new employment opportunities and raising productivity....

A final effect of government-provided welfare ... is inefficiency and waste.... Since bureaucrats are paid out of tax revenues, which are collected regardless of whether or not the bureaucracy does a good job, there is little incentive for them to maintain high standards. Since the amount of taxpayers' money that passes through their hands depends on the size and perceived importance of their programs, the bureaucrats have an incentive to expand the numbers encompassed by those programs and to find new reasons for increased funding. Since allocation of funds must for fairness' sake be by rule, a great deal of time and paperwork gets generated, and minimal scope is allowed for individual judgment about who deserves how much....

A look at the record

Are these potential problems realized in fact? If so, how bad are they? According to the U.S. government's figures, the answers to these questions are, respectively, "yes" and "very bad indeed."

In regard to government failure, to begin with, there is a rather impressive disparity between the amount of money

This article was written in 1984, before TANF was introduced. Under TANF most recipients must work after two years on assistance (see box on page 82).

The author's point about bureaucratic inefficiency can, of course, be applied to any government bureaucracy, not just welfare.

COMMENTARY: Welfare reform in the U.S.

In 1996 a welfare reform plan was put in place that changed the welfare system into one that requires work in exchange for time-limited assistance. Temporary Assistance for Needy Families (TANF) replaced the former Aid to Families with Dependent Children (AFDC) program. TANF requires that most recipients must work after two years on assistance, and families who have received welfare assistance for five years are ineligible for cash aid. To count toward the work requirement, recipients must participate in subsidized or unsubsidized employment, on-the-job training, work experience, community service, vocational training, or provide child care to people who are in community service. Tax credits are given to employers who hire long-term welfare recipients. Single parents with a child under six who cannot find child care are not penalized for failing to meet the work requirement.

In 2000 there were about 5.76 million people receiving TANF. Although data show that overall child poverty is at its lowest level since 1979, and poverty for female-headed families is the lowest ever, there is still concern about the most disadvantaged families. Critics point out that the decline in poverty has not been as steep as the decline in the number of welfare recipients. Deep poverty—defined as income below 50 percent of the poverty level—has been growing. Very low income earners appear to be worse off without welfare. Work expenses, such as child care and transportation, mean that some families are worse off, or no better off, despite their increased earnings. Critics also point that the strong economy has aided the apparent success of the reforms—but what will happen if (or when) the economy weakens?

spent for the stated purpose of relieving poverty, and the amount the poor actually receive. In an article entitled "Where Do All the Welfare Billions Go?" (*Human Events*, February 6, 1982) M. Stanton Evans points out some remarkable figures. In 1965 combined federal, state, and local outlays for "social welfare" totaled $77 billion.... In 1978 the total was $394 billion.... But the number of poor people in the country, according to official estimates, has remained nearly constant in those years, at about 2.5 million. Here I quote Evans at length:

> *One has to wonder how it is possible to spend these hundreds of billions to alleviate poverty and still have the same number of poor people.... Waive that objection for a moment, however, and simply compare the number of poor people with the dollars spent to*

help them: You discover that, if we had taken that $317 billion annually in extra 'social welfare' spending, and given it to the poor people, we could have given each of them an annual grant of $13,000—which is an income, for a family of four, of $52,000 a year.

A long quote is useful if it helps crystallize your argument.

In other words, with this colossal sum of money, we could have made all the poor people in America rich.… It prompts the more suspicious among us to ask: What happened to the money?… [A] tremendous chunk … goes to pay the salaries of people who work for and with the federal government—including well-paid civil servants and an array of contractors and "consultants"….

But we might expect ending poverty to be expensive. The crucial question is what has happened to poverty itself. That question is partly answered in the statistic above that the number of official poor has remained at about 2.5 million; clearly poverty has not been eliminated. But what of poverty as a percentage of population—are we at least decreasing the proportion of poor people?…

Do you think that governments should or could try to reduce poverty?

The problem persists

Since 1950 the number of (official) poor as a percentage of population was approximately 30 percent. From then until 1968 the figure dropped steadily, to about 13 percent. But then … when more money than ever was being spent to decrease poverty … the trend line flattened. After ten more years, marked by ever-increasing outlays, the percentage of poor in our population had dropped only to 11 percent. Two years later, in 1980, it was back up to 13 percent again. The more we spent, the less progress we made.

In short, despite doubled and redoubled outlays to try to do away with poverty, poverty is increasing in our country. We made much better progress when we were spending less.…

From 1996 to 2000 the welfare caseload dropped by 53 percent, partly as a result of the new regulations under TANF (see box on page 82).

Quit this business of relief

In any case, welfare, the dole, poor relief—call it what you will—is a spectacular failure. More than that, if the reasoning presented here is sound, it is one of the vast tragic ironies of our age. It springs from the desire of good-hearted people to see poverty diminished, but in practice, apparently, it augments poverty.… "To quit this business of relief," to end "the days of the dole," we might well find it best simply to do it.… Do away with policies.… Let care of the really needy be returned to individual responsibility—to genuine, private charity and efficient, private organizations.

OUT OF SIGHT, OUT OF MIND
The Economist

NO

A stroll down Wacker Drive, in Chicago, offers an instant snapshot of America's surging economy. Young professionals stride along, barking orders into mobile phones. Shoppers stream toward the smart shops on Michigan Avenue. Construction cranes tower over a massive new luxury condominium building going up on the horizon....

But there is a less glamorous side to Wacker Drive, literally below the surface. Lower Wacker is the subterranean service road that runs directly beneath its sophisticated sister, allowing delivery trucks to make their way through the bowels of the city. It is also a favorite refuge for the city's homeless, many of whom sleep in cardboard encampments between the cement props. They are out of sight of all that gleams above, and largely out of mind.

Do you agree that Americans find it easy to forget the poor?

As Wacker Drive, so America. Everywhere that is visible seems to be doing well.... The typical American family increased its net worth by 18 percent between 1995 and 1998 as house prices, stocks, and wages all rose.... Welfare rolls, long taken as the most obvious indicator of the number of poor people in America, have been halved since 1996, when new federal legislation ended the automatic entitlement to welfare and obliged the poor to take jobs. "I really think people think the problem [of poverty] is solved," says Susan Mayer, a poverty expert at the University of Chicago.

If they do, they are wrong. In 1998 ... America's official poverty rate—defined as an annual income of less than $16,660 for a family of four—was 12.7 percent. That figure is not markedly lower than its peak of 15.1 percent in 1993, and still higher than it was during any year in the 1970s....

In 2000 about 41 percent of TANF recipient children were black, 29 percent were white, and 24 percent were Hispanic.

Child poverty is far higher. Almost one in five American children lives in poverty, a rate about twice as high as in the big economies of Western Europe. One in four black American families is poor, as are nearly 40 percent of black children....

Always with us

American poverty has changed dramatically in the past decades, as has the approach—and coverage—of public antipoverty policies. In the 1960s, when Lyndon Johnson declared his war on poverty, America's poor were older, more rural, and even more overwhelmingly black than they are today. Roughly 30 percent of the elderly were poor in 1966. Half of the poor lived in rural counties, particularly in the South. And four out of ten black families were poor.

Increasingly generous payments from Social Security—the public pension program set up by Roosevelt in 1935—have made dramatic inroads into poverty among the old. Today only one elderly American in ten is poor. Progress in civil rights, migration to the cities, and, more recently, large-scale inward investment have reduced rural poverty, especially in the South…. Instead, 43 percent of the poor live in city centers. In short, today's poor are younger and more urban than they were a generation ago.

Single-parent families

Most striking, however, has been the concentration of poverty in families headed by single women. Such families are the largest and fastest-growing segment of the poor, making up over half of all poor families in 1998, compared with 21 percent in 1960….The breakdown in the traditional two-parent family does much to account for America's current poverty. Just over 30 percent of American children now live in single-parent families….

So are "the poor," as most Americans suppose, mainly single mothers on welfare? Until the mid-1990s this supposition was correct. Many poor families were headed by single women who did not work, relying instead on federal welfare payments. That has now changed. America's welfare regime was dramatically overhauled in the late 1990s; today recipients must work and no one can spend more than five years on welfare. The level and availability of public assistance for the nonworking poor have fallen sharply.

At the same time, public assistance for the working poor has soared. David Ellwood of Harvard University points out that changes in the law since 1984 have increased funds available to low-income working families almost tenfold, from less than $6 billion in 1984 to more than $50 billion in 1999. About half this rise comes from the Earned Income Tax Credit (EITC). Introduced in 1975 and expanded three times since then, this refundable tax credit tops up the earnings of poor Americans….

Public health insurance for the poorest (Medicaid) has also expanded greatly. Medicaid used to be limited mainly to those on welfare. Now states have to provide coverage for all poor children. Add in other new federal programs, such as tax credits for child care and a general child tax credit—as well

In 2000 more mothers than ever were working, and the average income of female-headed families was increasing. However, in general, single mothers are low skilled and will be the first to lose their jobs in a recession.

as vastly increased spending by the states on the working poor—and it is clear that incentives for the poor to work have multiplied....

Why they fail

Unsurprisingly, these changed incentives have altered the pattern of poverty. More than 60 percent of poor families have at least one person in the labor force some of the time. Yet despite the recent rise in wages across the board, and despite the massive rise in federal assistance, many poor single wage-earners have still not been able to lift their families out of poverty.

One obvious reason is low wages.... Single mothers, who are disproportionately low-skilled, face a triple disadvantage: they have only one worker, they earn low wages, and they pay all the costs of raising a child....

Economists attribute most of the stagnation in the wages of the low-skilled to rapid technological change, which has increased the demand for ... skilled workers and has made life harder for those without skills. Tougher competition from abroad, weaker unions, and a minimum wage that ... is much lower now in real terms than it was two decades ago have made a difference too....

But low wages may have less effect on poverty than the fact that the poor are not working full-time. Despite the boom, and despite the government's incentives, only 13 percent of poor adults worked full-time in 1998....

The poor and paid work

Does the cause of poverty affect whether the government should try to help the poor?

Why don't the poor work more? Some may not be able to. Not everyone can get or hold down a job, even in a booming economy. A stroll among the panhandlers of Wacker Drive shows that many of them suffer from mental illness, disability, or drug or alcohol abuse. Studies of welfare reform in the States show a similar picture: there is a hard-core group of mothers who are simply incapable of keeping a job, often because of substance abuse. Unfortunately, although alcoholism or drug addiction make people incapable of working, they do not qualify them for public assistance. The seriously mentally ill are eligible to receive both cash and medical treatment, but many are unable or unwilling to seek the benefits to which they are entitled....

The author's point here is that many people are falling through the welfare net because they cannot work.

For others, the constraints are less visible.... One long-term cost of America's love affair with incarceration will be a growing number of ex-convicts with even slimmer chances of finding a job than they had before they went to prison.

The second big hurdle is the logistics, and costs, involved in working.... Throughout America, the fastest job growth has been in the suburbs; but low-skilled workers now tend to live in cities.... Public transport rarely connects the two.

The chronic shortage of affordable housing exacerbates this problem. There is very little cheap housing in the suburbs where the jobs are. Worse, there is an increasing shortage of any cheap housing at all. Since the 1970s the number of low-income renters has increased by over two-thirds, while the number of low-cost rentals has fallen. This is partly the result of government policy; Congress drastically reduced the amount of money it appropriated for low-income housing in the 1990s, and has only recently begun to increase it. It is also a side-effect of a booming economy. As rents have risen across America, landlords are increasingly tempted to gentrify their low-income properties. At the least, a lack of affordable housing implies a long commute for the working poor. At worst, it means homelessness, which makes full-time work even harder....

Another huge constraint is the cost and availability of child care. In surveys, by far the most frequent reason unmarried women give for not working is that they are "taking care of home or family".... Since the federal child-care tax credit is not refundable, it does little for those who do not earn enough to pay federal income tax. According to [economist Isabell] Sawhill, over 1.5 million Americans live in working families that are poor because they have to pay for child care.

How could changes in policies such as transportation help the situation of the poor?

Figures from the Department of Health and Human Services reveal that families with annual incomes under $14,400 who paid for care for children under five spent 25 percent of their income on child care, compared with 6 percent for families with incomes of $54,000 or more.

Poverty traps

Even if these hurdles are overcome, another arises. Public incentives, such as the EITC, are phased out as incomes rise. Some women who successfully leave welfare for work find that, beyond a certain point, work does not pay. A woman earning as little as $10,000 can face a marginal tax rate of 100 percent as federal and state taxes kick in and benefits such as Medicaid and the EITC disappear....

Obstacles like these ... do much to explain why poverty has not fallen further in this boom. Another, more troubling, reason is that many poor families are not getting the public assistance to which they are legally entitled. Participation in food-stamp programs has fallen much faster than the poverty rate. As a result, only 40 percent of working poor families eligible for food stamps actually receive them, and only about one-third of children eligible for Medicaid benefits get them. This is because poor families, once they are off welfare, are less visible and less tied in to public-assistance programs.

Summary

The two articles here present very different views about welfare. In the first article, "Does Welfare Diminish Poverty?" Howard Baetjer Jr. argues that far from reducing poverty, government-provided poor relief actually increases it and that welfare is "a spectacular failure." He argues that poverty is only overcome when people are self-supporting and that an important way of reducing poverty is to increase production instead of wasting money on the bureaucracy necessary to keep the welfare system in place. Money spent on welfare could be spent on investment, which would create employment and raise productivity, he says.

In the second article, "Out of Sight, Out of Mind," *The Economist* argues for an expansion of the current system to help more of the nonworking poor. While incentives for the poor to work have multiplied, and welfare for the working poor has soared, there are still many hurdles to overcome in finding, and keeping, a job, and welfare for the nonworking poor has fallen sharply since the late 1990s. In many ways welfare has already been abolished. TANF has led to a situation in which people leaving welfare for work often have to survive on lower incomes. Thus welfare has become more necessary than before. The key map on the opposite page sums up the main points in this debate.

FURTHER INFORMATION:

Books:

Bane, Mary Jo, and David T. Ellwood, *Welfare Realities: From Rhetoric to Reform.* Cambridge, MA: Harvard University Press, 1996.

Bryner, Gary C. *Politics and Public Morality: The Great American Welfare Reform Debate.* New York: W. W. Norton & Company, 1998.

Articles:

Haskins, Ron, Isabel Sawhill, and Kent Weaver, "Welfare Reform." Welfare Reform and Beyond policy brief, Brookings Institution, January 2001.

Useful websites:

www.acf.dhhs.gov

Administration for Children and Families, Department of Health and Human Services website.

www.welfareinfo.org

Welfare Information Network website.

www.brook.edu

Brookings Institution website.

www.economist.com

Features articles on international welfare systems.

The following debates in the Pro/Con series may also be of interest:

In this volume:

Topic 2 Does capitalism inevitably lead to income inequality and environmental destruction?

Topic 7 Is the minimum wage fair?

Topic 8 Should wealth redistribution be part of government policy?

SHOULD WELFARE BE ABOLISHED?

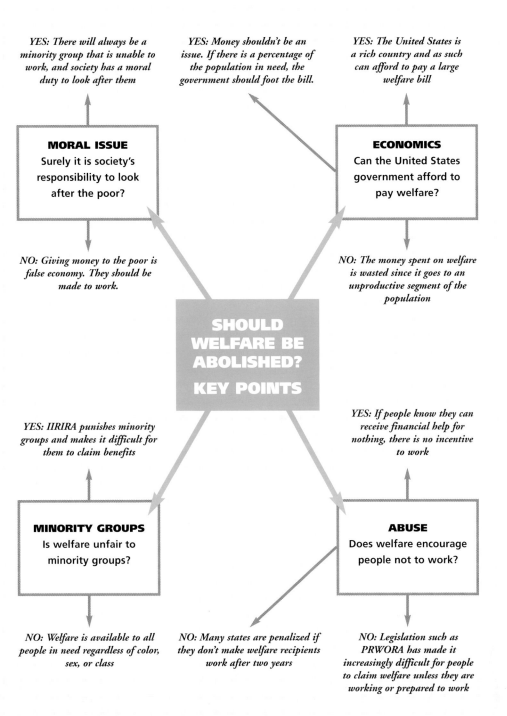

YES: There will always be a minority group that is unable to work, and society has a moral duty to look after them

YES: Money shouldn't be an issue. If there is a percentage of the population in need, the government should foot the bill.

YES: The United States is a rich country and as such can afford to pay a large welfare bill

MORAL ISSUE
Surely it is society's responsibility to look after the poor?

ECONOMICS
Can the United States government afford to pay welfare?

NO: Giving money to the poor is false economy. They should be made to work.

NO: The money spent on welfare is wasted since it goes to an unproductive segment of the population

SHOULD WELFARE BE ABOLISHED?

KEY POINTS

YES: IIRIRA punishes minority groups and makes it difficult for them to claim benefits

YES: If people know they can receive financial help for nothing, there is no incentive to work

MINORITY GROUPS
Is welfare unfair to minority groups?

ABUSE
Does welfare encourage people not to work?

NO: Welfare is available to all people in need regardless of color, sex, or class

NO: Many states are penalized if they don't make welfare recipients work after two years

NO: Legislation such as PRWORA has made it increasingly difficult for people to claim welfare unless they are working or prepared to work

Topic 7
IS THE MINIMUM WAGE FAIR?

YES
"THE NEXT STEP: THE NEW MINIMUM WAGE PROPOSALS AND THE OLD OPPOSITION"
THE ECONOMIC POLICY INSTITUTE, ISSUE BRIEF 130B, MARCH 8, 2000
JARED BERNSTEIN AND CHAUNA BROCHT

NO
"FULL EMPLOYMENT—A LESSON FROM THE DESERTS OF SAUDI ARABIA"
THE FREEMAN, VOL. 45, NO. 2, FEBRUARY 1995
KEITH WADE

INTRODUCTION

"Thomas Jefferson once said, in matters of principle stand like a rock."
—Bill Clinton, 42nd U.S. president, on the minimum wage

While approximately 76 to 80 percent of people in the United States apparently support a minimum wage, it remains a subject of debate. Its advocates argue that a minimum wage is essential for counteracting low wages and exploitative labor practices, and that it would help those sectors of the society that need it most—women, minorities, and the nation's poor. Proponents argue that a large percentage of workers in the United States, including the unskilled, single parents, immigrants, and women, work under exploitative conditions and earn wages that place them below the poverty line. These are the people that would benefit from a minimum wage.

However, not everyone agrees with this principle, and the cost of labor has always been an emotionally charged

issue. Those against the minimum wage say that the market price of an individual's labor—his or her wage—should be determined by supply and demand for that particular work. All things being equal, the more skilled the work is, the higher the labor cost will be, and vice versa. Employers attempt to purchase an individual's skills for the lowest or most competitive price possible, and the employee in return searches for the highest possible wage in the market. Those who are against the minimum wage believe it is a hindrance to this exchange between employer and employee, and that it actually deters people from employing unskilled or inexperienced workers.

Opponents go on to argue that far from helping the majority of low-wage workers, a minimum wage only helps a small minority and places the least experienced, least productive, and poorest workers at a disadvantage by pricing them out of the labor market.

So what is the history behind the minimum wage? It was introduced in

1938 by President Franklin D. Roosevelt as part of the New Deal Program. The wage—introduced by the Fair Labor Standards Act (FLSA)—was intended to alleviate the stress and poverty caused by the Great Depression and to encourage economic recovery.

The minimum wage has subsequently risen since the 1930s, and its supporters have included presidents Truman, Eisenhower, Kennedy, Johnson, Nixon, Carter, Bush, and Clinton. In real terms it reached its peak in 1968, when it was worth $6.92 in 1998 dollars. In the 1970s its value decreased, despite several increases, because of rapid inflation; and it deteriorated significantly in the 1980s, when there were no increases under the administration of Ronald Reagan.

"America's robust economy has created more than two million jobs since October 1996. Corporate profits and earnings will help to ensure that the lowest-paid Americans also share in this prosperity."

—ALEXIS M. HERMAN, SECRETARY OF LABOR

In 1991 it increased to $4.24 per hour, but remained at that level for five years. By 1996 around 10 million U.S. workers were earning between $4.25 and $5.14 per hour. Under President Clinton the federal minimum wage increased to $5.15 per hour on September 1, 1997 (Labor Day). By January 1, 2001, most states had a minimum wage policy; the exceptions included Alabama, Arizona, Florida, Louisiana, Mississippi, South Carolina, and Tennessee.

With this brief overview in mind, the argument for or against the minimum wage can now be better addressed. In the first of the following articles Jared Bernstein and Chauna Brocht argue for an increase in the minimum wage, since they believe that it would benefit the lowest-paid workers in society. The authors claim that around 10.3 million workers (8.7 percent of the workforce) would receive an increase in their hourly wage rate if the minimum wage were raised to $6.15. Since these workers earn, on average, $5.69 per hour, the average hourly increase would, they say, be no higher than $0.46. They argue that the "job-loss effect" would be either small or nonexistent. Ultimately, they believe that the benefits of a hike far outweigh the costs.

In the second article Keith Wade argues against this stance. In "Full Employment: A Lesson from the Deserts of Saudi Arabia" he outlines his belief that the minimum wage deters employers from employing unskilled or inexperienced workers. He uses the case of Saudi Arabia, which has a "hands-off" labor policy, to illustrate that when a contract is between the employer and employee, they are free to negotiate the terms and conditions of employment as they so wish. Wade therefore concludes that the minimum wage laws should be abolished, since they worsen the problem they are meant to solve.

THE NEXT STEP
Jared Bernstein and Chauna Brocht

YES

March 2000 saw further discussion by Congress over whether to increase the federal minimum wage from $5.15 to $6.15. The proposal by Rep. David Bonior (D-Mich.) would increase the minimum wage to $6.15 by 2001, while the proposal by Rep. Rick Lazio (R-N.Y.) would increase it to the same level by 2002.

How does this proposed increase fit with previous hikes in the minimum wage? Figure 1 (graft from the Economic Policy Institute) shows the inflation-adjusted minimum wage from 1955 to 2003 (projected). The figure clearly shows the sharp decline in the minimum wage over the 1980s, when Congress failed to adjust the wage floor for nine years. Even with the recent increases in the 1990s, the inflation-adjusted minimum is 21 percent lower today than in 1979.

Find out more about the decision to freeze the minimum wage in the 1980s at www.zmag.org/zmag/articles/sept94 mercier.htm.

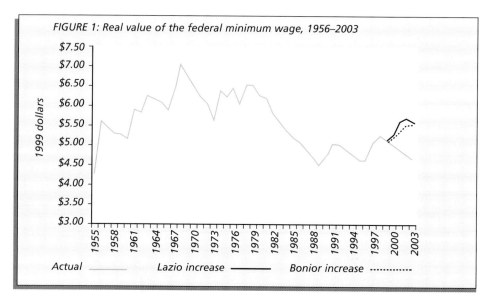

FIGURE 1: Real value of the federal minimum wage, 1956–2003

Actual ——— Lazio increase ——— Bonior increase ·············

The lines at the end of the figure show the impact of the new proposals. Without another increase, the real value of the minimum wage would fall to $4.67 (1999 dollars) by the year 2003 (according to inflation projections by the Congressional Budget Office). By 2003 the proposed increases would restore the wage floor to slightly above its 1983 level, still leaving it 15 percent below its 1979 peak.

Workers would initially see larger gains under the Bonior bill, which is phased in over two years, in comparison to the Lazio bill, which is phased in over three years. A full-time, year-round worker would gain an additional $1,000 over the course of three years under Rep. Bonior's proposal relative to the gains under the Lazio bill. By 2003 the Lazio proposal "catches up" to that of Bonior, leaving the minimum wage at $6.15 under both plans.

Who would be affected by the increase?

Around 10.3 million workers (8.7 percent of the workforce) would receive an increase in their hourly wage rate if the minimum wage were raised to $6.15. Since these workers earn, on average, $5.69 per hour, the average hourly increase would be $0.46.

Most of those workers directly affected by the increase in the minimum wage are female (59.7 percent), and 70.8 percent are adults (age 20 or older). Close to half (48.0 percent) work full time, and about another third (31.8 percent) work between 20 and 34 hours per week.

A disproportionate share of minorities would be affected by an increase in the minimum wage. While African Americans represent 11.7 percent of the overall workforce, they represent 15.7 percent of those affected by an increase; similarly, 10.8 percent of the total workforce is Hispanic, compared to 19.2 percent of those that would be affected by the minimum wage increase.

Minimum wage workers are concentrated in the retail trade industry and [are] underrepresented in the higher-paying manufacturing sector. An analysis by occupation reveals that those affected by the increase are concentrated in female-dominated occupations such as cashiers and food preparation. Minimum-wage workers are also the least likely group of workers to be represented by unions.

Various studies have found that, due to so-called "spillover effects," the group earning just above the minimum (perhaps as much as a dollar above) also benefits from the increase. Workers in this group … are more likely to be older (84.3 percent are adults) and to work more hours (65.4 percent are full time) than those in the directly affected range.

State-level results

As expected, states with lower wage levels, such as those in the Southern region, have larger-than-average shares of

For more information on David Bonior and his policies see www.cnn.com/US/ 9805/06/ minimum.wage/.

Why do women earn substantially less than men? Find out more at www.laborresearch. org/dis.shtml? paygap.txt.

For more information on the spillover effect see www.crfa. ca/sarlo.htm.

workers affected by the increase. In Louisiana (17.3 percent), West Virginia (15.3 percent), Arkansas (14.3 percent), and Mississippi (13.7 percent), relatively large shares of the workforce would be expected to benefit from the increase. Some Western states, such as Montana (14.5 percent), Wyoming (12.0 percent), and New Mexico (12.2 percent), also have relatively large shares of workers that would be affected by the proposed increase.

Higher-wage states, such as those in the Northeast and some in the West, typically have higher-wage levels and thus fewer workers affected by an increase in the minimum. In Colorado, for example, 4.8 percent of the workforce would benefit from the increase. Furthermore, some states have set minimum wage levels above the federal level, resulting in a smaller share of workers affected by the proposals. For instance, in Oregon, no workers will be affected by the current federal proposals to go up to $6.15 because the minimum wage in that state is currently $6.50.

Will the proposed increase cause job losses?

Opponents of minimum wage increases frequently argue that the policy is misguided, since it prices low-wage workers out of the labor market, forcing employers to lay them off after the increase takes effect. This claim has been carefully studied by labor economists interested in testing the actual impact of increases in the minimum wage among low-wage workers. This research, summarized in Bernstein and Schmitt (1998), has generally found the job-loss effect to be either small or nonexistent. The estimates from this literature unequivocally show that the benefits of minimum wage increases to low-wage workers and their families far outweigh the costs.

Why was the minimum wage increased at this time? To find out, see www.dol.gov/dol/esa/public/minwage/q-a.htm.

The most recent increase in the minimum wage—the $0.90 increase phased in over the 1996 to 1997 period—is a case in point. The study noted above examined the short-term effects of the increase and found that the policy had its intended effect—it raised the wages of low-wage workers from low-income families without leading to job losses.

Lack of evidence

However, many critics of the last increase argued that the negative effects take a few years to materialize. If so, the current low-wage labor market should certainly be providing this evidence. Yet, month after month, low-wage and minority workers post historic employment gains. In recent months, the unemployment rates of African Americans, Hispanics, and 16-to-24-year-olds (who are likely to be low-wage earners) all hit 30-year lows. Similarly, the employment rate of young (16–25-year-old) African American women with a high school degree increased by 7.8 percentage points in 1995 to 1999, and their unemployment rate fell by 6.4 percentage points. These gains are much larger than the average changes in these labor market indicators.

This last group (young minority females with high school degrees) is especially relevant in light of welfare reform, which has required many of these women to move from the welfare rolls and into the job market. Due to welfare reform and the growing economy, welfare caseloads have fallen precipitously since 1996, a trend that coincided with the most recent minimum wage increase.

Find out more about racial discrimination in the labor market at aspe.hhs.gov/hsp/lwlm99/holzer.htm.

Victims of wage increase?

The relevant question is whether the increase has made it more difficult for these women to find work. If this were the case, we would expect the growth in their employment rates to have been dampened by the wage increase. However, the data show that, even with the 1996 to 1997 minimum wage increase, the employment rates of single mothers, after stagnating for many years, rose steeply from 62 percent in 1995 to 71 percent by 1999. Of course, not all single mothers were on welfare, but among those who were, employment rates grew from 40 percent in 1995 to 56 percent in 1998, by far the highest level on record. Finally, Lazere (1998) presents direct evidence that, in Oregon, the increase in the minimum wage was associated with higher wages for former welfare recipients.

For more information about single mothers and social welfare see www.hec.ohio-state.edu/famlife/bulletin/volume.1/bull14b.htm.

Earning a fair share

Obviously, these dramatic improvements in the labor market conditions of historically disadvantaged groups stem largely from the tight labor market. But it is equally obvious that the last increase in the minimum wage did not prevent these gains from occurring. To the contrary, the last increase made sure that once they got to the labor market, low-wage workers would reap some of the benefits of the growing economy. Since then, the economy has continued to grow, but inflation has eroded the real value of the minimum wage. The proposed increase to $6.15 in 2001 would help ensure that those at the low end of the wage scale and those moving from welfare to work will continue to experience their fair share of the growth.

FULL EMPLOYMENT
Keith Wade

The United States has an unemployment problem.
While there are people out of work in every
segment of the population, the low-skilled worker has been
disproportionately out-placed. As the minimum wage rises
and guaranteed employer-subsidized health care looms
ominously on the horizon, more and more companies are
deciding that giving the teenager his or her first break is just
not worth it. The minimum wage has choked the life out of
many small businesses, forced many people who genuinely
want to work for a living onto the welfare rolls, and driven
up the cost of goods and services. The true minimum wage
is not $4.50; the true minimum wage is nothing at all!

Do you see any signs that this is true for you and your friends?

The pretty politics of compassion have convoluted and
obscured a simple fact of life—each individual has a unique
set of skills that have a certain value. The fact that some of
these skill sets cannot command the minimum wage is also
unavoidable. While the United States through its minimum
wage law has undertaken to make these unfortunate
individuals paupers, other nations have allowed these people
to work with dignity, resulting in positive results for the
worker, the employee, the consumer, and society at large.

Wages freely negotiated

As one of the 30,000 American professionals living and
working in Saudi Arabia, some of the economics of the Arab
world initially confounded me. A liter of water costs roughly
five times as much as a liter of gasoline.... Because most of
the markets are allowed to clear and prices are largely a
matter of negotiating between storekeeper and shopper,
pricing seems odd to the newcomer. The labor market is
no different. With every Saudi national who wants to work
guaranteed a job, there are still enough jobs to entice tens of
thousands of foreigners to flock to Saudi Arabia and find jobs
in a pay range from a few thousand dollars a year to hundreds
of thousands.

Do you think this kind of labor system suits everyone? What happens to a person who has no skills or qualifications and cannot find an employer?

The Saudi government has effectively separated wages from
the other elements of employment. The policy regarding
wages is "hands off;" wages are an issue between employee
and employer. Along with this policy, however, are a number

of exceptionally effective safeguards. Everyone working in Saudi Arabia has a contract that the employer is obligated to fulfil. Labor courts are quick and efficient…. So while the employee and employer are free to negotiate terms and conditions of employment, the "exploitation of workers" that we have been so long told would occur without government meddling just does not happen. The contract—as it once was in the United States—is law.

Employers, realizing the investment that they have in their workers (airfare, housing, paid leave), generally treat them like the valuable resource they are. Eliminating the minimum wage does not mean eliminating fairness or safety….

Saudi Arabian labor laws can be better understood by having a broader social and cultural knowledge of the country. Find out more at www.cia.gov/cia/publications/factbook/.

Clearing the labor market

The labor market in Saudi Arabia has been allowed to find its cost and has cleared. Those who opposed NAFTA were terrified that the borders would be overrun with people … seeking employment in the United States. These nay-sayers would do well to look at Saudi Arabia as an example of what happens when that occurs, for indeed a large part of the workforce here is foreign. Hundreds of thousands of workers have poured into Saudi Arabia (which is effectively impossible to enter without a guarantee by an employer of employment and return travel home). And these hundreds of thousands of workers have taken jobs ranging from senior managers to tea boy (women generally do not work outside of the professions of teaching and nursing) to ditch digger. In addition, all of the local inhabitants who wish to work have jobs ranging from senior manager … to goat-herder.

Why do you think that women in Saudi Arabia do not work outside of the teaching and nursing professions? Do you think that this is fair?

Because there is no interference with wages, each of these individuals is able to earn a living—something that they might not otherwise be able to do were the price for their labor set artificially high…. Large companies pay people to tear up confidential documents by hand as opposed to investing in paper shredders; many … merchants have at least one young man to bring tea to their customers; the … grocery store … (has) delivery boys to bring the shopper's packages home. Indeed—unlike the situation in the United States where the artificially high wages mandated by the minimum-wage law have driven millions out of the labor market and onto the welfare rolls—even someone with very meager skills, no education, and no ability to communicate in the local language, can get a job.

Whatever happened to shepherds in the United States? They found themselves priced out of the market. Barbed wire is cheap—no American farmer could afford to pay someone

Workers in Saudi Arabia, such as these market stallholders, are likely to suffer low wages because the government views wages as an issue between the employer and employee.

minimum wage to lean on a stick and watch a flock of sheep. Between the minimum wage, Social Security, FICA (etc.) … the cost is prohibitive. Consequently, people who would be perfectly content to watch sheep for a few dollars per day, read their philosophy books under the trees, and generally be happy with their lot are not allowed to do so. These people have been effectively made wards of the state by the highhandedness of the minimum wage laws….

Do you think Wade's example is a good one? Why else might shepherds no longer exist in the United States?

Everyone has a job

Without government interference the system is simple— everyone earns what he is worth and no one need worry about not being able to get a job…. In the United States we would purchase a paper shredder. We … do this … (because) it is cheaper to buy a paper shredder than it is to pay someone to tear papers to shreds. The U.S. government will not let us pay someone $100 per month to shred papers…. As a result, those members of society who can do nothing more valuable than tear up paper are unemployed and a burden on society.

Do you think that a social security system encourages people to accept handouts rather than look for work?

A simple rule that the supporters of the minimum wage law seemed to forget is that certain tasks are worth only so much. Consequently, parking lots are swept in Saudi Arabia and not in the United States for a very important reason— the U.S. government would make a criminal out of the store owner who gave someone $2.00 to sweep his parking lot….

All of society benefits from this natural clearing of the labor market. Obviously the worker benefits by being able to provide subsistence for their family by working as opposed to begging. Society benefits by not having to funnel its limited resources to supporting those who cannot command the minimum wage. Merchants benefit by being able to offer a variety of benefits that would be cost prohibitive in the United States—a coffee service to shoppers, a freshly swept parking lot, messengers, and a host of other services….

Wade's basic assumption is that any job is better than no job. Do you agree? And how might those who end up with the worst and cheapest jobs feel?

The United States should abolish minimum wage laws; they worsen the problem they were invoked to solve. There is an important lesson to be learned here—it is more dignified to allow people to work for less than a minimum wage than to force them to be paupers as a result of a high handed interpretation of what a minimum wage should be. It is better for society to have people happily working for less than minimum wage than to have these people forced into becoming ungrateful and involuntary wards of the state. It is better for the consumer to buy goods that are made with realistically priced labor than with artificially high-cost labor. And it is possible to accomplish all of these things.

Summary

The question of whether a minimum wage is fair is a difficult one that has elicited much debate over the years. Jared Bernstein and Chauna Brocht in "The Next Step: The New Minimum Wage Proposals and the Old Opposition" claim that there is no real evidence to show that a minimum wage results in job losses. With this in mind, they claim that there is no reason to deny financial assistance to those who most need it: minority groups that would otherwise not be able to earn a living. In their opinion the minimum wage does far more good than harm.

Keith Wade makes an alternative argument. He asserts that: "Employers, realizing the investment that they have in their workers generally treat them like the valuable resource they are. Eliminating the minimum wage does not mean eliminating fairness or safety." He argues that this practice creates a society of paupers, which is far less dignified than allowing people to work for less than what the minimum wage is perceived to be.

FURTHER INFORMATION:

Books:

Bernstein, Jared, *Making Work Pay: The Impact of the 1996-97 Minimum Wage Increase.* Washington, D.C.: Economic Policy Institute, 1998.
Ehrenreich, Barbara, *Nickel and Dimed: On (Not) Getting By in America.* New York: Metropolitan Books, 2001.
Gregory, Mary, Wiemer Salverda, and Stephen Bazen, (editors), *Labour Market Inequalities: Problems and Policies of Low-Wage Employment in International Perspective.* Oxford: Oxford University Press, 2000.
Kosters, Marvin H. (editor), *The Effects of Minimum Wage on Employment.* Washington, D.C.: AEI Press, 1996.
Levin-Waldman, Oren M., *The Case of the Minimum Wage: Competing Policy Models.* New York: State University of New York Press, 2001.
Nordlund, Willis J., *The Quest for a Living Wage.* Westport, CT: Greenwood Publishing Group, 1997.
Waltman, Jerold L., *The Politics of the Minimum Wage.* Champaign, IL: University of Illinois Press, 2000.

Useful websites:

www.dol.gov/dol/esa/public/minwage/main.htm
Historical overview of the minimum wage and minimum wage increases.
www.econ.umn.edu/~matheson/minwage1.html
A case for the minimum wage.
www.heritage.org/library/backgrounder/bg1162.html
A case against the minimum wage.
www.dol.gov/dol/esa/public/minwage/america.htm
Details of where minimum wage laws apply in U.S. states.
www.esc20.net/etprojects/formats/webquests/summer99/northside/Economics/default.html
Campaign to raise the minimum wage.
www.dismal.com/top25/t25_minimum.stm
An overview of both sides of the debate.
www.consumer.gov/endpoverty
Website dedicated to ending poverty in America.

The following debates in the Pro/Con series may also be of interest:

In this volume:

Topic 5 Does government intervention do more harm than good?

Topic 8 Should wealth redistribution be part of government policy?

IS THE MINIMUM WAGE FAIR?

YES: *As labor costs rise, they affect the general costs of production. Large businesses can absorb the rising costs, but small businesses often go out of business.*

YES: *It discourages employers who don't want to eat into their profit margin and thus exacerbates unemployment*

EMPLOYERS
Does the minimum wage discourage employers from employing low-paid workers?

SMALL BUSINESSES
Does the minimum wage work to the detriment of small businesses?

NO: *Recent studies have shown that it has very little effect since firms still need the workers in order to provide their goods and services*

NO: *It can work to their advantage since it puts them on an equal standing with larger businesses when competing for labor*

IS THE MINIMUM WAGE FAIR?
KEY POINTS

YES: *It allows unskilled workers to earn a decent, competitive wage in a dignified manner, while acquiring work experience*

EXPLOITATION
Does the minimum wage help stop the exploitation of low-wage workers?

NO: *Wages are only one way in which employers can potentially exploit their staff*

NO: *The minimum wage gives employers a legal right to exploit their workers by paying them a low wage for their work instead of a natural market level*

Topic 8
SHOULD WEALTH REDISTRIBUTION BE PART OF GOVERNMENT POLICY?

YES

"PULLING APART: A STATE-BY-STATE ANALYSIS OF INCOME TRENDS"
ECONOMIC POLICY INSTITUTE STUDY, JANUARY 2000
JARED BERNSTEIN, ELIZABETH C. MCNICHOL, LAWRENCE MISHEL, AND ROBERT ZAHRADNIK

NO

"PULLING US APART"
THE FREEMAN, VOL. 50, NO. 5, MAY 2000
CHARLES W. BAIRD

INTRODUCTION

Most governments in the world today practice some degree of wealth redistribution. Many raise more taxes from the richer members of society and spend some of the money to subsidize or support services such as free schooling or cheaper health care, or to provide monetary support in the form of welfare payments for the sick or the unemployed. Other nations have tried to improve the lot of the poor by enforcing minimum wage legislation.

Although wealth redistribution may be commonplace, it is by no means an inevitable part of politics. The classical laws of economics, as established by the 17th century economist Adam Smith, do not see the role of an economy as trying to achieve a more equitable balance between rich and poor. Smith's view of the free market argues that an economy functions most efficiently when factors such as production costs, output, and wages are determined only by market forces. In other words, prices and wages are set by demand for, and supply of, particular goods, services, labor skills, and so on. In the process some people become richer than others, while others lose out. Poverty is an incentive for the poor to get a better education, or move, or change jobs.

Smith's view dominated western society in the 18th and 19th centuries. Extremes of wealth and poverty were inevitable. In the latter part of the 19th century such an attitude was reinforced by the emergence of Social Darwinism. It applied to society the law of survival of the fittest put forward by the English naturalist Charles Darwin. In Darwin's view those species best adapted to their environment survived and reproduced, while those that were weaker became less dominant and eventually became extinct. As applied to society, Darwinism suggested that the existence of stronger and weaker citizens was not only inevitable but desirable. The stronger—the wealthy, powerful, or members of political élites—should not feel guilty about the weaker—workers, the sick, and servants. They were simply obeying natural laws and demonstrating their natural superiority. It was their job, however, to support the poor through providing jobs or through charitable donations and actions.

"We have to ask the wealthiest Americans to pay their fair share again. Their incomes went up in the 1980s and their taxes went down."

—BILL CLINTON,

42ND U.S. PRESIDENT

People have always argued against the unfair distribution of wealth. Early groups such as the Levellers in 17th century England proposed that private property should be abolished in favor of communal ownership. In the 19th century the grim conditions in the Industrial Revolution convinced more people that wealth redistribution was essential, both because it was moral and because it was economically efficient, encouraging the poor to buy more goods, and thus encourage industry.

Karl Marx and Friedrich Engels, in their 1848 book *The Communist Manifesto*, argued that the overthrow of the capitalist system would eventually come through violent revolution. During the 20th century a number of economies adopted a Marxist approach. In communist China, the Soviet Union, and other countries the government ran the entire economy in order, in theory, to produce a fairer distribution of wealth. Although these so-called planned economies often succeeded in getting rid of the most visible extremes of wealth, they did not necessarily improve the conditions of the poor.

In the western world, meanwhile, governments adopted a mixed economy in which they left much economic activity in private hands but were responsible for parts of it: running vital industries, for example, and creating welfare systems.

Pioneered in Scandinavia and other parts of northern Europe in the decades following World War II, welfare states endeavored to provide a safety net for the poor. Money raised through progressive taxation—in which the wealthy pay proportionately more— funded hospitals, dentist clinics, unemployment benefits, and public housing. Many such plans have proved highly successful and beneficial for their citizens, though others have been bitterly criticized as inefficient, expensive, and unfair in their own way. Progressive taxation, some people argue, discourages initiative and incentives to work hard.

In the first of these two articles the Economic Policy Institute describes how the gap between rich and poor is growing throughout the United States as the better off benefit more from economic prosperity. The paper argues that state governments should use labor market policies and progressive tax systems to address the disparities. Charles W. Baird, responding to the paper, argues that its authors are mistaken in their data and their conclusions. Gaps in income are inevitable and just, and are the results of economic choice.

PULLING APART
Jared Bernstein, Elizabeth C. McNichol, Lawrence Mishel, and Robert Zahradnik

Despite the strong economic growth and tight labor markets of recent years, income disparities in most states are significantly greater in the late 1990s than they were during the 1980s. The average income of the lowest-income families grew by less than one percent from the late 1980s to the late 1990s, a statistically insignificant amount. The average real income of middle income families grew by less than two percent, while the average real income of high income families grew by 15 percent.

What is the difference between average income and the average real income? Which do you think is more significant in the article's context?

The small growth in the incomes of low-income families over the last decade was not enough to make up for the decline in incomes during the previous decade. Nationwide, from the late 1970s to the late 1990s, the average income of the lowest-income families fell by over six percent after adjustment for inflation, and the average real income of the middle fifth of families grew by about five percent. By contrast, the average real income of the highest-income fifth of families increased by over 30 percent.

The authors commence their report using data from the late '70s, '80s, and '90s to illustrate how income disparities are growing in the United States. Do you think this use of statistics is effective?

The trend has been widespread. Income disparities between the top fifth of families and families at the bottom and the middle of the income distribution grew substantially in almost every state over the past two decades....

Widening gap between rich and poor

The resulting disparities between the incomes of high- and low-income families are substantial.

- In the United States ... the poorest 20 percent of families had an average income of $12,990 in the late 1990s, while the average income of families in the top 20 percent ... was $137,490, or more than 10 times as large....
- In the late 1970s, there was no state where high income families had average income that was ... 9.5 times larger than the average income of low-income families. By the late 1990s, 24 states had "top-to-bottom" ratios of 9.5 or greater....

The gaps between the incomes of high-income families and middle-income families also were not always as large as they are in the 1990s....

Prosperity not shared equally

The long-term trend toward increasing inequality has continued over the past decade, despite the economic growth of recent years. In only a handful of states was progress made toward reducing income inequality between the late 1980s and the late 1990s.

● … In two-thirds of the states, the gap in incomes between the top 20 percent of families and the bottom 10 percent of families grew between the late 1980s and the late 1990s. In 15 states, the average income of families in the bottom fifth … fell while the incomes of those in the top fifth grew.

● By contrast, the gap in income between the top 20 percent of families and the bottom 20 percent narrowed significantly in only three states.…

Families in the middle of the income distribution have [also] fallen farther behind upper-income families in most states over the past decade.…

Causes of rising inequality

Researchers have identified several factors that have contributed to the large and growing income gaps in most states. The growth of income inequality is primarily due to the growth in wage inequality. Wages at the bottom and middle of the wage scale have been stagnant or have declined over the last two decades. The wages of the very highest paid employees, however, have grown significantly.

Several factors have contributed to increasing wage inequality including globalization, the decline of manufacturing jobs and the expansion of low-wage service jobs, immigration, and the weakening of labor market institutions, the lower real value of the minimum wage, and fewer and weaker unions.…

In the last few years, persistent low unemployment, an increase in the minimum wage, and fast productivity growth have fueled real wage gains at the bottom. As a result, there has been a lessening of wage inequality at the bottom while the gap between middle- and high-wage workers continues to grow. However, even the recent wage growth for low-wage workers has not been sufficient to counteract the two-decade long pattern of stagnant or declining wages.

Besides wages, the other major source of income is investment income—[for example,] dividends, rent, interest, and capital gains. Since investment income primarily accrues to those at the top of the income structure, recent expansions of investment income have led to [even] greater income inequality.…

Free-market economists believe that wealth "trickles down" to the less well-off members of society during periods of economic growth. As the rich open more businesses and spend more money, everybody benefits.

Why might globalization—the shifting of domestic economic activity to other parts of the world—cause wage inequality?

A dividend is the amount of a corporation's profits that is distributed to shareholders. Capital gains are the increase in value of a capital asset, such as when a share is sold for more than it cost.

Another factor that explains some of the increased income inequality is the increase in the number of families headed by a single person. These families generally have lower income than two-earner families.

Role of government

Deregulation refers to a reduction of government control, most commonly over business activity. Trade liberalization, on the other hand, means the lifting of trade barriers—for example, tariffs and quotas on imports.

Government policies—both what governments have done and what they have not done—have contributed to the increase in wage and income inequality over the past two decades in most states. For instance, deregulation and trade liberalization, the weakening of the social safety net, the failure to have effective labor laws regulating the right to collective bargaining, and a minimum wage that has declined in real terms, have all contributed to growing wage inequality. In addition, changes in federal, state, and local tax structures and benefit programs have, in many cases, accelerated rather than moderated the trend toward growing inequality emerging from the labor market.

States can choose a different course

One consequence of the nation's prolonged economic recovery is that tax revenue has been growing at a faster rate than originally projected in most states, leaving states with surplus revenues. The strong economy also has played a part in reducing public assistance caseloads in many states. As a result, the current economic expansions provide state budgetmakers with the resources to mitigate some of the growing inequality through state policies.

During periods of high economic growth do you think policies to "mitigate ... growing inequality" are a valid use of taxpayers' money?

States have long played a major role in the establishment of labor market policies such as rules governing the formation of unions, the design of the unemployment insurance system, and the establishment of state minimum wages, all of which affect income inequality.

Minimum wage and social safety nets

The minimum wage, for example, has a direct bearing on individual earnings. The value of the federal minimum wage has fallen considerably since the late 1970s. One way that policymakers could help reverse or moderate the decline in wages for workers at the bottom of the pay scale would be to enact a higher minimum wage....

Since the 1970s, unemployment insurance protection has eroded as a result of both federal and state-level cutbacks. The proportion of jobless workers receiving unemployment insurance benefits has declined in recent years. These cutbacks have affected both middle- and low-income families.

Efforts to strengthen the unemployment insurance system ... are warranted in order to broaden the receipt of unemployment insurance among unemployed workers.

Changes in programs that provide assistance to low-income families have contributed to the increase in income inequality.... In the typical state, cash assistance benefits for a family of three with no other income fell 40 percent between 1975 and 1996, after adjusting for inflation....

There are a host of options state policymakers can consider to strengthen their social safety nets including the provision of supportive services such as transportation, child care, and health insurance coverage to low-wage workers. States can also provide intensive case management and a range of services to help current and former welfare recipients to maintain their present employment, move into better jobs, or obtain the education and training....

Regressive taxes

While the federal tax system as a whole remains progressive, nearly all state tax systems are regressive. States rely more on regressive sales taxes and user fees than on progressive income taxes and, therefore, take a larger percentage of income from low- and middle-income families than from the wealthy. In the past few years, when many states have sought to cut taxes, nearly all have chosen to make the majority of the cuts in the progressive income taxes, rendering their tax systems even more regressive.

Sales tax and user fees are regressive because everyone pays the same level of tax regardless of their income. This means that the poor are paying proportionately more of their income than the rich in these cases.

In order to narrow the gap between high- and low-income families, states can institute tax reforms that are progressive in nature and improve the after-tax distribution of income....

State policies constitute only one of a range of factors that have contributed to the increasing disparities in incomes over the past decade. If low- and middle-income families are to stop receiving steadily smaller shares of the income pie, state [and] federal policies will have to play an important role.

Do you think it is important that state and federal government address these increasing income disparities between low- and middle-income and high-income families?

PULLING US APART
Charles W. Baird

NO

Recently, two Washington, D.C., think tanks—the Economic Policy Institute and the Center on Budget and Policy Priorities—issued a study of the income gap between rich and poor American families titled "Pulling Apart." According to the authors, by the late 1990s average income among families in the top 20 percent (top quintile) of the income distribution was $137,500, while that of families in the bottom quintile was only $13,000—a gap factor exceeding ten. In nine states the gap factor exceeded 11, and since the late 1970s the income gap increased in 46 states.

The author lists the Economic Policy Institute's reasons for growing income inequality, but words them slightly differently. How does this lend strength to his argument?

The authors attribute the gaps to such factors as the growing importance of skilled labor relative to unskilled labor; the increasing value of higher education; the decline of low-skilled manufacturing employment; increased immigration; the stock market boom, which disproportionately benefits higher income people; and declining unionization. Except for the latter, all those factors have, indeed, affected the "distribution" of income.

The authors imply the gaps are unjust, and they propose remedies: "Through policies such as raising the minimum wage, strengthening unemployment insurance, implementing a wide range of supports for low-income working families, and reforming regressive state tax systems, state and federal lawmakers can help moderate the growing income divide."

Baird introduces the main points he disagrees with before proceeding to address them in detail.

There are at least three things wrong with this study. First, its authors have overstated the size of the gaps. Second, they ignore the fact that families and individuals move from quintile to quintile. Finally, gaps, no matter how large, if they are the result of voluntary exchange, are no cause for alarm. They are both desirable and just.

Exaggeration of gaps

The authors based their work on pre-tax data from the Census Bureau's Current Population Survey (CPS). In September 1999 the Heritage Foundation published a study that shows that CPS data systematically overstate income gaps. For example, in 1997, according to CPS data, families in the top quintile received 49.4 percent of total household income, while those in the bottom received only 3.6 percent.

When the data are corrected to take into account the effect of taxes, government subsidies, and capital gains, the two figures are 45.3 and 5.6 percent respectively. When the data are further adjusted to put an equal number of people, rather than families, in each quintile, the numbers are 39.7 and 9.4 percent, respectively. Therefore, all the gaps in "Pulling Apart" are exaggerated.

Are these changes to the CPS statistics justified? Do you think the revised figures give a more accurate picture?

Movement between quintiles

A quintile distribution of income is a snapshot of family income at a point in time. Suppose that the 1990 distribution indicates the top quintile received 50 percent and the bottom quintile 6 percent of total income, and that the 1999 distribution shows the same. This does not mean that the people in the bottom or top quintile in 1990 are still in the bottom or top quintile in 1999. Some people in the bottom in 1990 will have moved up to higher quintiles, even the top, by 1999. Similarly, some people in the top quintile in 1990 will have moved down to lower quintiles, even the bottom, by 1999. An unchanging quintile distribution is perfectly consistent with some poor getting richer and some rich getting poorer. A study reported by the Federal Reserve Bank of Dallas indicates that 29 percent of the families in the lowest quintile in 1975 had moved to the top quintile in 1991. Only 5.1 percent of those in the bottom in 1975 remained there in 1991. In a free-market economy there is constant movement—quintile distributions mean very little.

If families regularly move between quintiles, does this make the statistics giving quintile distributions meaningless, as the author suggests?

Hooray for gaps

The very term "income distribution" implies that there is a given total lump of income that belongs to everybody that must be divided up by some authority. But in a market economy, income is created by voluntary exchange between people. Each individual owns the income he creates. The distribution (use) of his income is for him to decide. Abstracting from sheer luck, in an economy based on voluntary exchange there is only one way to create income: giving other people opportunities to make themselves better off by agreeing to exchange with you. It is desirable for those who serve others well to have higher incomes than those who don't, because those differences provide incentives for people to try to serve others as best they can....

In the job market, for example, you can agree to exchange your labor and skills for a wage or a salary. If you are a producer, you agree to exchange your products for an agreed sum of money.

If you choose your occupation on the basis of what you like to do without regard to what other people are willing to pay you to do, you may end up happy but poor. I like to sing. But no one is willing to pay me to sing. So I talk and write for

COMMENTARY: Friedrich Hayek

Professor Friedrich A. Hayek (1899–1992) was one of the foremost defenders of the free market.

Friedrich A. Hayek, who won the Nobel prize for economic science in 1974, was one of the best-known defenders of the free-market and classical liberal economics of the 20th century. Born in Vienna, Austria, Hayek published 130 articles and 25 books, including his most famous work, the *Road to Serfdom*, in 1944.

In particular Hayek is remembered as one of the foremost opponents of the new theories of John Maynard Keynes in pre-World War II Britain. Keynes advocated government intervention in the economy to manage aggregate demand so as to maintain full employment. Hayek's criticism was that he failed to understand and take full account of interest rates and capital structure in his theories. However, Keynes' book *The General Theory of Employment, Interest, and Money* (1936), went on to become one of the most influential works on economic policy of the time.

During this period Hayek was also involved in debates regarding the problems of socialism. He believed that only a free market could coordinate an efficient allocation of resources to the production of goods and services. In a free market the price mechanism conveys information about supply and demand, and disperses this information to consumers and producers. In Hayek's view such information cannot be efficiently coordinated in any other way, for example, by planning mechanisms in a socialist economy. Hayek's critique of planned economies was that central planners would have no market prices to serve as guides and hence would have no way of telling which production possibilities were feasible.

Similarly, Hayek criticized any government intervention or planning that sought to redress the income balance between the rich and the poor. For the government to impose an income distribution different from the one that naturally emerges in a free market would be inefficient. Hayek also argued that those people who would rise to the top of a socialist regime would be those who were skilled at exercising discretionary power and who would be liable to run the system to their own advantage. That has political implications for income distribution.

a living. If I chose to sing for a living I would be justly poor. My poverty would give me no legally enforceable moral claim to the incomes earned by other people. I would have chosen to be poor.

Baird uses a striking personal analogy to make his point. But does his conclusion fit the story? Would it apply in every case?

Savers versus spendthrifts

Some people choose to save and invest part of the income they create. In doing so, they provide the means for entrepreneurs to undertake new ventures, create new products, and provide new employment and purchase opportunities for people. Other people consume most of their incomes. Savers and investors are likely to accumulate assets that will generate more income for them than the spendthrifts will have. Yet spendthrifts have no legally enforceable moral claim on the incomes of savers and investors. The authors of the study may want to grant people who make poor choices an enforceable claim to the incomes of people who make better choices, but there are no moral grounds to do so. Of course, anyone is free to redistribute his own income, but no one has a moral right to redistribute incomes created by other people without their consent.

Whose equality?

Jefferson proclaimed that it is "self-evident that all men are created equal." He meant that all people have the same natural rights and that a just government is one that enforces them equally for all people. It is also self-evident that all people are not created equal in terms of mental and physical abilities, alertness, attitudes, and other human attributes. In a market economy those natural differences inevitably result in different people creating different amounts of income and wealth. As Hayek [*see* box, left] pointed out, for government to impose an income distribution different from the one that emerges spontaneously in the market, government has to "treat unequal people unequally." Governments impose income distributions by taking from some people and giving to others. The victims of the takings are treated one way by government, and the recipients of the takings are treated another way. If a government wants to impose a more equal income distribution to mitigate the effects of natural human inequalities, it must discard Jefferson's principle that a just government must treat all people equally under the law. We have already gone far down that road, and it has already pulled us apart. The authors would have us go further. Like socialists around the world, they think there is never enough coercive redistribution.

The author is implying that it is unfair to take from the (deserving) rich to give to the (undeserving) poor. Do you think he is correct?

111

Summary

The authors of the influential Economic Policy Institute study "Pulling Apart" begin by analyzing economic trends in the United States in the 1990s. In a decade of prosperity the incomes of low-income families rose more slowly than those of high-income families. The result was to increase inequality in wages, a consequence encouraged by the policies of federal government, including deregulation and the failure to impose effective labor laws. State governments, the authors conclude, can do much to try to rectify the inequality. They can alter the labor market through policies on labor unions, unemployment insurance, and minimum wages; they can improve social security by providing services such as transportation and child care; and they can impose progressive taxes in which the rich pay more.

Charles W. Baird rejects the study altogether. Its data are wrong, he says, and the authors underestimate the constant movement in U.S. society as poorer families become better off. Above all, Baird argues, the gap between rich and poor is both desirable and just. Prosperity benefits all citizens; those who remain poor have, to some extent, chosen to be poor through various decisions about their jobs. Wealth redistribution also penalizes those who save and invest their money. The whole idea of redistribution, he concludes, is based on a misinterpretation of the idea of the equality of all humans. All people have the same natural rights, but this does not mean that they should all be the same—or that they should receive the same rewards.

FURTHER INFORMATION:

Books:

Collins, Chuck, and Felice Yeskel, *Economic Apartheid in America: A Primer on Economic Inequality and Security*. New York: New Press, 2000.

Haseler, Stephen, *The Super-Rich: The Unjust New World of Global Capitalism*. New York: Palgrave, 2000.

Sen, Amartya, and James E. Foster, *On Economic Inequality*. Oxford: Clarendon Press, 1997.

Shaffer, Harry G., *American Capitalism and the Changing Role of Government*. Westwood, CT: Praeger, 1999.

Useful websites:

www.epinet.org
The Economic Policy Institute is a nonprofit think tank that seeks to broaden public debate about strategies to achieve a fair and prosperous U.S. economy.
www.libertyhaven.com
The Liberty Haven website publishes articles from *The Freeman*, a broadly libertarian journal.

The following debates in the Pro/Con series may also be of interest:

In this volume:

Topic 1 Is the free market the best form of economic organization?

Topic 2 Does capitalism inevitably lead to income inequality and environmental destruction?

Topic 5 Does government intervention do more harm than good?

SHOULD WEALTH REDISTRIBUTION BE PART OF GOVERNMENT POLICY?

YES: *If people do not receive payments when out of work, they are more likely to take on any gainful employment they can find*

YES: *If people see that a large proportion of their income is going to the government for welfare payments, this acts as a disincentive to work*

INCENTIVES
Do income inequality and poverty act as incentives to make people work harder?

DISINCENTIVES
Does tax act as a disincentive to hard work?

NO: *Many people, such as the elderly, the sick, and mothers of young children, are not in a position to take on work and must receive welfare payments*

NO: *Tax rates have to be very high before they have any noticeable effect on people's motivation to take on employment and work hard*

SHOULD WEALTH REDISTRIBUTION BE PART OF GOVERNMENT POLICY?

KEY POINTS

YES: *Most people are poor because they have not studied or trained for jobs that pay well, or because they choose not to take the jobs that are available or to which they are best suited*

YES: *People who work hard, save, and invest deserve the wealth they accumulate*

UNDESERVING POOR
Do people deserve to be poor because of bad choices in life and work?

DESERVING RICH
Do the rich deserve their wealth?

NO: *People living in poor neighborhoods often do not have access to the necessary training, education, and other opportunities that will lead to employment*

NO: *People often become wealthy through having access to opportunities others do not have. It is fair that a proportion of that wealth should go to help those who are less fortunate.*

STOCK AND FINANCIAL MARKETS

In 1987 a stock market crash in New York and London led many economists and political commentators to believe that global economic collapse was imminent. Again in the late 1990s currency and stock market collapses in Southeast Asia, Russia, and Brazil seemed to threaten major economic imbalance and catastrophe. In fact no such economic collapse occurred—on a global scale at least—in either case.

"Money itself isn't lost or made, it's simply transferred from one perception to another."

—GORDON GEKKO IN *WALL STREET*, 1987

Barometers or catalysts?

Are the stock and financial markets merely barometers of what is going on in economies worldwide? Or are the markets themselves—prone as they are to speculators and the instant transfer of billions of dollars into and out of a particular firm's stock or a particular country's currency—the cause of major international destabilization? Commentators such as George Soros, the financier-turned-philanthropist, predict that the role of the financial markets will eventually be the cause of the fall of global capitalism itself.

Stock markets

A stock market has two parts: The primary market is for new stocks (shares) that are being issued by companies to raise funding, while the secondary market is for shares that have already been issued and are owned by investors. Ownership of stocks or shares denotes ownership of a part of the business that originally issued them. While payment for new stocks on the primary market goes to the company itself—to be used to expand its operations, say—payment for stocks on the secondary market simply causes the stocks to change ownership.

The size of the secondary market, in particular, is growing. At the end of 1998 U.S. households owned some $8.8 trillion in stocks and shares—although this was often through mutual funds that make large-scale investments using the small contributions of many individuals. That was around four times what was owned in 1990, much of the boost having come from the rapid expansion of the Internet and Internet dealing.

New breed of investor

Between 1965 and 1990 the number of Americans who owned stock increased from 10 to 20 percent of the population. This then doubled again, to 43 percent, by 1997. Many of these people are investors who are using the Internet to buy and sell shares. Often they have little experience and do not seek advice from professionals, hoping to "get rich quick" by buying the stocks of a company at a low price then selling them at a large profit. For example, investors may gamble that a stock price is low because the firm in question is currently performing badly but that this poor performance is only temporary, and the firm is likely to see an upturn in its fortunes in the future.

While increasing investment in stocks and shares has resulted in businesses being able to find more money for expansion and growth, some economists and others are concerned that it represents a high-risk form of investment for many people. During the 1960s and '70s investors preferred to invest in assets such as real estate rather than shares. Investors today may be setting themselves up to lose a lot of money should stock prices fall into a general decline.

Futures trading

Such speculation on the stock market is similar to futures trading, whereby an investor stakes his or her money on something that they believe will become more or less valuable on a specified date in the future.

The first futures market began in the United States in the 19th century. It was based on wheat, pork, and other commodities that people bought in advance at a fixed price. Investors gambled that by the time these commodities were ready for the market, the price would have risen, and they would make a profit.

Futures trading today is based on both commodities and money. Financial futures began with foreign exchange—investors would buy or sell Japanese yen, for example, gambling that the exchange rate for the currency would increase or decrease by some specified date. Although some investors trade in futures in order to speculate on the movement of money markets to make a profit, others do so in order to protect themselves from changes in the price in the future.

Self-fulfilling prophesies

A characteristic of both stock and financial markets is that investors may actually cause events by thinking something is going to happen. For example, if people start to buy shares in a particular firm, others may follow suit and buy shares in the same firm themselves. That drives the firm's share price up. Likewise, if many investors decide to sell, that may have the opposite effect. A similar effect can be seen with the financial markets. George Soros and others worry that the destabilization of whole countries might result from such speculative swings. This effect was seen in East Asia between 1990 and 1995, when a "speculative boom" in economic growth in the region was followed by the swift withdrawal of funds from local businesses and currencies, which precipitated major destablilization in the region.

PART 3
TRADE AND GLOBAL ECONOMICS

Trade lies at the heart of economics and is traditionally not one of the areas of most economic controversy. However, after 1999 regular clashes between protesters and police marked the meetings of the World Trade Organization (WTO) and other international bodies concerned with shaping global economic development. There are numerous issues behind these clashes, including some that are domestic rather than international; but they all crystallize in the idea of globalization. That is the name given to the phenomenon whereby the world's national economies seem to be growing more closely linked. Partly it is the result of technology, and partly it reflects the way in which the world's industrialized nations seek to find new sources of materials, new markets for their products, and cheaper locations for their operations.

Closely connected with globalization is the issue of free trade. International bodies largely encourage free trade. Numerous regional arrangements, such as the North American Free Trade Agreement (NAFTA), the European Union (EU), and Asia Pacific— as well as the World Trade Organization itself—are results of a tendency away from economic isolationism and protectionism toward the opposite, integration and liberalization.

Since the start of classical economics with Adam Smith in the 18th century some economists have argued that all international trade should be free of restrictions in the form of tariffs or quotas. Smith and his followers, such as David Ricardo, argued that unrestricted international trade benefited all nations. It allowed them to concentrate on those economic activities in which they enjoyed some advantage—raw materials, suitable setting, worker expertise—and trade the results with other countries that specialized in different sectors.

At the same time, however, other economists and some politicians supported a policy of protectionism. As its name suggests, the purpose behind the policy was to protect the domestic economy. By restricting imports from other countries or imposing taxes that raised their prices, governments sought to ensure that domestic consumers bought domestic goods. Not only would that protect jobs; it also prevented the country's financial reserves being sent abroad in return for goods. In the 17th and 18th centuries this was a central part of an influential economic policy called mercantilism.

In the continuing debate on free trade versus protectionism both approaches have their critics. Free trade, some people argue, allows richer countries to exploit poorer ones. Meanwhile, for all the apparent common sense that lies behind protectionism, it has rarely worked. On one occasion, when the United States introduced the Smoot-Hawley Tariff in 1930—against the opposition of more than 1,000 economists—it helped produce a global depression. The tariff increased import duties by an average of 60 percent. More than 60 of the United States' trading partners retaliated with even higher duties, and world trade declined.

Global economics

This section of the book introduces some of the debates at the heart of international trade in the 21st century. It highlights not just attitudes toward global trade but also the ways in which international considerations affect U.S. economic policy and influence the economic fortunes of its citizens.

Topic 9 Is Globalization Inevitable? addresses the issue of globalization. It does not ask directly whether globalization is good or bad, but instead concentrates on whether anything can be done to halt the phenomenon. The report of a panel brought together by *Time* magazine is optimistic that free trade at a local and global level is the best way to bring economic growth. Leading antiglobalization commentator Naomi Klein, however, reporting on the World Social Forum, held at Porto Alegre in Brazil, discusses ways in which local democratic initiatives can resist the forces of globalization.

Economic protectionism

Topic 10 Are Protectionist Trade Policies Ever a Good Idea? considers this traditional debate in the context of current trends toward globalization. In a candid overview Steven Suranovic supports protectionism by reference to NAFTA. By contrast, the prestigious but free-trade British magazine *The Economist* argues a more traditional case that protectionism is bad for economic growth. It suggests that the international trend toward antidumping cases constitutes a covert form of creeping protectionism.

WTO justification

A key player in international economics is the World Trade Organization. Set up as a forum to promote free trade among nations, it has been bitterly criticized as a tool of the richest economies. *Topic 12 Is the WTO Fair to Poor Countries?* presents the arguments the WTO itself uses to counter such accusations. Its critics misunderstand its purpose and its standing, it argues. George P. Brockway dismisses such claims and seeks alternatives to globalization, like Naomi Klein, in initiatives to increase local democracy.

Topic 13 addresses one of the most high-profile issues in international economics, *Should Rich Countries Cancel "Third World Debt"?* Many of the world's poorer nations are deep in debt to governments, banks, or international finance organizations. They incurred the costs during a period of improving their infrastructures, encouraged by lenders, but are now unable to repay the loans and are often crippled by the interest incurred. Jubilee 2000 puts the case for canceling the debt. It was instrumental in raising awareness of the issue in the late 1990s, after which western governments agreed to cancel some of the debt. The opposing piece argues that international loans must be repaid. If they are not, the global economic system will break down.

Topic 9
IS GLOBALIZATION INEVITABLE?

YES

"FORUM ON THE FUTURE: A TIME PANEL AGREES THAT THE FTAA IS THE BEST BET FOR
REGALVANIZING THE HEMISPHERE"
TIME, APRIL 19, 2001
GEORGE RUSSELL

NO

"A FETE FOR THE END OF THE END OF HISTORY"
THE NATION, MARCH 19, 2001
NAOMI KLEIN

INTRODUCTION

The meetings of such international bodies as the World Trade Organization and the G8, the world's leading industrial nations, have become the occasion for tens of thousands of citizens to gather to protest what they see as problems in the world economy. Their targets range from abolishing Third World debt to improving women's rights, but their chief target is summed up in one word: globalization.

Globalization is one of the most controversial issues in economics. At its most basic the term refers to the tendency for economic and cultural influence to spread from one country to others. It reflects the spread of multinational corporations throughout the world and the dominance of western, particularly American, culture. Opponents of globalization predict a nightmare world in which main streets have the same stores all over the globe; in which local economies are pushed aside by multinationals; in which everyone listens to the same music and watches the same TV shows, so that much regional culture dies out; and in which large corporations are beyond the influence of national governments and far more powerful in people's lives. Above all, these opponents argue, globalization allows the developed world to exploit poorer countries but without giving those countries the possibility of growing wealthy.

Supporters of globalization argue that its effects can be highly beneficial. The advance of communications and computer technology—on both of which the phenomenon of globalization rests—will result in the disappearance of national boundaries. The developing world will be able to share in the knowledge and prosperity of the western world; and far from being forces of oppression, multinationals can be forces for good. Consumer pressure on companies to behave in ethical ways will lead to corporations helping raise working conditions and minimum wages for people in countries where they would otherwise live in poverty. They point to documented success stories, such as the remarkable rise of the Indian computer sector, to show that developing countries can achieve prosperity as a result of being involved in the global marketplace.

It remains to be seen whether globalization will be a positive or negative force in world economics. About the only thing that both sides agree on is that it is happening now. But is it inevitable?

"There's no society that's able to withstand commercial western culture....
But that's going to be the challenge now, whether democracy is going to be up to it."
—RALPH NADER,
CONSUMER ADVOCATE

Some economists argue that globalization is inherent in the idea of the marketplace. In general terms businesses create goods and services as efficiently as possible and try to sell them for as much profit as they can. In ancient times merchants traded goods over thousands of miles, introducing silk from China and Japan into markets in Europe, for example. Later, European nations established colonies throughout America, Asia, and Africa, seeking cheaper raw materials and markets.

When transportation, computing, and telecommunications allowed businesses in the late 20th century to set up international operations, relocating their factories to take advantage of cheaper labor and materials, the corporations involved were simply acting as businesses act. The result might be lost jobs in developed countries but also cheaper prices for consumers— and higher profits for corporations.

As for the dominance of western companies worldwide, some people assert that, again, it is inevitable. The laws of supply and demand that underlie classical economics argue that such businesses exist only because consumers want what they sell. In this reading, customer demand fuels globalization; the phenomenon is an inescapable part of capitalism in a developing world.

Those people who want to stop globalization do not see it as inevitable. They look on it as the artificial creation of the corporations and governments of developed countries. They point to the role of international bodies in protecting the ability of the richest countries to gain influence in poorer countries, largely by forcing those countries to allow free trade. In this view it is the economic might of the developed world that powers globalization. Markets are successfully generated by marketing products in societies that neither need nor can really afford them.

In the first article economists on a panel enlisted by *Time* magazine discuss a limited example of globalization, the creation of a Free Trade Area of the Americas. They conclude that it will bring economic growth in the region, even among the poorest. Naomi Klein sees globalization as a crisis for democracy. She reports on a conference that put forward various initiatives to replace globalization with local democratic alternatives.

FORUM ON THE FUTURE
GEORGE RUSSELL

The FTAA, still under negotiation at the time of writing, is intended to consist of the 34 countries of North, Central, and South America and the Caribbean, except Cuba.

In general terms fast-track authority is designed to assure potential U.S. trading partners of a swift response to an agreement. It enables the U.S. president to negotiate a trade deal and pass it to Congress for speedy approval or rejection, bypassing regular procedures.

There are plenty of minefields ahead before agreement is reached on a Free Trade Area of the Americas (FTAA). In the wake of the U.S. economic slump, many of the hemisphere's vulnerabilities are more apparent than ever: wildly uneven income distribution in Latin America; a dramatic financial crisis in Argentina; rising levels of crime and pollution; deterioration of such institutions as public education and health in many nations. No agreement is possible without a meeting of the minds between Brazil and the U.S., and that did not seem probable on the eve of the Quebec City summit. Even if that sea change came about, the process of negotiating the deal is one of the most challenging in modern history. In short, the odds on building a new trade framework before the 2005 deadline look forbiddingly long.

And yet, in a world beset by economic slowdown and turbulence, political fragility, and growing social challenges, no tool is likely to have greater success in regalvanizing growth and prosperity than a successful FTAA negotiation. Despite their differences, the countries of the Americas have never been more firmly committed to promoting such a deal, or to helping smaller, poorer nations cope with the consequences. Many of the widely publicized differences over the FTAA are more tactical than strategic. And many elements that seem to be obstacles to a deal, like the absence of U.S. congressional fast-track approval for trade negotiations, may not be obstacles at all.

Those were among the main conclusions of a panel of distinguished economists and trade experts who met at *Time*'s behest in Miami to consider the prospects for the FTAA....There was a strong tone of optimism among most panelists about prospects for the deal and its beneficial effects in a faltering economic climate. There was also a firm conviction that the countries of the hemisphere are more strongly committed to the free-trade process than they often appear to be....

Global convergence

While fully aware of the difficulties, [Charlene] Barshefsky, [who served as U.S. Trade Representative—chief trade

negotiator—during the Clinton administration, and is]
now a visiting public-policy scholar at the Woodrow Wilson
Center in Washington, argued that the FTAA talks reflect
"a convergence in our hemisphere along the lines of
market economics, democracy, shared ideals, and common
aspirations." She was hopeful about the will of the Bush
administration to support the FTAA process, and even
try to push it faster by agreeing to put such controversial
U.S. practices as antidumping legislation on the table
for improvement....

Most of all, perhaps, Barshefsky was optimistic on account
of the widespread consensus that renewed economic growth
is vital to the region—and that free trade is the best and
fastest way to that growth. This view got strong endorsement
from Andrés Velasco, Sumitomo professor of international
finance and development at Harvard's John F. Kennedy School
of Government and a former adviser to Chile in free-trade
talks with the U.S. "Growth is the key question facing Latin
America today," Velasco said. Analyzing the ways that
developing nations could achieve more rapid growth,
he said a "great bet for the next decade" was to "integrate
yourself into a richer area"—precisely the path of the FTAA.
"You import the institutions and procedures of that richer
area, and then you grow. That works," he said, citing such
cases as Portugal, Ireland, and Greece in Europe, "countries
that have caught up very quickly to the income of that area."
The economic success of Mexico in the wake of the NAFTA
accord also proves the case. "There is a very tight link
between the growth prospect for Latin America, the payoff
associated with reform and FTAA success," Velasco said. "It
is the big chance Latin America has for jumping on the fast-
growth bandwagon."

New vehicles for economic growth

The need for new vehicles for growth is great, according to
Kenneth Courtis, the Canadian-born vice-chairman for Asia
of the Goldman Sachs International investment firm. "We
are not in a U.S. slowdown. We're in an OECD slowdown,"
he said, referring to the 30-member association of advanced
industrial nations. Europe, the U.S., and Japan are all losing
momentum; that could put at risk economic and political
stability in parts of the Americas and set back the entire
process of globalization, which Courtis credited with
providing much of the economic progress of the 1990s.
"There's little sign yet in the leading indicators that we
have a bottom coming soon. It's become a rough landing."

In a trade context "dumping" is the sale, often abroad, of goods at lower than normal prices. This activity can harm the business of producers in the country where dumping is taking place. Antidumping laws give these producers a means of seeking redress.

The North American Free Trade Agreement (NAFTA) between the U.S., Canada, and Mexico came into effect on January 1, 1994. Under its conditions most trade barriers between the partners are to be gradually removed.

The members of the Organization for Economic Co-operation and Development (OECD) produce some 60 percent of the world's goods and services. The OECD itself fosters the development of economic and social policy among its members.

"It's important to build a momentum to move ahead," Courtis said, "because if you don't, we risk losing a lot of what we spent 20 years building. We're in a new game, and basically that new game can be played only if Brazil and the U.S. join and drive this process." If they do, and the FTAA is realized, Courtis said, it would lead to a substantial increase in investment in Latin America, higher growth, lower inflation and, over time, much better fiscal positions for the whole region....

A "free-trade mood"

Courtis's assessment drew a mixed response from Herminio Blanco, who was Mexico's trade minister from 1994 to 2000.... For one thing, Blanco agreed emphatically that the FTAA is a powerful engine for prosperity. "Who could have thought in 1991, when we were negotiating NAFTA, that we would become the second customer and second supplier of the U.S.?" he asked rhetorically. "For Mexico, NAFTA has meant more than 1 million jobs." In the interim, Mexico has negotiated free-trade agreements with 12 other countries in the hemisphere, as well as with Europe. Blanco sees these not as impediments to the FTAA but rather as a reason why there is a "good chance" of securing the hemispheric deal. "Through these bilateral negotiations, countries are getting trained, let's say, for the FTAA," he said. "There is a free-trade mood in the hemisphere, and I believe the best for everybody, including Mexico, is to have one agreement in the whole of the hemisphere."

"Bilateral" means between two parties; in this case between two countries. "Multilateral" means between many parties at the same time.

...Blanco was skeptical about the likelihood that the U.S. Congress would give up such powerful weapons as its punitive antidumping laws and agricultural subsidies to secure a trade deal. And he was adamant that Mexico and other nations would not accept the inclusion of environmental and labor guarantees in any free-trade pact, and that they should not. These, he said, amounted to protectionism by other means, aimed at countries with lower standards of living. Even though Barshefsky believes labor and environmental agreements are politically necessary for the U.S., she agreed to the extent that these should not be used to create a "debtor's-prison mentality: we won't trade with you until you get those standards right." But she also pointed out that so far, negotiators have been highly creative in making deals that did not add new burdens to trading partners but instead left the onus on them to enforce their own labor and environmental standards. The same could be true, she implied, in the FTAA....

Why do you think countries might be wary of environmental and labor guarantees? How might they be interpreted as protectionist?

"Just make up your mind one way or another and do it," she said, "and the rest of the world will adjust."

Antiglobalization demonstrators during the G8 summit in 2001 in Genoa, Italy, after the death of a protester who was shot by the Italian police.

A FETE FOR THE END OF THE END OF HISTORY
Naomi Klein

NO

ATTAC is the Association for the Taxation of financial Transactions for the Aid of Citizens. Founded in France in 1998, it is a pressure group opposed to globalization.

The World Social Forum referred to took place in the city of Porto Alegre, southern Brazil, in January 2001.

Established on January 1, 1995, the World Trade Organization (WTO) supervises the rules of international trade. In July 2001 it had 142 member countries.

..."The failure of Seattle was the inability to come up with a common agenda, a global alliance at the world level to fight against globalization," says Christophe Aguiton of ATTAC, who helped organize the forum.

Which is where the World Social Forum came in: ATTAC saw the conference as an opportunity to bring together the best minds working on alternatives to neoliberal economic policies—not just new systems of taxation but everything from sustainable farming to participatory democracy to cooperative production to independent media. From this process of information swapping ATTAC believed its "common agenda" would emerge....

In workshops and on panels, globalization was defined as a mass transfer of wealth and knowledge from public to private—through the patenting of life and seeds, the privatization of water, and the concentrated ownership of agricultural lands. Having this conversation in Brazil meant that these issues were not presented as shocking new inventions of a hitherto unheard-of phenomenon called "globalization"—as is often the case in the West—but as part of the continuum of colonization, centralization, and loss of self-determination that began more than five centuries ago.

This latest stage of market integration has meant that power and decision-making are now delegated to points even further away from the places where the effects of those decisions are felt at the same time that ever-greater financial burdens are off-loaded to cities and towns. Real power has moved from local to state, from state to national, from national to international, until finally representative democracy means voting for politicians every few years who use that mandate to transfer national powers to the WTO and the IMF [International Monetary Fund].

In response to this democratic crisis, the forum set out to sketch the possible alternatives—but before long, some rather profound questions emerged. Is this a movement trying to impose its own, more humane brand of globalization, with taxation of global finance and more democracy and transparency in international governance? Or is it a movement against centralization and the delegation of power on principle, one as critical of left-wing, one-size-fits-all ideology as of the recipe for McGovernment churned out at forums like Davos (cut taxes, privatize, deregulate, and wait for the trickle-down)? It's fine to cheer for the possibility of another world—but is the goal one specific other world ("our" world, some might say) or is it, as the Zapatistas put it, "a world with the possibility of many worlds in it?"

...In the end, the conference did not speak in one voice; there was no single official statement (though there were dozens of unofficial ones). Instead of sweeping blueprints for political change, there were glimpses of local democratic alternatives. The Landless Peasants Movement took delegates on day trips to reappropriated farmland used for sustainable agriculture. And then there was the living alternative of Porto Alegre itself. The city has become a showcase of participatory democracy studied around the world. In Porto Alegre, democracy isn't a polite matter of casting ballots; it's a contact sport, carried out in sprawling town hall meetings. The centerpiece of the Workers Party's platform is something called "the participatory budget," an initiative that gives residents, through a network of neighborhood councils and a shadow city council, a direct say in such decisions as how much of the municipal budget should go to sanitation versus transportation.

"This is a city that is developing a new model of democracy in which people don't just hand over control to the state," British author Hilary Wainwright said at the forum. "The challenge is, how do we extend that to a national and global level?"

Perhaps by transforming the anticorporate, antiglobalization movement into a pro-democracy movement that defends the rights of local communities to plan and manage their schools, their water, and their ecology. In Porto Alegre, the most convincing responses to the international failure of representative democracy seemed to be this radical form of local participatory democracy, in the cities and towns where the abstractions of global rule become day-to-day issues of homelessness, water contamination, exploding prisons, and cash-starved schools. Of course, this has to take place within a context of national and international standards and resources. But what seemed to be emerging organically out of the World Social Forum (despite the best efforts of some of the organizers) was not a movement for a single global government but a vision for an increasingly connected

The Swiss city of Davos hosts the annual meeting of the World Economic Forum, at which leading businessmen and politicians meet to discuss global issues.

The author suggests a movement that defends people's rights to manage their own local services instead of having them controlled by organizations divorced from local life. How might such a movement manifest itself?

The author explains that opponents of globalization are faced with a choice—to campaign for the inclusion of labor and environmental clauses in international trade agreements or to attempt to prevent the agreements themselves from becoming fact.

international network of very local initiatives, each built on direct democracy....

With a sweeping new round of WTO negotiations set for the fall, and the Free Trade Area of the Americas (FTAA) being negotiated in April [2001], these questions about process are suddenly urgent. How do we determine whether the goal is to push for "social clauses" on labor and environmental issues in international agreements or to try to shoot down the agreements altogether? This debate ... is now very real. U.S. industry leaders, including Caterpillar and Boeing, are actively lobbying for the linking of trade with labor and environmental clauses, not because they want to raise standards but because these links are viewed as the key to breaking the Congressional stalemate over fast-track trade negotiating authority. By pushing for social clauses, are unions and environmentalists unwittingly helping the advancement of these negotiations, a process that will also open the door to privatization of such services as water and more aggressive protections of drug patents? Should the goal be to add onto these trade agreements or take entire sections out—water, agriculture, food safety, drug patents, education, healthcare? Walden Bello, executive director of Focus on the Global South, is unequivocal on this point. "The WTO is unreformable," he said at the forum, "and it is a horrible waste of money to push for reform. Labor and environmental clauses will just empower an already too-powerful organization."

NGO means nongovernmental organization.

But that is not the strategy leading up to the Summit of the Americas in Quebec. Several large labor organizations and NGOs have taken government money to organize a parallel People's Summit during the official week of meetings, and have yet to issue clear statements on the FTAA. Not surprisingly, there were tensions about these issues at the forum, with those favoring direct action accusing the People's Summit organizers of helping to make the closed FTAA process appear open to "civil society"—perhaps just the public relations gloss Bush needs to secure fast track.

There is a serious debate to be had over strategy and process, but it's difficult to see how it will unfold without bogging down a movement whose greatest strength so far has been its agility. Anarchist groups, though fanatical about process, tend to resist efforts to structure or centralize the movement. The International Forum on Globalization—the brain trust of the North American side of the movement—lacks transparency in its decision-making and isn't accountable to a broad membership. Meanwhile, NGOs that might otherwise collaborate often compete with one another for publicity and funding. And traditional membership-based political structures like parties and unions have been reduced to bit players in these wide webs of activism.

Perhaps the real lesson of Porto Alegre is that democracy and accountability need to be worked out first on more manageable scales—within local communities and coalitions and inside individual organizations. ...What has become clear is that if the one "pro" this disparate coalition can get behind is "pro-democracy," then democracy within the movement must become a high priority. The Porto Alegre Call for Mobilization clearly states that "we challenge the elite and their undemocratic processes, symbolized by the World Economic Forum in Davos."

The Porto Alegre Call for Mobilization, a summary of the proposals adopted during the World Social Forum 2001, was signed by delegates of 144 organizations.

Despite the moments of open revolt, the World Social Forum ended on as euphoric a note as it began. There was cheering and chanting, the loudest of which came when the organizing committee announced that Porto Alegre would host the forum again next year. The plane from Porto Alegre to São Paulo on January 30 was filled with delegates dressed head-to-toe in conference swag—T-shirts, baseball hats, mugs, bags—all bearing the utopian slogan: Another World Is Possible...

Klein concludes with a familiar image for an upbeat ending.

Summary

The panel of economists brought together by *Time* magazine discusses the chances of the Americas avoiding the worst effects of a global economic slowdown and concludes that the best chance lies in the creation of a free-trade area, the Free Trade Area of the Americas (FTAA). Free trade would galvanize growth and prosperity throughout the region. Involvement with the prosperity of the United States would bring the chance for Latin America to jump on "the fast-growth bandwagon." One of the interviewees quoted sees a parallel in the creation of the North American Free Trade Agreement (NAFTA), which came into effect in 1994. NAFTA made Mexico the second most important customer for American trade and the second most important supplier of American imports. NAFTA brought Mexico a million jobs; FTAA would do the same for other poorer countries.

Naomi Klein reports on a conference in Brazil of groups seeking alternatives to globalization. There was no consensus, she admits, but an agreement that globalization was not only about economics but also about democracy. It removed ownership and political power from local people to the extent that democracy was in crisis. She reports on various local projects such as initiatives for land reform. In particular, she describes the site of the conference, Porto Alegre, as a city in which local democracy has been reinvigorated by the involvement of citizens in their own government. The way forward for the antiglobalization movement, she argues, is to transform itself into a prodemocracy movement to defend the rights of local communities. The experience of Porto Alegre suggested that such initiatives must first be launched at a local level.

FURTHER INFORMATION:

Books:

Lechner, Frank, and John Boli (editors), *The Globalization Reader*. Oxford: Blackwell Pub., 1999. O'Meara, Patrick, Howard D. Mehlinger, and Matthew Krain (editors), *Globalization and the Challenges of the New Century: A Reader*. Bloomington, IN: Indiana University Press, 2000.

Useful websites:

www.attac.org/ang/
ATTAC website (English language version).
www.ftaa-alca.org/alca_e.asp
Free Trade Area of the Americas official home page.
www.pbs.org/globalization/home.html
Overview and access to transcript of PBS TV show on Globalization and Human Rights.

The following debates in the Pro/Con series may also be of interest:

In this volume:

Topic 2 Does capitalism inevitably lead to income inequality and environmental destruction?

Topic 3 Does privatization always benefit consumers?

Topic 11 Is the WTO fair to poor countries?

IS GLOBALIZATION INEVITABLE?

YES: Workers producing for the global economy are better off than those who are not

YES: Integration into a richer area can bring rapid economic growth to poorer countries

YES: Consumer pressure for companies to behave ethically can lead to improved working conditions and pay

ECONOMICS
Is globalization a force for good for the poorer countries of the world?

NO: The developed world exploits poorer countries, taking advantage of cheap labor and forcing the sale of products there that people neither want nor can afford

DEMOCRACY
Does globalization give people control over their destiny?

NO: Globalization leads to local economies being marginalized by multinationals

NO: Globalization takes power and decision-making farther away from the individual, centralizing them in distant corporate and organizational headquarters

IS GLOBALIZATION INEVITABLE? KEY POINTS

YES: It is part and parcel of the notion of the marketplace and has been around, more or less, since ancient times

YES: Technology will transcend national boundaries, bringing knowledge and prosperity to all

INEVITABILITY
Is globalization inevitable?

LIFESTYLE
Will globalization have a beneficial effect on people's lifestyles?

NO: It is the creation of the corporations and developed world governments

NO: An all-pervading single culture will replace diversity, creating a homogenous world

Topic 10
ARE PROTECTIONIST TRADE POLICIES EVER A GOOD IDEA?

YES
"WHY ECONOMISTS SHOULD STUDY FAIRNESS"
CHALLENGE, VOL. 40, ISSUE 5, SEPTEMBER/OCTOBER 1997
STEVEN SURANOVIC

NO
"UNFAIR PROTECTION"
THE ECONOMIST, NOVEMBER 5, 1998

INTRODUCTION

Trade is at the heart of economics. By being able to swap their labor or the goods they produce for other services or goods, individuals are able to specialize, so that some produce food but others make furniture or practice law. Trade, however, means that all of them have food to eat, chairs to sit on, and legal advice if they need it. The same is also true of trade among nations. Some have supplies of particular resources or become leaders in certain industries, such as computers.

How trading nations should relate to each other is a matter of continuing debate for economists and politicians, however. There are three main options. Free trade leaves all imports and exports free of any restriction beyond the laws of the market, or supply and demand. Protectionism, on the other hand, places tariffs on exports or, more usually, imports, thus raising their prices. The logic behind protectionist policies is that they protect a country's domestic industries by preventing a

flood of imports from countries that can produce goods more cheaply. The third option is the establishment of trading blocs or alliances in which certain countries—often in the same geographical region—agree to a mutual reduction or abolition of trade duties.

Classical economics, as formulated by Adam Smith (1723–1790) in the mid-18th century, argues that a country should specialize in the things it does well and export some of the goods. That allows it to buy a greater number and variety of goods than it could have produced itself without trade. Such exchange, however, depends on unrestricted trade.

While economic theory promotes free trade, however, governments have at various times practiced greater or lesser degrees of protectionism. They impose taxes on trade or other barriers in the form of quotas that will encourage domestic production for domestic consumption. The main result of such policies is to increase the cost of imports or to reduce their availability. The main political purpose behind protectionism is most often to protect jobs by guaranteeing markets for domestically produced goods.

Although common sense seems to suggest that protectionism must work, and many workers and voters pressure governments to impose protectionist measures, most economists continue to argue, like Adam Smith and his successors such as David Ricardo, that tariffs and restrictions harm an economy. Such economists argue that restrictions limit a country's ability to specialize and make its economy efficient by concentrating on those things that it does best. Rather than protect "inefficient" jobs, governments should redeploy labor resources to other sectors of the economy.

"Trade and commerce, if they were not made of India-rubber, would never manage to bounce over the obstacles which legislators are continually putting in their way."

—HENRY DAVID THOREAU, PHILOSOPHER AND WRITER

Opponents of protectionism argue that it should only be justified on social or political grounds. Many people, for example, would concede that it is desirable for a country to have its own defense industry rather than relying on imports from countries that may become hostile. This is different, however, from preferring protectionist policies on economic grounds. Indeed, according to classical theory the political preference would bring a loss of economic welfare by diminishing the potential gains from trade.

In the first article, "Why Economists Should Study Fairness," Steven Suranovic puts a subtle and balanced economic case for reconsidering and reopening the questions of tariffs. He accepts the traditional premise that trade will make both countries better off, overall, but he argues that this is not the end of the story. The benefits from trade are not equally distributed. He shows that the traditional story is too simple: Although consumers may benefit, some workers—especially those with low skills in traditional industries—will be most vulnerable to competition and are likely to lose out. Suranovic asks whether the groups who gain most from the gains in trade have a responsibility to compensate the losers.

A key argument for opponents of trade protection is put forward in the second article, "Unfair Protection," from *The Economist*. This article seeks to highlight one of the dangers of subtler forms of protectionism designed to stop only "unfair" trade. Trade protection by one country soon leads to retaliation by others. The most famous example is that of the world economic depression in the 1930s. As the 1920s boom turned to depression, all countries sought to protect their own economies and jobs against competition. The Smoot–Hawley Tariff Act passed in the United States in 1930 provoked tit-for-tat responses. The resulting collapse of world trade pitched each country further into an economic depression that arguably moved the world closer to World War II.

WHY ECONOMISTS SHOULD STUDY FAIRNESS
Steven Suranovic

NAFTA came into force in the U.S., Canada, and Mexico on January 1, 1994. The agreement, designed to increase trade and investment among the partners, aims to eliminate nearly all tariffs on trade in goods between the three countries by January 1, 2003.

Economic policies almost invariably create losers. But how does one assess when the losses that result from one policy are more acceptable than the losses from another? There is no way to avoid the importance of trying to assess the fairness of one policy over another.

In the 1996 Republican presidential primaries, Pat Buchanan argued that the North American Free Trade Agreement (NAFTA) is causing the loss of American jobs. That spring Buchanan visited a closed textile plant in South Carolina to emphasize his belief that free trade agreements cause factories to close and jobs to be lost. Buchanan argued that continuing movements to free trade will put many other … jobs at risk. On the same day Senator Bob Dole visited a new BMW plant in South Carolina. He argued that the new jobs at the plant are precisely the kind of opportunities one can expect from free trade. Each of these candidates was trying to convince voters that his argument was right. Unfortunately for voters, economic theory suggests both are right.

Free trade v. protectionism
In the continuing public debate between free trade and protectionism, the lessons that economic theory teaches are often misunderstood or misrepresented. Perhaps the reason is that each side in the debate tends to emphasize the positive aspects of their position while virtually ignoring the negative aspects. For example, free trade advocates tend to emphasize the opportunities that free trade will open up for exporters and consumers…. Opponents of free trade, on the other hand, tend to emphasize the threats to our import-competing industries posed by open competition with low-wage countries. More specifically they will argue that free trade will cause painful job losses for already low-paid workers in our economy.

This article explains why both positions are consistent with economic theory. Trade theory does not tell us that free trade is good for everyone or bad for everyone. Instead, free trade (or trade liberalization) is likely to cause a redistribution of income. Some individuals will gain from trade, while others will lose....

The effects of free trade

When barriers to trade are removed, increased foreign competition in a product line, such as cotton shirts, will lower the prices of imports. In the case of cotton shirts, lower import prices will stimulate domestic demand for imported shirts while reducing demand for domestically produced shirts. To minimize the drop in sales, the home firms will have to cut their prices, causing revenues to fall. To reduce costs, local shirt factories may reduce employee bonuses, initiate smaller wage increases, and perhaps even make wage reductions. The result is a drop in income for some employees at the home shirt factories as a direct result of free trade. Since revenues are down, profits will likely fall as well, adversely affecting the owners and shareholders in the company.... In time, firms may be forced to reduce output. Some workers facing uncertain wages and uncertain future employment will begin searching for alternative employment....

In 2000 the U.S. had a trade deficit of $74.6 billion with the other NAFTA countries. That is, it imported more goods and services from Canada and Mexico than it exported.

Of course, economic models also predict positive effects. When the price of cotton shirts and other importables fall with the reduction in trade barriers, millions of consumers who buy these products will now have a little money left over to spend on other goods in the economy. Although for any particular consumer the savings may seem negligible, when summed up over millions of consumers, it can represent a sizable amount of additional purchasing power. This increase in purchasing power will raise demand and prices for other products in the economy. Exactly which markets will be affected will depend on how those with extra money decide to spend it. In addition, foreign cotton-shirt exporters and others like them will now have larger dollar incomes that will either stimulate demand for our export goods or increase savings in the U.S. financial sector. If the latter occurs, more funds will become available for loans, which, once made, will stimulate demand and raise prices of investment goods (or other consumption goods) in the domestic economy.

Many economic theories seem difficult because of this discrepancy between what individuals experience and the experience of the economy as a whole.

Regardless of the combination of effects that occurs, higher demand and prices for other sectors' goods and services will stimulate the growth of these sectors.... Industries that expand will require a different mix of labor and capital than industries that are contracting.... Some workers who lose their jobs in declining industries will not be in demand in the expanding sectors. This will have two long-term effects. First, excess labor demand for the technically skilled workers will permanently bid up their wages compared to pre-free trade wages. Second, excess labor supply of [less skilled] workers … will permanently bid down their wages.…

Lessons from trade theory

A number of important lessons emerge from this story of trade liberalization. First, economic analysis shows that trade liberalization will result in gains in income and well-being for some individuals and losses in income and well-being for others. Second, the gains and losses will be spread out over time. Some people will lose initially but will be better off in the long run; some will suffer losses for the rest of their lives; some may gain in the short term and lose in the long term; some will never experience losses, only gains. Third, for many individuals losses will precede the gains … Fourth, the losers will be easier to identify than the winners. This is because the losses occur in industries that are directly affected by the removal of trade barriers, and these losses occur first. The gains generally arise indirectly, after a series of effects that begin in the import sector. Fifth, the gains will more likely be experienced by the higher-skilled, younger, or more adaptable workers.…

Improvements in aggregate economic efficiency can be of two kinds: production—more goods and services are made with the same resources— and consumption— consumers will have more satisfying choices available to them.

The economic case for free trade

Most economic models demonstrate that trade liberalization will raise aggregate economic efficiency. Thus, free trade will benefit everyone on average, or the country benefits in the aggregate. However, both of these statements mask the income redistribution effects caused by freer trade.

A more accurate way to relate the efficiency improvements of trade liberalization is to say that the sum of the gains will exceed the sum of the losses. Thus, it is clear that the net effect of trade liberalization is positive, but a redistribution of income, with some individuals winning and others losing, will also result.… In general … some firms will experience price, production, and employment increases while other firms will suffer price, output, and employment reductions.…

A new question

These theories and realities should lead us to the following question. Under what circumstances is it appropriate for a government policy (trade liberalization in this case) to cause uncompensated losses to some individuals?…. How do you tell the families of steelworkers that the town they grew up in will die a slow death? How do you explain to farmers across America that the days of the family farm will end? These things matter to people because they form the basis of their hopes and dreams, for themselves, their children, and their grandchildren. Would it really make sense for them to accept the economic efficiency argument that their losses are appropriate since others will gain even more than they lose? Can the losers be convinced that the government would step in and compensate them for their losses to assure that everyone will indeed gain from trade? To both of these questions the answer is unequivocally no.

Some modern economists argue that economic judgments must take account of nonfinancial factors, such as tradition, community spirit, and so on. What other factors might be useful in such judgments?

The effects of protectionism

Indeed, it is these very arguments about the losses likely to arise from trade liberalization that convinces many people that protectionism is warranted. However, upon further reflection, protectionism could just as easily be discredited. When trade barriers are raised, most of the effects described above are simply reversed. That means that an increase in protection, as advocated by Pat Buchanan, will also result in a redistribution of income. Those who benefited from free trade ... would now lose from additional protection. Those who had lost before would now gain....

Overall, economic efficiency will probably decline with the increase in protection ... [but] the main difference between protectionism and free trade is that the gains from protection will be obvious while the losses will be much more obscure. Clearly this is one of the reasons protectionism is so popular.

Gains and losses with both methods

Nevertheless, in one important respect, the effects of protection are really much the same as the effects of trade liberalization. Protection will also generate uncompensated losses, in the form of higher prices to consumers or lost opportunities to some individuals in the economy.... Whether a government moves to free trade or chooses to raise barriers to trade, its actions will effectively take money away from some people within the country and give it to others. Trade policy actions, then, are just as much a story about who wins and loses domestically as it is a story about one country versus another. If free trade is chosen, workers ... have every reason to ask why they must suffer income losses in the name of aggregate efficiency. If more protection is chosen (fully informed) workers have a reason to ask why their opportunities must be limited (and their incomes reduced) in order to save other workers' jobs....

The author is saying that fairness is an important part of evaluating international trade policies. Since any policy brings losses as well as gains, how might fairness be judged?

UNFAIR PROTECTION
The Economist

NO

"Dumping" is the sale of a commodity on a foreign market at a price below marginal cost.

Protectionism is on the rise in a new guise: antidumping cases are multiplying in America, Europe, and around the world. "Foreign competitors are destroying an American success story. Hundreds of thousands of American jobs are threatened. Foreign steel is being dumped on our shores at cut-throat prices. It must be stopped," clamor full-page ads in American newspapers. America's steel makers may shout the loudest. But they are far from alone in calling for limits on imports. As economic gloom spreads to America and Europe, and once-emerging economies try to export their way out of a slump, protectionism is on the rise—but in a new form. Instead of raising import tariffs or cutting quotas, countries are slapping "antidumping" duties on imports they claim are too cheap.

Antidumping on the rise

The most prominent antidumpers are in the United States. Twenty-five new cases have been launched so far this year [1998], up from 16 in the whole of 1997. The steel industry is going after imports from Japan, Brazil, and Russia. South Korean memory-chip makers have been hit with heavy duties. Their Taiwanese counterparts are now under fire; and many other cases are pending in industries such as machine tools, textiles, and clothing, and even apple juice.

Where America leads, others follow. Canadian steel makers are preparing antidumping actions against four countries. The European Union is investigating 13 steel cases from Slovenia to South Korea. It has just extended duties on magnetic disks from Japan, Taiwan, and China, and on electronic scales from Singapore. And firms in such sectors as chemicals, consumer electronics, textiles, and forestry are threatening to bring cases.

From January 1995 to June 2000 the U.S. was the third most popular target of antidumping measures worldwide—after China and Japan.

But perhaps the most worrying new trend is that developing countries are retaliating with antidumping actions of their own. Mexico, Argentina, and Brazil have launched a bevy of cases, many against the United States. So has South Africa. And Asian countries are at last hitting back. Antidumping actions are multiplying in China and South Korea. India is setting up a new body to cope with an upsurge in cases. Even Thailand and Indonesia are getting in on the game.

Antidumping is popular mainly because world trade rules allow it. Countries have slashed their tariffs on industrial goods in successive rounds of trade talks. If they were to raise them again, other countries could demand compensation at the World Trade Organization (WTO) or retaliate with higher tariffs of their own. But WTO rules allow countries to impose antidumping duties on foreign goods that are being sold cheaper than at home, or below the cost of production, when domestic producers can show that they are being harmed.

For a discussion about the WTO, see Topic 11 Is the WTO fair to poor countries?, *pages 144–155.*

Manipulating the figures

Antidumping measures are not only legal, they are also very flexible. Only some firms in an industry need complain for an investigation to be launched; it can be directed at specific firms and countries; and they can be hit with differing duties. Perhaps most important, antidumping duties can be presented not as protection but as redress against "unfair" competition. In one sense, "dumping" is common, since companies often charge less in more competitive foreign markets than they do at home. The figures can easily be manipulated to show dumping, because it is so hard to make sensible comparisons across borders. To prove injury, it is enough for companies merely to show that sales are being dented by rising imports.

America's dumping rules, copied by many countries—and the basis for the WTO code—allow plenty of helpful wiggle-room. So does Europe's more opaque system; in its recent (unsuccessful) effort to impose duties against unbleached cotton imports, the European Commission decided for purely political reasons to remove Turkey from its hit-list. Often new cases are filed as soon as old ones have been rejected—on the basis that, eventually, one will succeed. Between 1980 and 1997, 71 percent of antidumping claims in the EU [European Union] did indeed succeed, as did 80 percent of those in America.

Antidumping duties are not just easy to secure; they also tend to be hefty and long-lasting. In the EU they averaged 29 percent between 1991 and 1995—a huge margin on a product such as steel. America's averaged 57 percent, and can be ludicrously big: a 454 percent duty was slapped on supercomputers made by Japan's NEC last year. And while market conditions change quickly, antidumping duties are reviewed only after five years. By then, they may no longer be wanted; but they can easily be extended.

There are also huge indirect costs. Even unsuccessful dumping cases are a tax on trade: they typically tie companies up for over a year, and impose huge legal costs, particularly in

A steel worker in Lorrain, Ohio, stands by a furnace pouring a river of molten steel. The U.S. steel industry has suffered from the dumping of cheap foreign steel.

America. Moreover, a case against one foreign company may deter others from competing too fiercely. And the mere threat of action is often enough to spur foreign producers to raise prices or curtail sales. Russian and Japanese steel makers, for instance, are already negotiating to limit their exports to America. In effect, antidumping measures encourage domestic and foreign producers to collude to raise prices. Patrick Messerlin, an economist at the Institut d'Etudes Politiques in Paris, estimates that, because of this pro-cartel effect, antidumping duties are generally twice as costly to the economy as equivalent import tariffs.

> A "cartel" is an association of industries or firms that together establish a national or international monopoly by price fixing or by controlling the supply of goods.

Supporters of antidumping claim two merits. It is said to prevent "predatory pricing," in which foreign firms—especially those that earn fat profits in protected home markets—undercut domestic producers so as to drive them out of business. They then raise prices and recoup their losses. The second alleged justification is political: that antidumping is a safety-valve for countries that are otherwise opening up their markets.

But predatory pricing is an unconvincing excuse. It is not mentioned in the WTO's antidumping code, nor indeed in American or European law. And it is rarely a winning strategy, because when predators raise prices again, they invariably attract new competitors. According to Mr. Messerlin, only 3 percent of antidumping cases in the EU and 4 percent in America might involve predation as defined in domestic antitrust rules.

The political argument does not hold up either. WTO rules already allow countries to use "safeguard" measures for temporary protection against import surges, so long as compensation is paid. But countries nearly always resort to antidumping instead, suggesting that their real aim is not to ease the adjustment to freer trade but to bring back protection by the back door.

The new wave of antidumping cases is particularly alarming because protectionists are pushing at an open door. America's top trade negotiator, Charlene Barshefsky, says her country's current-account deficit—which she sees ballooning to $300 billion next year [1999]—is "politically unsustainable." Already the American government is encouraging antidumping suits, promising to vet them faster. It is so keen on antidumping that it is loth to complain when other countries retaliate in kind. In the 1930s, the Smoot-Hawley tariff provoked tit-for-tat responses and a collapse of world trade. According to Gary Horlick, an antidumping lawyer at O'Melveny & Myers, in Washington, D.C., we may now be witnessing "Smoot-Hawley in slow motion."

> The Smoot-Hawley Tariff Act became law in the U.S. in 1930. It raised tariffs on imports, which brought retaliatory tariff rises from foreign countries. U.S. trade suffered a sharp decline, and the Great Depression, which had started in 1929, intensified.

Summary

In the first article presented here, "Why Economists Should Study Fairness," Steven Suranovic argues that the principle of fairness should be taken seriously when evaluating international trade policies. There are winners and losers with both a free trade system and with protectionism. Economists need to establish under what circumstances it is appropriate for a government policy to cause uncompensated losses to some individuals, he says. The benefits of trade tend to benefit a very large number of people by relatively small amounts for each, while the disadvantages are more obvious to more concentrated groups such as an industry and its workers who are likely to lose out significantly. His argument in effect puts forward a case for reconsidering a tariff system.

The second article from *The Economist*, "Unfair Protection," argues that the rise in antidumping measures in the United States, Europe, and elsewhere in the world is an unfair form of trade protection. It encourages domestic and foreign producers to collude in order to raise prices, deters other foreign suppliers from competing, and is costly to the economy. The article points to the dangers of some subtle forms of protectionism and uses the world economic depression of the 1930s as an example of countries making tit-for-tat responses to trade protection moves from other countries, which can result in even deeper economic depression.

FURTHER INFORMATION:

Books:

Batra, Raveendra N. and Ravi Batra, *The Myth of Free Trade: The Pooring of America*. Carmichael, CA: Touchstone Books, 1996.

Gomory, R. E., and W. J. Baumol, *Global Trade and Conflicting National Interests*. Cambridge, MA: MIT Press, 2001.

Roberts, Russell D., *The Choice: A Fable of Free Trade and Protectionism* (revised edition). Upper Saddle River, NJ: Prentice Hall, 2000 .

Useful websites:

www.freetrade.org
Center for Trade Policy Studies (CATO Institute) website.
www.epinet.org
Economic Policy Institute website.
www.independent.org
The Independence Institute is a nonprofit research and educational organization that sponsors comprehensive studies on political economy.

The following debates in the Pro/Con series may also be of interest:

In this volume:

Topic 1 Is the free market the best form of economic organization?

Topic 5 Does government intervention do more harm than good?

Topic 9 Is globalization inevitable?

Topic 11 Is the WTO fair to poor countries?

ARE PROTECTIONIST TRADE POLICIES EVER A GOOD IDEA?

YES: Free trade agreements lead to lower profits and wages

YES: Free trade agreements create a higher demand for foreign goods, leading to domestic factory closures and job losses

THE ECONOMY
Does protectionism aid the economy?

JOBS
Do protectionist trade policies protect jobs?

NO: Free trade agreements lead to lower prices, which stimulate consumer demand and create increased purchasing power

NO: Under free trade agreements expanding domestic industries will require more highly skilled workers

ARE PROTECTIONIST TRADE POLICIES EVER A GOOD IDEA?

KEY POINTS

YES: Expanding domestic industries will have higher profits under protectionism—they can afford to sell their goods and services more cheaply overseas

YES: Some measure of protectionism is healthy for the economy, which stimulates demand for our exports

EXPORTS
Can our export trade prosper under protectionism?

NO: Under free trade foreign exporters have a greater dollar income, which can stimulate demand for our export goods

NO: Raising tariffs on imports will cause foreign countries to retaliate, which in the past has led to a decline in exports and even economic depression

INTERNATIONAL ECONOMIC ORGANIZATIONS

World recession, such as that following the Wall Street Crash of 1929, and the economic upheaval of World War II led to the founding of various international economic organizations to work with the interests of the world community in mind. The history of such organizations is charted below.

1929 Wall Street Crash and the recession that follows stimulate debate about how such a future global crisis can be avoided.

1939–1945 World War II results in huge loss of life and resources. To avoid such conflict in the future, the Allies conceive the idea of a "new world order" that is based on consensus rather than mutual mistrust.

1944 The United States and its allies meet at Bretton Woods, New Hampshire, to establish

a global monetary system. The gold standard is restored for the U.S. dollar, and other nations fix their exchange rates to the dollar.

1946 The International Monetary Fund (IMF) and the World Bank are set up to support the rebuilding of war-torn Europe.

1948 The General Agreement on Tariffs and Trade (GATT) is established for countries to discuss and agree on the easing of trade restrictions such as tariffs and import quotas.

THE IMF AND THE WORLD BANK

The IMF began with 35 member countries. Today it has its headquarters in Washington D.C., and the membership comprises 182 nations. It is funded by loans from member states' reserves and lends this money to members experiencing financial difficulties. Richer countries pay (loan) more toward their IMF membership than poor countries, but can also borrow more and have greater voting rights. Loans above a certain level require the borrowing nation to demonstrate the economic reforms it intends to apply so that it will be able to pay back its debt within a specified period of time.

The World Bank, whose full name is the International Bank for Reconstruction and Development (IBRD), soon shifted its emphasis from the reconstruction of Europe to helping countries in the developing and underdeveloped world. Today only such countries can borrow from the bank. The World Bank membership is the same as that of the IMF, and member countries "subscribe" money to the bank's capital fund on the basis of economic strength. Loans are made to developing countries on the condition that certain economic reforms are instituted—for example, that the government in question reduce public expenditure, improve its monetary policy, open up to trade and foreign investment, or sometimes that it privatize less efficient state industries.

1959 The Inter-American Development Bank (IDB) is established to promote development in Latin America and the Caribbean. The initial membership comprises 18 Latin American and Caribbean nations plus the United States. Loans are made to finance a variety of economic and social programs. Today the IDB has 46 member states, including 16 in Europe, Japan, and Israel.

1967 An informal meeting takes place between the finance ministers and governors of the central banks of the world's most powerful countries: France, Germany, Japan, the United Kingdom, and the United States. This is the beginning of the Group of Eight (G8) summits.

1975 The first G6 meeting takes place in Rambouillet, France, as the five countries that met in 1967 are joined by Italy. The summit discusses stabilizing exchange rates, promoting international trade, and monitoring loans to the developing and underdeveloped world.

1976 G6 becomes the Group of Seven (G7) in Puerto Rico as Canada joins the six nations.

1977 The London summit of the G7 takes place, the name being retained although the entire European Community is now represented at the meetings.

1989 The Asia-Pacific Economic Cooperation (APEC) group is formed to foster cooperation among economies of the Pacific Rim. Membership today is 21 countries, including Australia, Canada, China, Indonesia, Japan, Malaysia, the Philippines, and Russia.

May 1990 The European Bank for Reconstruction and Development (EBRD) is established to aid in the transition of Eastern European countries to free-market economies.

December 1992 The North American Free Trade Agreement (NAFTA) is signed, expanding on a free-trade agreement that already existed between the United States and Canada. The terms of the agreement stipulate the gradual removal of nearly all restrictions on trade and investment between the United States, Canada, and Mexico.

January 1, 1994 NAFTA comes into effect. There is strong opposition both from U.S. labor unions worried about jobs being lost as firms relocate to cheaper Mexico and from Mexico, worried that its economy may be dominated by multinational corporations.

January 1, 1995 The World Trade Organization succeeds GATT as the foundation of the world's trading system. By 2000 the WTO has 135 member states. The aims of the WTO are similar to those of GATT—to liberalize world trade through negotiating the reduction of tariffs, duties, and quotas on goods traded between member countries.

April 1998 Representatives of 34 states, including Brazil, Chile, Argentina, and Colombia, meet to begin negotiations to set up a Free Trade Area of the Americas (FTAA) to exist alongside NAFTA and other agreements.

1998 Russia fully participates in a G7 summit for the first time, and G8 is born. The summit's mandate has broadened to include such issues as terrorism, drug trafficking, the environment, and the Internet.

December 1999 The WTO summit in Seattle is disrupted by demonstrators, and talks are abandoned without agreement on key issues.

July 2001 The G8 summit in Genoa, Italy, is the scene of violent "antiglobalization" protests. Leaders leave the summit questioning the future of such talks.

Topic 11
IS THE WORLD TRADE ORGANIZATION FAIR TO POOR COUNTRIES?

YES
"SEVEN COMMON MISUNDERSTANDINGS ABOUT THE WTO"
FROM *TEN COMMON MISUNDERSTANDINGS ABOUT THE WTO*
WORLD TRADE ORGANIZATION

NO
"WHY FREE TRADE IS NOT FAIR"
NEW LEADER, VOL. 83, ISSUE 1, MARCH/APRIL 2000
GEORGE P. BROCKWAY

INTRODUCTION

The World Trade Organization (WTO) was created in 1995. It grew out of the General Agreement on Tariffs and Trade (GATT), which was the result of rounds of negotiations that had been taking place among world governments since the 1940s. The aim of GATT, inherited by the WTO, was the reduction of trade barriers between nations. The member countries of the WTO—some 138 in 1999 and still growing—meet regularly to discuss the promotion of free trade, the reduction of protectionist measures, and other aspects of international trade.

The WTO claims to operate in the interests of all member countries, and that this is vital for the developing world: "A fair global trading system based on rules which all observe will help the weakest most." Without the WTO, its supporters argue, international trade would be subject only to "the law of the jungle," under which the strongest—the industrialized nations— would set the rules to suit themselves.

The GATT talks and later the WTO conferences received little public attention until the WTO met in Seattle in November 1999. Violent riots, a heavy police response, and images of a devastated downtown propelled the WTO onto the front pages and into the center of political debate. Since 1999 every meeting of the WTO has been met by tens or even hundreds of thousands of protesters.

Opponents to the WTO are highly varied. Some are labor activists, concerned that U.S. jobs are being lost as businesses shift operations to poorer countries. Some are more radical and claim against globalization and against the unfairness of capitalism itself. They argue that the WTO is a front behind which multinational corporations are subverting democracies and inflicting the damaging effects of capitalism on the developing world. Most of the protesters against the WTO are from the developed world. They claim to speak for the developing world, however, arguing that those people are excluded from the debate by their own governments and elites.

The protesters say that the WTO, by reducing barriers to trade, makes it easier for multinational companies to exploit cheaper costs in the developing world. They point to the alleged poor conditions, low wages, and child workers in overseas factories that supply branded companies such as Nike or Gap. They also object to the "westernizing" of local cultures. The removal of restrictions to trade, they argue, also results in the removal of restrictions on the influence of the world's richest countries—notably the United States—over the poorest.

> "The progress in lowering trade barriers since World War II marks the triumph of putting an important idea into practice—that international trade benefits all nations."
>
> —ALAN GREENSPAN, CHAIRMAN, FEDERAL RESERVE

Yet not everyone agrees with this, even in the developing world. There, many see trade with the developed world as vital to improving their own economies. Orthodox economic theory agrees that increased trade with the West will bring an improvement in living and working conditions—and increased markets for western goods.

Many people in developing countries fear that those in the industrial nations who oppose the WTO, like the labor unions, actually intend to prevent cheap imports into the United States. They want to do this not to help the poorer countries but rather to protect jobs in the developed world from "unfair" competition. Many such commentators are critical of what they perceive to be the double standards of the anti-WTO protesters. Those who protest have all of the advantages of global trade, from branded sneakers to mobile phones, but demand that others should remain "unspoiled" and be denied these same opportunities.

Not everyone in developing countries, however, believes that the WTO works for their benefit. At Seattle some developing countries—many of whom were taking part in WTO talks for the first time—complained that they were excluded from informal talks in which the major countries sought to make the real decisions on their own. And developing countries are still denied access to many of the most important western markets. For example, industrialized nations offer subsidies to their domestic agriculture producers worth more than the entire economic output of sub-Saharan Africa.

The following articles study both sides of the question. In the first the WTO itself focuses on dispelling the myths that surround it. It says it is controlled by governments seeking to advance prosperity in developed and developing nations alike. George P. Brockway, on the other hand, argues that the WTO reflects the interests of developed nations, and that its changes to trade exploit developing nations and make the future of developing nations dependent on the developed world.

SEVEN COMMON MISUNDERSTANDINGS ABOUT THE WTO
World Trade Organization

YES

1. The WTO dictates governments' policies

Not true. The WTO does not tell governments how to conduct their trade policies. Rather, it's a "member driven" organization. This means that:

- the rules of the WTO system are agreements resulting from negotiations among member governments, and they are ratified by members' parliaments, and
- decisions taken in the WTO are generally made by consensus among all members.

The only occasion when a WTO body can have a direct impact on a government's policies is when the Dispute Settlement Body (which consists of all members) adopts a ruling by a disputes panel, or an appeal report. Even then, the scope of these rulings is narrow: they are simply judgments or interpretations of whether a government has broken one of the WTO's agreements—agreements that the infringing government had itself accepted. If a government has broken a commitment, it has to conform.

In all other respects, the WTO does not dictate to governments to adopt or drop certain policies.... In fact, it's the governments who dictate to the WTO.

2. The WTO is for free trade at any cost

Not true. Yes, one of the principles of the WTO system is for countries to lower their trade barriers and to allow trade to flow more freely. After all, countries benefit from lower trade barriers. But just how low those barriers should go is something member countries bargain with each other. Their negotiating positions depend on how ready they feel they are to lower the barriers, and on what they want to obtain from other members in return.

The WTO provides the forum for negotiating liberalization. It also provides the rules for how liberalization can take place. The rules written into the agreements allow barriers to be lowered gradually so that domestic producers can adjust. They also spell out when and how governments can protect their domestic producers, for

The WTO claims to be an entirely democratic body, run by governments for governments.

Free trade is a policy by which government restrictions or interference with imports or exports is reduced or removed. The WTO maxim that free trade is good is raised in this paragraph; look for its reappearance later in the article.

example from dumped or subsidized imports. Here, the objective is fair trade.

Just as important as freer trade—perhaps more important—are other principles of the WTO system. For example: nondiscrimination, and making sure the conditions for trade are stable, predictable, and transparent.

Trade policies in which global standards are adopted can expose the smallest countries to risk. The WTO says it looks after those countries at risk.

3. The WTO's concern for commercial interests takes priority over development

Not true. Developing countries are allowed more time to apply numerous provisions of the WTO agreements. Least developed countries receive special treatment, including exemption from many provisions. The needs of development can also be used to justify actions that might not normally be allowed under the agreements, for example, giving subsidies.

At the same time, underlying the WTO's trading system is the fact that freer trade boosts economic growth and supports development.

4. In the WTO, commercial interests take priority over environmental protection

Not true. Many provisions take environmental concerns specifically into account. A range of subsidies are permitted for environmental protection. Environmental objectives are also recognized specifically in provisions dealing with product standards, food safety, intellectual property protection, etc.

What's important in the WTO's rules is that measures taken to protect the environment must not discriminate against foreign goods and services. You cannot be lenient with your own producers and at the same time be strict with foreigners. Also important is the fact that it's not the WTO's job to set the international rules for environmental protection. That's the task of the environmental agencies and conventions.

5. The WTO dictates to governments on issues such as food safety, and human health and safety

Not true. Remember, the agreements were negotiated by WTO member governments. Key clauses in the agreements (such as GATT Article 20) specifically allow governments to take actions to protect human, animal, or plant life, or health. Both these actions are disciplined, for example to prevent them being used as protectionism in disguise. Some of the agreements deal with product standards, and with health and safety for food and other products made

Article 20 allows exceptions from trade rules for reasons of environmental protection.

Protectionism is a policy by which a country sets trade barriers to protect domestic producers.

from animals and plants. At the same time, the agreements are also designed to prevent governments setting regulations arbitrarily in a way that discriminates against foreign goods and services. Safety regulations must not be protectionism in disguise.

One criterion for meeting these objectives is to base regulations on scientific evidence or on internationally recognized standards. Again, the WTO does not set the standards itself.... Governments are free to set their own standards provided they are consistent, are not arbitrary, and do not discriminate.

6. The WTO destroys jobs and widens the gap between rich and poor

Not true. But take a closer look at the details. Freer-flowing and more stable trade boosts economic growth. It creates jobs and helps to reduce poverty. When a country lowers its trade barriers, it is itself the biggest beneficiary. The countries exporting also gain, but less.

Clearly, producers who were previously protected face new competition when trade barriers are lowered. Some survive by becoming more competitive. Others don't. But that's not the end of the story. Freer trade creates more jobs than are lost. And the boost it gives to the economy allows adjustments to be made (such as preparing people for new jobs) more easily. That's why the trade agreements allow changes to be made gradually—to give governments and producers time to make the necessary adjustments.

The OECD was founded in 1961 to stimulate world trade and economic growth. Members are drawn mainly from the developed nations.

There are also many other factors behind recent changes in wage levels. Why, for example, is there a widening gap in developed countries between the pay of skilled and unskilled workers? According to the OECD [Organization for Economic Cooperation and Development] imports from low-wage countries account for only 10 to 20 percent of wage changes in developed countries. Much of the rest is attributed to "skill-based technological change." In other words, developed economies are naturally adopting more technologies that require skilled labor.

In fact, protection is expensive because it raises costs and encourages inefficiency. According to another OECD calculation, imposing a 30 percent duty on imports from developing countries would actually reduce U.S. unskilled wages by 1 percent and skilled wages by 5 percent. One of the costs of protectionism is lower wages in the protectionist country. At the same time, the focus on goods imports distorts the picture. In developed countries, 70 percent of economic activity is in services, where the effect of foreign competition on jobs is different—if a foreign telecommunications company sets up business in a country, it will naturally employ local people, for example.

Finally, while about 1.5 billion people are still in poverty, trade liberalization since World War II has contributed to lifting an estimated 3 billion people out of poverty.

"Critics of free trade argue that poor people within a country lose out when it liberalizes. Not so. The new WTO study finds that the poor tend to benefit from the faster economic growth that trade liberalization brings. It concludes that 'trade liberalization is generally a strongly positive contributor to poverty alleviation— it allows people to exploit their productive potential, assists economic growth, curtails arbitrary policy interventions and helps to insulate against shocks.'"

—MICHAEL MOORE, WTO DIRECTOR GENERAL, 2000

---

7. The WTO is undemocratic

Not true. Decisions in the WTO are generally by consensus. In principle, that's even more democratic than majority rule because everyone has to agree. It would be wrong to suggest that every country has the same bargaining power. Nevertheless, the consensus rule means every country has a voice, and every country has to be persuaded before it joins a consensus. Quite often reluctant countries are persuaded by being offered something in return.

Inevitably, strong countries like the United States have the greatest bargaining power. Do you suppose this would affect the democratic nature of the WTO decision-making process?

Consensus also means every country accepts the decisions. There are no dissenters. What is more, the WTO's rules, which were the result of the Uruguay Round negotiations, were ratified in members' parliaments.

WHY FREE TRADE IS NOT FAIR
George P. Brockway

NO

The meeting in Seattle in 1999 was marked by violent protests against the globalization of world trade.

Let me say at once that aside from a few broken windows, I believe the recent World Trade Organization (WTO) meeting in Seattle, because of the demonstrations it sparked, was as near perfect as could have been expected. Perfection would have been for the WTO to abolish itself and start over, and with luck we may come to that.

Let me say next that I'm not impressed … with the argument that it's wrong to oppose child labor in India … on the grounds that if the children didn't work, their parents would starve. Arguments of that kind have been used since the beginning of time to justify every conceivable example of man's inhumanity to children, to women, and even to other men. If it is impossible to make rugs of the highest— that is, most traditional—quality unless the knots are tied by juvenile fingers, it would be no hardship for us to walk on broadloom carpets.

For reasons he will explain, the author defends support for domestic producers, despite the claims of critics that buying American goods damages producers in developing countries who have come to depend on exports to the United States.

I am not, furthermore, abashed by the debater's point that if I want to protect several million American jobs, I can do so only by throwing several million (and probably more) workers out of work on the other side of the world.… I am willing to entertain … the exceedingly remote possibility that American environmentalists thought up dolphin-safe tuna nets and turtle-safe shrimp nets to interfere with the ability of Central American fishermen to compete with ours. Whether the new nets impede trade or not, though, they certainly promote diversity of life and so, in the general interest, should be required by any responsible authority.

On the other hand, I submit that it is none of our business where France buys its bananas.… It is preposterous … that we should have the right, because France insists on buying bananas from its former colonies, to impose tariffs of 100 percent on brie and foie gras and other delicacies.

A done deal

All such nonsense, and much more, was foreseen by Ralph Nader, Senator Ernest F. Hollings (D–S.C.), and others who testified against Congressional approval of the World Trade Organization.… Brief hearings were … held over a few days around Thanksgiving in 1994. Unfortunately, it was agreed that the question would go to the floor on a "fast track" basis, with limited debate and no opportunity for amendment: just a simple vote up or down. The whole thing was a done deal by December 8. It would not be outrageous to suggest that few legislators had a detailed understanding of what the WTO was about … and most citizens did not know how their senators and representatives had voted, let alone why.

The trouble was, and is, not that the WTO has a few sloppily drafted passages of the sort that are almost unavoidable in any large piece of legislation. No, the trouble is that the World Trade Organization is not merely foolish, but dangerous. Unhappily, what's done is not so easy to undo, especially in an organization that was conceived in secrecy, does most of its business in secret ad hoc committees, and can overturn its secretly arrived-at decisions only by a unanimous vote. (A vote of 148-to-nothing is hard to achieve in the best of conditions, and is practically certain to prove impossible when the "ayes" must include both the plaintiff and the defendant.)

Somewhere on the desk before me I have suggestions for an alternative approach. My idea was designed to protect the interests of workers and consumers in both developed and underdeveloped nations.

An alternative for the developed world

We begin with the workers in the developed countries, for the WTO is taking away something they once had—namely, reasonably decent jobs.… I say the way to protect is to protect directly and openly. First, we recognize that a few of our important (not necessarily our largest) industries are threatened in their home market by severe competition from foreign industries. Second, we determine whether that competition is made possible by wages or working conditions that we should consider exploitative or dangerous. Third, we simply and absolutely refuse admittance to commodities produced under such conditions. We don't fiddle with the tariff on foie gras or any thing else; we simply forbid the importation of offending stuff.

The proposal … does not cover all industries or any other nation (although we would not object if the possibility helps improve conditions in other countries anywhere in the world). It does not dictate where France buys its bananas. It does not require elaborately contentious cost accounting, as do the WTO rules against "dumping." It turns on straightforward questions of fact. What are the working conditions? Is child labor employed? What are the wage

What measures could be taken to protect Congress against such accusations that it rushed through legislation it does not understand?

The author mocks the supposedly democratic decision-making process of the WTO.

Brockway is proposing a limited, ethically responsible, and national (i.e., not global) trade policy. How does this compare with the WTO?

Does the United States, as the world's largest economy, have a duty to help improve other nations' economies?

scales?.... The proposal does not interfere with ... trade anywhere else in the world. In every respect it is analogous to laws currently in effect that refuse entry to contaminated foods or drugs we consider dangerous.... Such laws protect Americans as consumers and citizens. The proposal will protect Americans as workers and as entrepreneurs.

An alternative for the developing world

Now consider the situation of the underdeveloped countries and peoples of the globe. Today, as in the 18th and 19th centuries, the more developed countries need the less developed countries as sources of raw materials.... The multinational corporations also use certain less developed countries as sources of cheap labor and working conditions. The banks of the First World have found the weak nations of the Third World eager borrowers of money at high interest rates. What was imperialism before independence has become neoimperialism. The social and political domination of imperialism is largely gone, but the economic extraction of neoimperialism grows and festers.

High interest rates on loan repayments are crippling the economies of many developing countries.

"Editorial pronouncements that people do not understand the 'abstract complexity' of 'globalized free trade' are mocked by the millions who understand perfectly the destructive manipulation of their lives by monetarist ... governments, institutions like the WTO, and piratical corporations."

—JOHN PILGER, JOURNALIST, DECEMBER 1999

The irony is that what is mainly extracted is labor power. This comes about because the goods the multinationals manufacture in the Third World are sold in the First World.... American textbooks printed in Hong Kong are studied in British classrooms. California sports shirts stitched together in China are sold in resorts on the Florida keys. As a result of all this activity, the Third World has goods to export, but never seems to have enough. The reason is that the exports to the

First World are paid for with imports from the First World.... Many times more labor goes into the exports as into the imports. The wage differential varies from industry to industry, from country to country, and from time to time, but a rough idea of comparative wage scales can be gathered from the Gross National Product per capita. Today that figure is $2,800 in the Peoples' Republic of China, $1,350 in Nigeria, and $3,300 in Brazil. In the United States it is about $32,000. On the basis of these figures, we will not be overstating the case if we say that a dollar commands at least five times as much labor in the Third World as it does in the First World. Thus when the two "worlds" exchange goods, the Third World is the net loser of four-fifths of the labor involved. This four-fifths is extracted and gone forever.

The Third World nations will escape from neoimperialism only when they are able to sharply reduce manufacturing [goods] for the First World and increase manufacturing [goods] for trading with one another.

The Third World has been enticed, by faulty economic theory, into producing primarily for export. On such a foundation, they can have little hope of an early escape from neoimperialism. Providentially, they can be helped if we help ourselves. That is to say, they may be nudged into trading among themselves if we reduce our labor-extracting trade with them. It is in our interest to protect ourselves from such trade because it hurts our fellow citizens.

Producing for export, Brockway argues, enslaves developing countries to the demands and trade policies of the developed nations.

Respect for citizenship

The citizens of a nation have ... certain rights, privileges, and immunities that are denied to foreigners. If we who are citizens are not distinguished in this way from outsiders, of what meaning is citizenship to us? ... the well-being of our fellow citizens has to be vital to us. We can't demand respect for our own well-being unless we ... respect theirs.

In contrast, the theory of free trade is concerned only with commerce. Like classical economics, it has no respect for persons, except possibly as consumers. It sees no need for government beyond minimal police protection. As was demonstrated in Seattle, the World Trade Organization is not prepared even to consider questions concerning human rights, labor rights, the environment, or the use of natural resources. Even after the financial debacle of Southeast Asia, no attempt will be made to rationalize the surge and countersurge of money around the globe. In a free trade world, politics stops at the cash register.

Brockway refers to the meltdown of Southeast Asian economies in 1997.

Summary

At the heart of the debate about the WTO are broad issues about the nature of globalization, capitalism, and development. Even if everybody agreed to focus policy on improving conditions for the world's poorest (the 40 percent of the world's population who live on less than $1 a day), then there would remain major debates about how that would be achieved.

The WTO argues that it is a democratically governed organization working for a better deal for developing countries in particular, within the limitations of its central credo—that free trade is economically beneficial for rich and poor countries alike. It maintains that it places importance on development, environmental protection, and such issues as health care and food safety—again, within the confines of an essentially capitalist economic system.

Brockway argues that to seek to develop through trade is a historic mistake, and that developing countries will make progress only if they stick to trading with each other. He would have the WTO scrapped in favor of regional trade controls that restrict imports produced under sweatshop conditions. This not only helps drive human rights and economic reforms in those exporting countries, but also protects domestic U.S. workers, who are then liberated from the severe pricing competition imposed by the import of such goods (which are inevitably cheap to produce).

FURTHER INFORMATION:

Books:

Chossudovsky, Michel, *The Globalization of Poverty: Impacts of IMF and World Bank Reforms*. London: Zed Books, 1997.

Weisbrot, Mark, *Globalization: A Primer*. Washington, D.C.: The Preamble Center, 1999.

Useful websites:

www.wto.org/
The Official World Trade Organization website.
www.usinfo.state.gov/topical/econ/wto99/
The U.S. Department of State's WTO information site.
www.wtoaction.org/
An anti-WTO site.
www.seattlep-i.nwsource.com/wto/
A Seattle-based news source featuring news stories arising from the violent 1999 WTO conference.
www.ifg.org/newissues.html
Article by Martin Khor, Director of Third World Network: "Why Developing Countries Cannot Afford New Issues in the WTO Seattle Conference."

www.twnside.org.sg/trade.htm
Third World Network's website on the WTO.

The following debates in the Pro/Con series may also be of interest:

In this volume:
Part 1 Economic Systems, pages 8–9

Topic 1 Is the free market the best form of economic organization?

Part 3 Trade and Global Economics, pages 116–117

Topic 9 Is globalization inevitable?

IS THE WORLD TRADE ORGANIZATION FAIR TO POOR COUNTRIES?

YES: No WTO ruling can be passed without a unanimous vote; the decision-making process is therefore democratic

YES: Exemption clauses are built into WTO rules to help developing countries work around such concerns

EQUAL VOTE
Do all member nations have equal voice in WTO policy-making?

EXEMPTIONS
Does the WTO take development, health care, and environmental concerns into account?

NO: Stronger countries set the agenda and then force the hand of smaller countries; the process is undemocratic

NO: The WTO gives leeway only so long as such considerations do not interfere with commercial interests

IS THE WORLD TRADE ORGANIZATION FAIR TO POOR COUNTRIES? KEY POINTS

YES: Opportunities for trade with industrialized nations provide a vast export market for developing nations

YES: Classical economic theory argues that trade benefits all of the countries involved

FREE TRADE IS BEST
Is free trade the best way to economic growth in developing countries?

NO: Free trade favors the wealthy nations but not the poor on account of inequalities in GNP and labor/wage costs

NO: The cost of importing goods from developed countries eclipses any economic growth that developing counties can make from their own exports

155

Topic 12
SHOULD RICH COUNTRIES CANCEL "THIRD WORLD DEBT"?

YES
"THE DEBT BURDEN ON IMPOVERISHED COUNTRIES: AN OVERVIEW"
WWW.J2000USA.ORG/DEBT/EDPAC/DEBT.HTML
JUBILEE 2000/USA

NO
"PAYING ONE'S DEBTS"
NATIONAL REVIEW, VOL. 42, ISSUE 24, DECEMBER 17, 1990
CHRISTIE DAVIES

INTRODUCTION

The developing world—once widely known as the Third World—owes the developed world trillions of dollars: $2 trillion (thousand billion), to be precise. Most is owed to richer governments, the World Bank, the International Monetary Fund, and various aid agencies. The money was originally loaned for various purposes—to improve living conditions, to modernize industry or infrastructure, or to help newly independent countries find their financial feet. Now, however, even finding the money to pay the interest charges on their loans is difficult for some of the world's poorest nations. If they borrow to pay the interest, they become trapped in a spiral of increasing debt.

Of the total debt, some $375 billion is owed by 52 of the world's poorest and most indebted countries, and that is the debt whose cancellation is most strongly debated. The combined interest payments on this share of the

debt amount to $20 billion a year, which could otherwise be spent on frequently underfunded health or medical provision.

While $20 billion would mean a lot to poor economies, critics argue, it would hardly be missed by the lenders. They further argue that some $300 billion of the initial debt has been written off by lenders who already realize that it will never be repaid. Therefore, it would not be expensive to cancel the debt, but it would help the Third World develop.

The case for dropping the debt gained momentum between 1997 and 2000 thanks to the international campaign organized by Jubilee 2000, later renamed Drop the Debt. The campaign, which used the millennium to promote the idea of a new beginning, attracted considerable public and political support. It argued that enforcing debt repayment often harmed new and vulnerable democractic governments that had replaced the corrupt governments that had wasted the loans in the first place. It also argued that those who loaned the money in the first place had to take some responsibility for what were evidently bad lending decisions.

The campaign culminated in December 1999, when the G7 group of the world's largest economies promised $110 billion of debt cancellation. A year later, however, just $7 billion had been canceled. Initial debt rescheduling efforts had proceeded with 21 of the 52 countries, but had covered only a small amount of their debts. Sixteen of the 52 were still, in 2001, spending more on debt than health—for example, Mauritania is paying $63m on servicing its debt, but only $51m on education and $17m on health. Tanzania is paying out $168m in debt servicing compared to $87m on health.

Many of the issues of whether and how debt can be fairly canceled remain unresolved. Not everyone agrees that the debt should be canceled. The first argument against cancellation is that those countries that have borrowed money have a responsibility to pay it back. If they could not afford the loan, they should not have taken it. The only reason some countries are poor, critics argue, is because their governments squandered much of the money borrowed in the past. Although such arguments may be true in essence, they ignore both the impact of Third World debt on the global economy—if poorer countries became richer, they would buy more goods from developed countries—and the unfairness of making a country's citizens suffer for spending in the past, often on military projects that did not benefit them.

The main economic argument against debt cancellation—"moral hazard"—suggests that countries will have no incentive not to waste the money they have borrowed if they believe that debt forgiveness might become the norm. To make an analogy with personal finance, if you were to pay off a credit card over many years, why should somebody who had made no plans to do so simply have their debt written off?

Cancellation might also have profound implications for the global economy. International borrowing has long been central to investment and infrastructure plans. If it becomes apparent than international debts might not be repaid, what countries or institutions would be prepared to lend money in the future?

The following arguments put the case for and against canceling the debt. The Jubilee 2000 article explains how its coalition of development charities, churches, trade unions, and community organizations tried to address the traditional objections to debt cancellation. The extract from the *National Review* argues that those countries that have incurred debts must remain responsible for them and should consider new ways of paying what they owe, such as selling off economic assets or trading parts of their territory.

THE DEBT BURDEN ON IMPOVERISHED COUNTRIES
Jubilee 2000/USA

YES

"I called long ago for the cancellation of the crippling debt we have had to bear for so long.... There are others who have joined their voices in this campaign. There is something called Jubilee 2000. We ask our friends who have stood by us in the dark days of oppression and injustice. This is the new moral crusade to have the debt cancelled following the Biblical principle of Jubilee. Basically [this principle] says everything belongs to God; all debts and mortgages must be cancelled in the Jubilee Year to give the debtors a chance to make a new beginning."
—Archbishop Desmond Tutu in a speech to the General Assembly of the All Africa Conference of Churches, October 1997

Desmond Tutu was elected Archbishop of Cape Town in April 1986, the highest position in the South African Anglican Church. He is a tireless campaigner against racism and social inequality.

This "new moral crusade," as Archbishop Tutu calls the Jubilee 2000 campaign, is a worldwide movement to cancel the crushing international debt that poor countries owe to the developed world. Why is this crusade so important? This piece describes the origin and nature of indebtedness and its impact on people living in poverty.

Poor pay the price of debt

Poor countries owe a vast amount of money to rich nations and international financial institutions (IFIs) like the World Bank and the International Monetary Fund (IMF). For developing countries as a whole this debt is over $2 trillion. Most of this is owed by "middle-income" developing countries. But some of the lowest-income countries in the world are also heavily indebted, owing around $250 billion.

Hundreds of millions of people living in poverty in low and middle-income countries alike are paying the price for their countries' enormous international debt. Ordinary people did not benefit from many of the loans that gave rise to this debt, yet they bear the principal burden of repayment. Without major debt reduction, poor countries are trapped, making unending interest payments on their debts. This requires them continuously to divert large amounts of scarce resources from health care, education, and food security. The debt burden inhibits the social and economic development that is needed to lift people out of poverty.

To be sure, international debt is not the sole cause of poverty in many developing countries. Nor would cancelling the debt automatically result in improved conditions for people living in poverty. But this burdensome debt makes conditions worse for the poor. Its cancellation—if carried out in ways that benefit ordinary people—can bring a new opportunity for hope to millions who are currently unable to meet their basic human needs.

The countries of sub-Saharan Africa, for example, spend more each year on repaying their debts than they spend on all primary education and health care. Latin American and some Asian countries suffer as well. In Nicaragua, debt repayments exceed the total spending on social programs, yet three out of four people live below the poverty line and one out of four children under five suffers from malnutrition. Honduras—where over half the population lives in abject poverty—spends more on debt service than on health and education combined.

What are the other causes of poverty facing the developing world? See www.oxfam.org for further news and information.

The origin of the debt

The debt crisis burst onto the international agenda in the fall of 1982 when Mexico announced it could not pay the interest and principal due on its foreign debt. This was unthinkable—countries did not go bankrupt, and not to service the debt meant banks had to show a loss on their books. Many of these banks had overlent, and did not have the reserves to cover even a short period of nonpayment by a major borrower.

Many parts of the developing world, particularly Africa, Latin America, and parts of Asia, soon followed Mexico. The general causes were the same, although regions differed depending on the major creditors. For example, most countries of Latin America had large debt to commercial banks. Africa, on the other hand, owed more to donor governments such as the United States and to "multilateral" creditors such as the World Bank.

The common background of debt consists of actions taken by the wealthy northern economies during the 1970s for their own domestic reasons. But, those actions had great impact on poorer southern countries' economies. The United States had been spending vast sums to promote growth in

The World Bank is a consortium of five autonomous agencies providing loans, advice, and an array of customized resources for developing countries and countries in transition.

post-World War II Europe and Japan, on the Cold War, on the Vietnam War, and on various domestic concerns. This meant that international markets were awash with dollars. President Nixon took the dollar off the gold standard, ushering in variable interest rates on all lending, including domestic home mortgages and loans to foreign governments. These actions lowered the dollar's value. The major oil producing nations (OPEC) raised the price of oil—which is only paid for in dollars—in part because, with the dollar worth less, their oil earnings were able to buy far fewer ... imports.

The oil price hike earned the OPEC countries more money than they could absorb, so they deposited it in commercial banks in Europe, the United States, and Japan. These banks had to earn enough interest to attract the OPEC depositors, so they lent to developing countries who had to pay high oil bills, and who wanted to maintain their rates of economic growth. Commercial loan officers would in some cases get promoted based on the amount of money they moved, quite apart from the merits of the loans themselves. Governments borrowed because interest rates were relatively low and the banks put few conditions on their loans. Banks thought countries were secure risks since the economies were growing, and their belief was firm that countries could not go bankrupt.

Caught in a vicious circle

The 1973 oil price hike triggered inflation in the United States and other northern countries. When the second oil price hike of 1979 occurred, the U.S. Federal Reserve Board raised interest rates very high to halt inflation. International interest rates skyrocketed as well. In reducing inflation, the northern economies went into severe recession. As a result they purchased fewer products from southern producers. The southern economies became desperate: How could they pay higher interest rates when they could not earn more by selling their products to the northern markets?

Bitter medicine

The Latin American countries and two African countries, Nigeria and Cote d'Ivoire, had borrowed mainly from commercial banks. By 1989, through the Brady Plan, commercial banks agreed to reduce some of the demands for repayment in exchange for guarantees that they would be repaid the reduced amount. The World Bank and governments such as Japan and the United States guaranteed repayment of the remaining debt.

The Organization of the Petroleum Exporting Countries (OPEC) was created in Iraq in September 1960. Its purpose is to limit supplies to keep prices high.

The 1973 oil price hike has been identified as a trigger for Third World debt. See why by looking at www.multiline.com. au/-johnml/3rd world.htm.

The Brady Plan was a U.S. strategy that emphasized debt-forgiveness for highly indebted developing countries. See www.emta.org /emarkets/brady. html for more information.

Latin America's debt problems did not end with the Brady Plan. In order to pay off their commercial bank loans, Latin American countries borrowed from donor governments and multilateral agencies (IMF, World Bank, and Inter-American Development Bank). These loans came with strict economic conditions ... designed to stop inflation, balance budgets, and open (the developing countries') economies to trade.

However, these adjustment policies weighed heavily on people living in poverty, the majority of the population in most debtor countries. Basic investments in social programs and infrastructure dried up and private investment fled. In the 1990s private investment has gradually returned to Latin America, but largely in primary exports such as mining and agriculture, which create relatively few jobs. The governments still have large foreign and domestic debts that they must service before they can fund education, health, basic sanitation works, roads, and other public services.

Other factors have worsened Africa's debt problems. During the Cold War, donor governments were more interested in gaining allies than in whether the governments served the people or the money went to productive purposes. Newly independent African nations were led by inexperienced governments. Many projects financed by donors were poorly designed and unproductive—roads that went nowhere, factories that never produced, and power plants that were left uncompleted. This mis-spending left nothing behind except debt.

Africans with money kept their wealth overseas ("capital flight"). Civil wars and natural famines caused additional devastation. The African Development Bank, where the borrowers maintain a majority of decision making power, continued to make high interest loans to desperately poor countries. Neither these market rate loans nor low interest loans have been repaid, but the debt continues to grow as interest is charged for unpaid principal and unpaid interest. Because of inadequate resources to reduce Africa's debt, governments built up huge arrears.... Compounding the problem, international financial institutions and donor governments gave African governments poor advice on how to reform their economies. Ordinary Africans were excluded from having a voice in the decisions about debt relief while rich donor governments dominated the discussion.

Africa has been trapped by the past—old debt drains new sources of development funds. Ridding Africa from the debt burden will not eradicate poverty. It can free Africa to address the present and future needs of its people and its land.

Find out more about loans to Africa—and their consequences— offered during the Cold War at www.africapolicy. org/action/debt. htm.

"Capital flight" occurs when the citizens and businesses of a country are not confident of the future of their economy or their currency—they tend to send their savings outside of the country to keep them safe.

PAYING ONE'S DEBTS
Christie Davies

Rarely has so much humbug been written as on the subject of the "Third World debt crisis." Professional leftists want the debts of these countries, owed to Western banks or Western governments, to be written off altogether, and even the moderately progressive are urging a suspension of the payment of interest on these loans and a rescheduling of the repayment of the capital.

Banks not to blame

Find out more about Tanzania's economic history at www.bot-tz.org/bot/details.asp?ItemID=9

It is very difficult to take these arguments seriously, for banks are not to blame for the recklessness with which underdeveloped countries like Tanzania, industrializing countries like Brazil, Mexico, or Greece, and even wealthy nations like Sweden borrowed enormous sums of money abroad and then squandered it. So why should the banks or other foreign lenders be expected to pay for the corruption, incompetence, and lack of foresight of these politicians?

Why do we have an obligation to act charitably to others? What examples of this principle can you think of?

Those who think that banks should abandon the debt owed to them argue that the poverty of the peoples whose unrepresentative rulers borrowed so recklessly will be exacerbated if the debt is not cancelled. True, we have a duty to act charitably toward those who are living in poverty, but is it really wise to reward countries that hid their talents in the ground while failing to assist the more prudent poor?

It is probably the case that some of the Third World borrowers will default and welsh on their foreign debts, much as the state of Pennsylvania did in the early 19th century, to the disgust of British investors and the scorn and ridicule of the famous moralist and humorist, the Reverend Sydney Smith.

Sydney Smith did not wring his hands like modern clerics, but forthrightly called the Pennsylvanians thieves and swindlers. Many other borrowers defaulted in the course of that century, notably Peru. However, the only real penalty for the defaulters was that no one would lend them money until the memory of their sin had faded from the minds of the creditor nations.

Today we fear that such massive defaulting would lead to bank failures and even the collapse of the entire financial system. The Third World politicians know this and attempt to use it as a blackmail weapon against Western banks and governments. Yet there is no real reason why they should not be treated like any other debtor—that is, declared bankrupt with the proviso that their assets shall be seized to the amount of the debt.

Something roughly similar to the above occurred to the independent Dominion of Newfoundland, which went bankrupt in the 1930s and was to all intents and purposes taken over and run by the British Treasury for several years. Newfoundland never regained its independence, and in 1949 its citizens chose in a referendum to become a part of Canada.

The taking game

Given the tendency of the rulers of Third World kleptocracies and schnorrocracies to seize the possessions of their own citizens and foreigners alike, there exists in many countries a large pool of state-owned land, capital, and mineral rights that could be used to pay off their international debts. Eastern European countries such as Bulgaria are already offering an equity stake in their state corporations as a means of paying off their debts to the West, which ultimately means foreign private ownership of their manufacturing and extractive industries. It is only the hysterical pride of the underdeveloped politicians that prevents their countries from settling their obligations on the same basis and bringing their debt crisis to an end.

A "kleptocracy" is a type of government that is fundamentally based on theft and dishonesty. A "schnorrocracy" is a government that relies on the support of other countries.

Repayment terms and conditions

Some countries of course may not have a sufficiently large or profitable state-owned sector for their creditors to take over, and it would be quite wrong to encourage them to sequester the private property of their own citizens. Instead, deals between states should be struck in which changes of frontier occur without changes in the ownership of property. Just as in the past the United States bought Alaska from Russia or made the Gadsden Purchase from Mexico, so today it should seek further territory for cash on the understanding that those who live there would be immediately entitled to American citizenship. It would make more sense to purchase sparsely inhabited northwestern territory in Mexico than to continue to permit illegal immigration to undermine America's safety and integrity.

Find out more about the 1854 Gadsden Purchase at www.progress.org /gads.htm.

Similarly, a "territory-for-debt" swap would permit a just and peaceful solution to the problem of the future frontier between a united Germany and Poland. It is now clear that

Demonstrators calling for debt cancellation rally outside the U.S. embassy in Manila, Philippines, in June 1999. The giant octopus shown above symbolizes the U.S. and Japan.

the transfer to Poland of the German territories of Prussia and Silesia to compensate Poland for the Nazi–Soviet aggression of 1939 was only a means of extending the Soviet military empire. Many of the Germans living there were driven out by force or threats, and other "Germans" of mixed German and Polish ancestry stayed and called themselves Poles to appease their new masters. Now they want to be Germans again.... However, these regions have also received large numbers of new Polish settlers from those parts of eastern Poland annexed by the Soviet Union, and these people have a right to the land they have acquired and the homes they have built.

Resolving problems

If Poland were to agree to transfer some of the old German territories back to Germany in exchange for Germany's paying off all Polish debts to Western countries, a problem that has vexed Europe throughout the twentieth century could be resolved peacefully. Germany would have purchased the reunification of its lands and people, and Poland would have found a route from its present poverty and pollution to a state of freedom and prosperity. Those Poles who became German citizens as a by-product of the deal would have all the rights and privileges of that citizenship and a place in Europe's most dynamic economy and most stable democracy. Their lives and possessions would be as secure as those of the millions of people with Polish names already listed in West German phone books.

Did you know that Germany has one of Europe's most stable economies? Find out more at http://tiss.zdv.uni-tuebingen.de/webr oot/sp/spsba01_W9 8_1/germany1b.htm

Market solutions to debt

The market processes that can provide a solution to the problems of national indebtedness could also be used as a means of unfreezing other chronic conflicts involving disputed territory or ethnic minorities in, say, Israel and Palestine, or Kashmir. If we had in the past created a market in territory and citizenship, many devastating and expensive wars could have been avoided.

India and Pakistan have been fighting for possession of the state of Kashmir for around 50 years.

For a sum of money far smaller than the cost of the 1982 Falklands war, Argentina could have purchased the remote Islas Malvinas from Britain and given compensation of several million dollars to each and every British resident (there were 1,200 of them in total) who chose to leave. In most areas of life in advanced countries, buying and selling has long since replaced coercion as a means of settling disputes. If this is true, why can't we transform international relations in the same way?

In 1982 Britain and Argentina went to war over the tiny Falkland Islands, a British dependency in the South Atlantic off the Argentine coast.

Summary

Campaigners to "drop the debt" have succeeded in shifting international political debate. But will debt relief happen—and how much difference will it actually make to the lives of the poorest?

The Jubilee 2000 piece sets out a complex political and economic explanation of the debt crisis, arguing that the poorest developing countries would not be able to help themselves without debt relief. By acknowledging that "international debt is not the sole cause of poverty in developing countries," it raises the issues of what else needs to happen for debt relief to make a difference.

Should donors insist that the money is spent on poverty reduction, health, and education, or is this simply an excuse to slow down urgently needed action? Would canceling debt discharge the responsibilities of the developed countries, or are other actions as or more important, from development assistance to access to markets?

Christie Davies, writing in the *National Review*, takes a more robust approach to the issue. He attacks "professional leftists" and proposes that a purely market-based solution can put the poorest countries of the world back on track. Davies' attitude to canceling Third World debt is traditional: The countries that have built up debts are responsible for them. He suggests that they consider alternative ways of paying what they owe. Although many developing countries are in the process of privatizing and selling off assets, the idea of trading territory is not on the political agenda.

FURTHER INFORMATION:

Books:

Klein, Naomi, *No Logo: Taking Aim at the Brand Bullies*. New York: Picador, 2000.

Dent, Martin, and Bill Peters, *The Crisis of Poverty and Debt in the Third World*. Burlington, VT: Ashgate Publishing Co., 1999.

Payer, Cheryl, *The Debt Trap: The International Monetary Fund and the Third World*. New York: Monthly Review Press, 1975.

Tavis, Lee A. (editor), *Rekindling Development: Multinational Firms and Third World Debt*, Notre Dame, IN: University of Notre Dame Press, 1988.

Useful websites:

www.worldwatch.org/alerts/010426.html
For article entitled "'Forgive and Forget' Won't Fix Third World Debt."

www2.gol.com/users/bobkeim/money/debt.html
Information about the Third World debt crisis, with information on linked sites. .

The following debates in the Pro/Con series may also be of interest:

In this volume:

Topic 11 Is the WTO fair to poor countries?

Topic 14 Should companies be more ethical in their dealings?

SHOULD RICH COUNTRIES CANCEL "THIRD WORLD DEBT"?

YES: The burden of debt repayment inhibits the social and economic development necessary for alleviating poverty

YES: The ordinary people of the developing world should not be held responsible for the corruption of their past or present government

DROP THE DEBT
Is the developed world morally and socially obliged to cancel debt repayment?

REPAY THE DEBT
Should repayment of the debt be rescheduled to make repayment easier?

NO: Countries that borrow will have an incentive to waste money if they believe that debt forgiveness is the norm

NO: Developing countries can pay the debt in kind by handing over national industries, assets, or territory

SHOULD RICH COUNTRIES CANCEL "THIRD WORLD DEBT"?

KEY POINTS

YES: Banks are not responsible for the mismanagement of Third World spending—countries in debt should repay what they owe

YES: Lenders believed that developing countries were secure risks while their economies were growing; they did not think that countries could go bankrupt

BORROWERS
Should developing nations accept responsibility for their debts?

LENDERS
Were banks originally right to offer loans to developing countries?

NO: Some lenders should acknowledge that they gave developing countries bad advice about reforming their economies and therefore renegotiate debt repayment

NO: Lenders offered money to some countries to make allies during the Cold War—they were not genuinely motivated to help the developing world

THE EAST ASIA CRISIS

Between 1990 and 1995 six of the top 10 quickest growing economies in the world were in East Asia: China had an average growth rate in Gross Domestic Product (GDP) of 12 percent, while Malaysia, Singapore, South Korea, Thailand, and Vietnam all had growth in the region of 7.5 to 8.5 percent. The economies of these countries were buoyed by a combination of cheap labor and strong government backing, so they were able to manufacture electronic equipment, cars, and other products at prices the West could not match.

Tigers' Achilles' heel

The so-called tiger economies had an Achilles' heel, however: Their financial institutions were relatively undeveloped and weak. This became apparent in July 1997, when a regional crisis began. The Thai government floated the Thai currency, the baht. Before this the baht had been tied to the U.S. dollar on the international currency exchanges, its value rising and falling with that of the dollar. The Thais hoped that given their booming economy, international confidence in the baht would be maintained even without the backing of the dollar. When the baht was floated, however, its value plummeted as speculators sold their holdings of the currency.

A drama turns into a crisis

The fall of the baht caused a wave of panic selling of other East Asian currencies as investors pulled their money out of Indonesia, Malaysia, and South Korea, as well as Thailand. Most currency values across the region fell by between 40 and 60 percent, while the Indonesian rupiah dropped by some 80 percent. As their currencies fell, the East Asian countries found it increasingly difficult to pay their debts abroad. Economic growth slowed to a standstill, unemployment soared, and some 70,000 businesses went bust.

Reasons behind the crisis

In addition to the underdeveloped nature of many of East Asia's financial institutions, a number of other factors lay behind the crisis. Indonesia, for example, was governed by the corrupt President Suharto and his family. Some responsibility could also be laid at the door of U.S., European, and Japanese banks, corporations, and financial speculators. During the early 1990s they poured money into the tiger economies, and foreign investment averaged 37 percent of GDP in the region, fueling what is termed a speculative boom. This meant that wealth was created on the basis of confidence alone, without the economies in question being strong enough to warrant the amounts of money that were being put into them. When the crisis in Asia hit, foreign governments and investors panicked, pulling their money out of local firms and businesses, and rushing to convert any local currency holdings they had back into U.S. dollars and other safe currencies. In doing so, foreign investors, although they perhaps did not actually cause the crisis they so feared, exaggerated it far beyond the initial fall of the Thai baht.

Lucky escapes, rescue, and recovery

Indonesia, South Korea, Malaysia, and Thailand bore the brunt of the crisis. The older and more stable economies of Hong Kong, Singapore, and Taiwan escaped its impact. China, too, was able to actually take advantage of the situation—many of its firms and businesses were now able to move into the export markets for certain goods vacated by the crisis-stricken countries.

Eventually, the International Monetary Fund (IMF) stepped in with rescue packages. Despite the aid, the stricken countries continued to suffer in 1998, with GDP in Indonesia falling by 14 percent, by 6 percent in Malaysia, and by 8 percent in Thailand. It was two years before foreign investors began to reappear in the region, exports began to recover, and the stricken East Asian economies began to show signs of modest growth and recovery.

JAPAN

Japan is the largest economy in the East Asia region and was, until recently, by far the strongest. So what was happening in Japan while the tiger economies were reeling from currency devaluations, investment withdrawal, bankruptcies, and soaring rates of unemployment?

Following the destruction in World War II, Japan set itself on the road to recovery, combining a strong and highly interventionist government sector with heavy investment in, and efficient use of, technology. By the 1990s Japan looked set to take over from the United States as the world's largest economy.

Much of Japan's investment, and its subsequent growth during that decade, however, was the result of heavy borrowing. Crisis finally hit in the late 1990s with a stock-market crash of more than 50 percent. The traditionally interventionist government attempted to spend its way out of the collapse—even giving out money in 1998 as part of a trillion-dollar package of rescue measures in the hope of stimulating demand and spending. Still, many businesses collapsed, the banking sector fell into crisis, and the much-needed increase in consumer spending failed to materialize.

Finally, in July 2001, with new prime minister Junichiro Koizumi at the helm, the government announced a far-reaching economic restructuring plan. Reforms included the elimination of bad debt from the banking sector, privatization, and large cuts in public spending. However, the economic stagnation and slowdown look likely to worsen before any significant recovery is likely to take place. Meanwhile, reforms could have a devastating impact on living standards.

PART 4
BUSINESS ETHICS

Business ethics is a relatively new issue in economics. Whether firms act ethically or not has not traditionally been a prime consideration for consumers or a major consideration in economic theory. In the main, consumers, classical theory argued, wanted to buy the best goods possible at the cheapest possible price. The hourly wage of the miner who dug their coal or the hot working conditions of a laundress did not come into their decision to purchase or not. Most people who protested such things did so primarily as workers in labor unions, rather than as consumers. In other circumstances, in which it was the consumers themselves who suffered from unethical conduct, the prevailing attitude was summed up in the ancient Roman warning "caveat emptor"—"let the buyer beware."

In the last decade this situation has changed dramatically. How businesses behave is now seen as being an important component of how an economic system functions as a whole. Fairness, environmental protection, exploitation, working conditions, sustainable development, chemical treatment of foods, involvement with industries such as arms manufacture: Increasing numbers of consumers are making decisions based on such considerations. Businesses seem to be rushing to embrace a morality that can mean success in the marketplace.

One of the fundamental causes of the increasing importance of business ethics lies in increasing consumer awareness of choices and issues. The influence of such awareness is seen, for example, in the popularity of organic foodstuffs, which sell well in supermarkets despite often costing considerably more than nonorganic produce. Another sign of consumer awareness was the worldwide 1980s boycott of South African exports, a powerful consumer rejection of that country's policy of apartheid.

More recently, consumers have joined with shareholders, labor unions, development advocates, and nongovernmental organizations (NGOs) to protest corporate involvement in globalization. Leading companies such as McDonalds, Nestle, Nike, Shell, and Gap have come under pressure from consumers and other campaigning groups because of their perceived exploitation of the developing world, either in terms of aggressive marketing campaigns or in the shape of exploitation of low-paid workers.

Business reactions to such charges are varied. Some firms are eager to be associated with positive moves such as the ethical standards set out by the International Standards Organization. A further response has been the evolution of ethical investment opportunities by stock exchanges, pension funds, and mutual funds.

The smoking debate

If the issues surrounding globalization are some of the most significant in business ethics today, one of the most controversial is the debate about smoking. The sole purpose of tobacco companies is to sell tobacco, and in order to do this, they must convince people to become smokers. Since 1964, however, Americans have been told by the Surgeon General that smoking damages their health. Should tobacco companies therefore be liable for not warning their customers about the possible health risks associated with the habit? Numerous court cases resulting in tobacco companies being ordered to pay substantial compensation suggest that they should. The companies themselves argue that they are not— and continue to fund advertising campaigns to try to convert new smokers. Are they behaving unethically? Or are they simply meeting a need for society—and in many nations also raising a great amount of tax, which is traditionally high on tobacco products?

Consumers and companies

The question of smoking arises in *Topic 13 Should Governments Intervene to Protect Consumers?* The health warnings that tobacco manufacturers are forced by law to display on packets of cigarettes are a positive form of government intervention, argues Jack Beatty. Consumers should not always be expected to know their own most beneficial course of behavior. Joseph S.

Fulda believes that if consumers are provided with information, the market will react to their demand, rather than to state rules or corporate ethics.

Topic 14 asks an apparently simple question—*Should Companies Be More Ethical in Their Dealings?*—but produces two contrasting viewpoints. *The Economist* argues from a purely practical point of view that in the current consumer climate, paying more attention to ethics will actually make companies more successful, meaning more profitable. John Hasnas believes, on the other hand, that companies have one duty, which is to make money for their shareholders. Other considerations are little more than diversions.

Ethics and adverts

One of the most questionable parts of business in ethical terms is advertising, as discussed in *Topic 15 Does Advertising Benefit Both Consumers and Producers?* Traditional economic theory is based on laws of supply and demand, making consumer wants central to economics. But advertising sets out to get consumers to want things that in many cases they do not need and in some they cannot afford. So the producer is not meeting a real demand at all, only one that it has created for itself. Israel Kirzner argues that advertising is a vital means of providing information to consumers. Robert Berner, however, argues that advertising at best patronizes and at worst intentionally misleads consumers.

Topic 13
SHOULD GOVERNMENTS INTERVENE TO PROTECT CONSUMERS?

YES
"THE SEARCH FOR THE SMOKING GUN"
ATLANTIC MONTHLY, FEBRUARY 7, 2001

NO
"CONSUMER PROTECTION THROUGH THE WORKINGS OF THE FREE MARKET"
JANE LANIGAN

INTRODUCTION

What role does a government play in the economy? There are a whole range of possible answers: Classical economic theory stresses the need to reduce regulation of free trade; at the other end of the scale communist and dictatorial governments have established so-called command economies in which every detail of economic activity is controlled by a central office. The majority of industrial nations today—including many countries of the former Soviet Union—practice a certain degree of government intervention in the economy. In the United States it takes the form of the application of federal policies to change the way in which business is conducted, products are made and sold, or industry is regulated.

The collapse of communism in the Soviet Union and eastern Europe in 1989 marked a significant failure of experiments with command economies. China still retains a large amount of centralized economic planning, but most of the industrialized world is strongly committed to a capitalist economic system. According to economic theory, capitalism thrives in a free-market economy in which industries are given as much freedom as possible to innovate, develop products, and initiate profitable marketing and sales procedures.

One of the central problems with nonregulation, however, is that the free market is not always the most efficient form of economic organization. In the last decades of the 19th century, for example, successful businesses in the United States were able to buy up their competitors to establish monopolies in which only one company supplies a commodity, or they formed alliances called trusts that worked in much the same way. Trusts could artificially raise prices because they had no competition. From early in the 20th century the U.S. government has intervened in the economy by using antitrust laws to prevent unhealthy monopolies becoming established.

Government intervention may be necessary for other reasons. There may be inefficiencies in the market, such as the lack of power plants that caused a series of serious power shortages in California in the spring of 2001. There may be secondary consequences of industrial process, such as pollution, to clean up and control. The government in the United States has accepted an obligation to step in and enforce efficient and environmentally responsible practices.

"Here's [tobacco] that cuts short the lives of millions of Americans, and it's totally unregulated. And here's the premier consumer-protection agency in the world [the FDA]. Why isn't it doing its job?"

—JEFF NESBITT, FORMERLY OF FDA

This topic concentrates on a particular aspect of intervention: consumer protection. A good case of government involvement, for example, is smoking. Within a year of the 1964 Surgeon General's report, which was the first official warning that smoking was a serious health hazard, cigarette packages had to carry a health warning. The government intervened to protect the consumer in this case. A similar example might be the labeling of foodstuffs. Producers have little to gain by informing consumers of the contents of food, such as a high level of salt, that might damage sales. However, the public has a right to know what it eats. The government can force manufacturers to reveal that information.

Critics of intervention say that it infringes the freedom of both producers and consumers. A "nanny state" that protects its citizens through regulation can lead to consumer irresponsibility. If government is going to warn people of unhealthy products, why should consumers bother to conduct their own research? The outcome of this complacency is likely to be an uninformed public and increased exposure to risk.

The two articles in this topic address entirely different themes, but raise many of the important issues of consumer rights and intervention. The first praises the unsuccessful attempt by David Kessler, formerly of the Food and Drug Administration (FDA), to have nicotine classed as a drug. This would have enabled the FDA to control the promotion and sale of tobacco products. At the core of this issue is the question of whether the industry has deliberately "hooked" smokers, or whether smokers have only themselves to blame for having gambled knowingly with their health.

In the second article Jane Lanigan argues for greater market freedom, since it is the market, rather than the state, that can and should produce most goods and services. She suggests that consumer information be provided only if the market demands it, rather than as a requirement of state regulation. Lanigan's perspective assumes that consumers have the time and money to engage with firms and to invoke legal and other rights. Producers will also regulate and provide product information themselves, because they are acting in competition with other businesses that will do the same.

THE SEARCH FOR THE SMOKING GUN
Jack Beatty

Philip Morris is a U.S. holding company that owns several major companies, notably Philip Morris Inc., with diversified interests in tobacco and food products.

The FDA can control the sale of drugs: hence Kessler's attempt to have nicotine classed a drug and thus brought under FDA regulation.

Repetition for emphasis is an effective tool in written and spoken debate.

YES

Imagine my shock on discovering that Philip Morris considered buying *The Atlantic Monthly*, along with several other media outlets, in order to "influence the public policy agenda and the information flow to the populace," to quote from an early 1990s in-house document. Big Tobacco was desperate to change the antismoking climate of opinion. And David Kessler would add a new dimension to their desperation. During his tenure as the head of the Food and Drug Administration (FDA), from 1991 to 1997, Kessler did more to advance the health of Americans than any other public servant in U.S. history. His politically courageous (but ultimately unsuccessful) campaign to have nicotine classified as a drug is the story grippingly told in his new memoir, *A Question of Intent: A Great American Battle with a Deadly Industry*.

More money than God

That Philip Morris thought of acquiring the *Atlantic* illustrates one of the main points of the book: the tentacular reach of the tobacco industry. "You don't know what you are up against," an industry flack once told a would-be opponent. "We have more money than God." That money has tainted the most unlikely hands. Not just members of Congress from tobacco-growing states and white-shoe Washington law firms like Covington & Burling. Not just former officials of the FDA, including at least one former commissioner. But also the Sloan-Kettering Institute for Cancer Research, one of whose former directors "publicly expressed his doubt that smoking is implicated" in cancer, according to a Philip Morris memo. And the American Medical Association, which took money from tobacco to finance its lobbying campaign against Medicare in the 1960s.

Seeking to manage "the social climate for tobacco use," the industry has contributed to the Heritage Foundation, the Manhattan Institute, the Hoover Institution, the National Association of Manufacturers, and the National Journalism Center, which Philip Morris claimed gave them access to "journalists … throughout the country … which has resulted in numerous pieces consistent with our point of view." Big

Tobacco sought to influence Islamic mullahs to put a prosmoking gloss on their interpretation of the Koran.

Friends in high places

Kessler made these and like discoveries while sifting through tobacco-company documents … and the book tracks his sadness and outrage and finally cynicism as he finds name after prominent name—former Senate Majority Leader Howard Baker, Margaret Thatcher, leading cancer researchers, former lawyers for the FDA, congressmen at FDA hearings reading questions prepared for them by Big Tobacco—who have taken money from an industry that has killed 12 million Americans since 1964, when the famous Surgeon General's Report on smoking and health was released and we knew and they knew, past all but conscienceless denial, that cigarettes meant death.

The author is tacitly accusing leading figures in society of taking bribes from Big Tobacco to ignore the lethal effects of smoking.

"Individuals have a right to be protected from known or unwarranted promotions that will negatively impact their health."

—ARTICLE 12, INTERNATIONAL CONVENTION ON ECONOMIC, SOCIAL, AND CULTURAL RIGHTS

Kessler was a physician, hospital administrator, and lawyer who had taught FDA-related law. He had also briefly served on Capitol Hill as a volunteer for the Labor and Human Resources Committee working on FDA issues. Kessler's mettle was tested early on during his tenure at the FDA. Embroiled in a controversy with the Agriculture Department over accurate food labeling, he pledged to resign on principle if the Administration did not side with the FDA. (It did.)

A question of industry intent

It was a former aide to Dan Quayle, Jeff Nesbitt, who, after witnessing Kessler's grit in the labeling fight, challenged Kessler to take on tobacco. "I thought Jeff was crazy," Kessler writes. The federal courts had held that cigarettes could not be regulated as a drug, which the FDA's enabling statute defines as "articles (other than food) intended to affect the structure or function of the body." Nicotine might fit that definition, but the statute also requires a finding of intent—

David Kessler spearheaded an FDA initiative to bring tobacco under drug regulation. That he failed testifies to the power of the tobacco giants and the hazards of the free market.

The key question— that of intent—was whether the FDA could prove that big tobacco was selling the cigarette as a drug-delivery system.

the manufacturer of the drug must intend to purvey it through his product for the FDA to exercise jurisdiction. Should the FDA attempt to regulate cigarettes by trying to establish industry intent? Soon after he was appointed, Kessler put the question to his staff. Some members feared congressional retaliation against the FDA. (Indeed, the GOP takeover of the House in 1994 would confirm their fears. In an airport interview with NBC days after the election, Newt Gingrich, the new House Speaker, called Kessler a "bully and a thug," a hint of congressional hostility to come. "When I later saw the clip of the Brokaw interview," Kessler recalls, "I watched Gingrich step from the tarmac onto a plane owned by a tobacco company.") But at Kessler's fateful staff meeting one FDA official voiced the spirit that would inform the agency's seven-year battle to prove industry intent. "This is the most important thing we can do," she said. "If we take it up, I'm willing to spend the rest of my career working on it."

Defeat in court

In Kessler's deft telling the search for intent becomes a moral, scientific, political, and administrative detective story, a "policy thriller," *Business Week* calls it, with informers, false leads, threats, dead ends, and revelations—the story of a race against premature death for the 3,000 U.S. teenagers who start to smoke every day. The race ended in defeat when the Supreme Court, in December, 1999, ruled … that the FDA did not have the authority to regulate tobacco. Even though Philip Morris, in a historic reversal just weeks before the Supreme Court hearing, had publicly admitted that nicotine was a drug, and even though the FDA thickly documented its contention that "the manufacturers … engineer their products to deliver the precise doses of nicotine that consumers need to obtain its powerful effects," the conservative justices did not get it. Chief Justice Rehnquist said that previous FDA commissioners had told Congress that the FDA did not have the statutory authority to regulate tobacco. Despite the Kessler-led FDA's new findings, he saw nothing new: the government had known since the early sixties that smoking was dangerous…. Categorical conservative antipathy toward government regulation drove the ruling, Kessler believes. He writes, "I was convinced there was no evidence we could have presented to sway those five justices."

Ninety percent of new smokers are children and teens.

Civil actions to follow

But the evidence … that cigarette companies deliberately try to addict customers has and will cost the industry billions in civil suits. "The industry that once boasted of having more money than God [is] in trouble," Kessler writes. Hoping to sway opinion, it has made a series of welcome concessions. It has even signaled that it may support raising the minimum age to buy cigarettes to twenty-one. But this is not enough for Kessler … who fears concessions will breed complacency. Regulation of the existing industry always faced a conceptual ambiguity he did not—perhaps could not, politically— acknowledge while at the FDA.

Kessler has moved closer to that position as the industry has moved to accommodate some regulation. He now wants tobacco companies spun off from their corporate parents and made separate entities under strict congressional scrutiny, with no promotions allowed and no profits. "[I]t's too easy to be swayed by the argument that tobacco is a legal product and should be treated like any other. But a product that kills people—when used as intended—is different. No one should be allowed to make a profit from that."

Big Tobacco agreed in 1999 to pay $206 billion in annual installments to 46 states in lieu of facing endless crippling lawsuits. See Media volume, Topic 9, Should tobacco advertising be banned?

CONSUMER PROTECTION THROUGH THE WORKINGS OF THE FREE MARKET
Jane Lanigan

NO

The role of government in modern society has long been debated among economists, politicians, and others. However, it is generally accepted that even the most free-market of governments still need to intervene in cases where some kind of market failure occurs. So, for example, it is often argued that governments should at least provide public goods, such as policing and national defence, should legislate to protect the environment, should regulate certain business activities, and so on. It is also argued that government should intervene to protect consumers against unscrupulous firms that seek to exploit the fact that it is seldom possible to obtain perfect information about products, another instance of market failure.

But is this really the case with consumer protection? Is this really an instance where bureaucratic interference will go toward making the situation more, rather than less, efficient? I don't believe so. In the following article I will show that in the case of consumer protection, if the market is allowed to work freely, without outside interference, not only will the most efficient outcome result, but it will also be the outcome that serves the best interests of consumers.

Buyers and sellers are said to have "perfect information" when they are fully aware of all the characteristics (including the prices and output) of the products being sold by different firms in an industry. Perfect information is one of the conditions of perfect competition.

Consumer protection

The conventional argument goes as follows: In most circumstances consumers have limited knowledge of what they are buying prior to purchasing a particular good or service. Because of this, it is possible that people will sometimes buy products that are in some way defective or harmful. It is also possible that consumers may be dissatisfied with the after-sales service for a good, or they may feel that the firm from which they bought a product withheld or suppressed important information about it.

What products can you think of for which it might benefit the manufacturer to withhold information?

As a result, numerous consumer-protection agencies have been established by governments to provide consumers with information about the products they intend to purchase, to warn people about health and safety issues, and to inform consumers of bad business practices. In the United States agencies of this type include: the Federal Trade Commission: Bureau of Consumer Protection, an agency that works to protect consumers against unfair, fraudulent, or deceptive practices; the Consumer Product Safety Commission, a federal agency established to protect the public against unreasonable risks of injury that might arise from the use of products or services; and the Food and Drug Administration (FDA), which acts in the interests of public health.

But are these agencies really necessary? And do they really provide consumers with the best and most efficient sources of information and protection?

Product information

In actual fact, product information can be seen as an economic good just like any other, subject to market forces—that is, to the forces of supply and demand. As such, it will be provided to consumers if it is profitable for the business in question to research and disseminate that information. Whether or not this is the case depends on whether consumers value the information enough to pay the increase in price that will result from its provision.

One of the characteristics of a free market is that if there is a demand for a particular good at a particular price, then producers will find a way to supply it.

So, for example, we can look at the case of food labeling. Pressure from government consumer protection agencies has meant that food processors in the United States have long been forced to test their products extensively so that they are able to provide accurate labeling of the cholesterol, fat, and caloric content of every product they sell.

However, without this government interference would consumers be denied that information? Not necessarily. When the demand for such precise and accurate information about a product is high enough to support the necessarily higher price, normal, healthy competition will ensure that it is supplied. If the demand is not there, on the other hand, the information will not be provided.

Other sources of protection

But how can it be guaranteed, critics contend, that the information producers provide via this scenario will be neutral? Surely it is in the interests of unscrupulous firms to hide defects in their products, or to suppress any information that will make their products look bad? Surely it is necessary for the government to regulate in cases such as these?

If you were going to buy a new CD-player, how might you protect yourself from buying a faulty, poor-quality, or unsuitable product?

Again, not necessarily. The consumer actually has several other, more efficient, sources of protection from suppliers who choose to suppress non-neutral information: The law, other competitors, other consumers, and him- or herself.

If some form of outright fraud is committed by a supplier, consumers can obviously seek redress through the courts. However, recourse to the law is a time-consuming and expensive process. Not only this but, critics point out, it is a process necessarily undertaken only after whatever damage or injury has already been suffered. Nonetheless, preventative measures can also be left to the workings of the market.

Information as a dimension of competition

The actions of each supplier in a marketplace are circumscribed by the actions of other competitors in that market, and by consumers and the degree of risk those consumers wish to bear. Every consumer prefers to purchase under circumstances where the information on the product they are buying is maximum, so keeping the risk of buying the product to a minimum. As a result, information becomes an aspect over which firms will compete. A producer may wish to offer his or her product for sale without information, but consumers are then likely to go to other producers who are willing to provide that information.

Would you be willing to pay more for goods that are sold with clear and accurate information or for food products that are labeled with a clear list of ingredients? In which products is the provision of neutral information most important?

To return to the example of food, a producer of pork sausages may decide not to label his or her product with the percentage of pork that goes into the sausages compared to cereals and other ingredients. However, many consumers will decide that the risk is too great for them to buy those sausages, preferring instead to go to food manufacturers who provide that information, albeit at an increased price. However, this decision is left, ultimately, up to the consumer.

The role of insurance

It is often pointed out that there exist cases where important information cannot be confirmed by consumers, and that lack of this information could prove dangerous. Undoubtedly this is the case with medication. Is there not then an argument for government intervention here?

In such cases the damages that would be exacted by the law and the loss of future sales actually make the provision of inadequately tested and labeled medication too high a risk for a drugs manufacturer to take. Any drugs company, particularly an unscrupulous one, would certainly take out insurance against having to pay the kind of damages that might result from the sale of harmful medication.

However, it is also in the interests of insurance companies to ensure that the minimum of claims are made on their policies. The inspections that an insurance company would carry out on a firm prior to insuring it, with millions of dollars at stake, will surely be more thorough than those carried out by bureaucrats working for an indifferent government agency?

In addition, any firm or business attempting to market a dangerous drug or some other harmful product would find itself in the position of having to pay very high insurance premiums. This event would soon result in its having to charge higher prices than its competitors, eventually forcing the firm out of business. Any firm without insurance, meanwhile, would be boycotted by the majority of consumers.

If a company's record affects the cost of its insurance, then there is an incentive for that company to keep a clean record. But such incentives are the result of the free market, not of government intervention.

> *"The real and effectual discipline which is exercised over a workman is ... that of his customers. It is the fear of losing their employment which restrains his frauds and corrects his negligence."*
>
> —ADAM SMITH, *THE WEALTH OF NATIONS*

Guarantees

Another mechanism that is provided by the free market to protect consumers is the guarantee. Given that prior information about the quality of some goods and services is difficult for consumers to obtain, guarantees have become a useful substitute. Although a guarantee works only after the transaction has taken place, it takes away the incentive for a firm to make a sale under false pretenses, and also provides a cost on that firm of making such a sale.

Despite all these mechanisms, no system can completely eliminate fraud, misrepresentation, or the omission of damaging information. However, it can be seen from the preceding discussion that the operation of the free market, without government interference, will at least minimize such abuse. The best evidence that such a system works better than one whereby the government seeks to protect consumers itself, can be seen in the quality and safety of goods and services provided under command economies where every stage of the production of a good is under government control.

Summary

Jack Beatty's tribute to David Kessler doubles as an argument for government intervention when there is a perceived benefit to society—in this case the saving of thousands, maybe millions of lives through control of tobacco products. Beatty explains the method by which Kessler sought, albeit unsuccessfully, the right to apply that intervention. In doing so, he also exposes the pervasive spread of Big Tobacco's influence in the media and on politicians and lawmakers—an influence that, he asserts, accounts for the failure of Kessler's campaign.

Jane Lanigan argues for the free market by explaining the various regulating mechanisms that protect the consumer, with special regard to product information. She claims that product information is itself a measurable product that can be bought and sold, and that acts on pricing policy. She places responsibility for acquiring such information firmly in the court of the consumer: It is consumer activism (or the lack of it) that directly affects how much product information is supplied. But information is also regulated by the "invisible hand" of the free market acting on manufacturers, which give information on their own product or inform negatively on competitors' products. Allied with this is the establishment of insurance and guarantees to meet the mutually beneficial self-interest of consumer and producer.

FURTHER INFORMATION:

Books:

Kessler, David, *A Question of Intent: A Great American Battle with a Deadly Industry.* New York: Public Affairs, 2001.
Stigler, George, *The Citizen and the State: Essays on Regulation.* Chicago: University of Chicago Press, 1975.

Useful websites:

www.mises.org/efandi.asp
A page at the Ludwig von Mises Institute explaining the principles of interventionism.
www.nationalcenter.org/NPA280.html
An essay by Amy Ridenour on how government intervention harms consumers.
vlad1mir.tripod.com/index.htm
An independent site providing economic models.
www.dailybruin.ucla.edu/db/issues/99/10.13/view.lalas.html
An international perspective on U.S. interventionism.
www.econ.iastate.edu/classes/econ536/lence/lect11b/
An easy-to-follow slide show on the purpose and method of government intervention.

The following debates in the Pro/Con series may also be of interest:

In this volume:

Topic 1 Is the free market the best form of economic organization?

Topic 5 Does government intervention do more harm than good?

Topic 8 Should wealth redistribution be part of government policy?

Topic 9 Is globalization inevitable?

SHOULD GOVERNMENTS INTERVENE TO PROTECT CONSUMERS?

YES: Intervention is necessary to break monopolies, supply certain public goods (i.e., utilities, defense), and deal with pollution, waste, and other spillover costs

YES: Consumers cannot be expected to find out everything about all products; government must meet them halfway (i.e., in such cases as tobacco and health, or drug information)

FOR THE ECONOMY
Does government intervention improve the state of the economy?

FOR SOCIETY
Does government intervention improve societal well-being?

NO: State regulation of industrial and technological processes inhibits development and competition, impeding economic growth

NO: Government action is not always impartial and therefore not always in the wider public interest

SHOULD GOVERNMENTS INTERVENE TO PROTECT CONSUMERS?

KEY POINTS

YES: The free market abandons both public and producers to the law of the jungle; intervention provides the necessary checks and balances on the naturally destructive and wasteful symptoms of self-interest such as pollution, misinformation, fraud, and corruption

FREE MARKET
Is intervention a better option than the free market?

NO: The free market is self-regulating; competition between producers and profit incentives lead to technological innovation and to guarantees and insurance that protect public and producer; production naturally meets desired targets of supply and demand

Topic 14
SHOULD COMPANIES BE MORE ETHICAL IN THEIR DEALINGS?

YES
"DOING WELL BY DOING GOOD"
THE ECONOMIST, APRIL 20, 2000

NO
"THE SOCIAL RESPONSIBILITY OF CORPORATIONS AND HOW TO MAKE IT WORK FOR YOU"
THE FREEMAN, VOL. 44, NO. 7, JULY 1994
JOHN HASNAS

INTRODUCTION

The issue of ethics and of companies having some sense of "social responsibility" in the way in which they go about their day-to-day business is becoming an increasingly important one for both consumers and producers.

This has come about partly as a result of a number of major health and safety scandals. For example, in the United States and elsewhere people are asking themselves just how much information tobacco companies held on the hazards of smoking as long as 40 years ago. Were firms knowingly selling products that were a serious risk to health (without the warnings on the packets that are now required by law)? If so, did the industry have some kind of moral responsibility to at least inform its customers? Or is a firm answerable only to its shareholders (owners)? Should it have a wider responsibility toward other "stakeholders"—customers, workers, and society more generally?

A less obvious area than health where many companies have started to draw up codes of practice is industrial, or human, relations. For example, does a firm have the right to conduct random drug tests on its staff members? Does it have the right to screen personal e-mails? Are these practices ethical?

The question of corporate ethics has also come to the fore in recent years because of increasing public concern about human rights and environmental issues. For example, the role of the large multinational oil company Shell in exploiting oil reserves on homelands of the Ogoni people in Nigeria came to public attention when the Nigerian human rights activist and author Ken Saro-Wiwa was executed by the Nigerian military government in 1995 following his protests on behalf of the Ogoni. Shell made no protest when Saro-Wiwa and eight of his fellow activists were hanged, and people began to ask questions of the corporation, including what kind of consultation was carried out between Shell and the people living on the land where it wished to drill?

Other prominent examples of public concern on this issue include sports clothing manufacturer Nike sourcing much of its production out to factories in the developing world. Increasingly, people want to know if the sport shoes they are wearing have been produced by people being paid a pittance for working long hours under poor conditions, or if the expensive, hand-woven carpets they are walking on have been made by young children.

"These guys commit their crimes with a pencil instead of a gun."

MARIO MEROLA, DISTRICT ATTORNEY, *NEW YORK TIMES*, 1985

In terms of investments and pension funds, many people are also eager to know how their money is being used by the companies they have invested in. Are their funds going toward investments in firms that produce arms and weaponry, for example, or in well-known polluters of the environment?

In the following articles both authors note that the concepts of "business" and "ethics" can be seen as a contradiction in terms. Yet, increasingly, ethical corporate behavior is becoming an important part of business policy for firms. That is not only because firms and corporations wish to avoid legal penalties, but also because they do not want to attract the bad publicity that often results from poor ethical behavior toward workers or the community.

In the first article *The Economist* authors outline some of the moral pitfalls that might befall businesses today. They range from questions of staff relations within the firm itself, to meeting local environmental standards when firms are operating overseas, and more complex issues, such as whether companies should continue operating in countries that have a poor record on human rights. The article states that good corporate ethics and profitability are often connected, although the authors recognize that it is difficult to prove that ethical virtue will somehow bring financial rewards. However, even if it were not for this link, the authors conclude that it is worthwhile for companies to be concerned about their ethical behavior and reputation.

By contrast, John Hasnas's article takes the opposing view—that the only social responsibility of business is to use the money advanced by its stockholders in accordance with their wishes. Under normal circumstances, then, the only responsibility of business management is to manage the firm in such a way as to increase profits. For the firm to use company cash for the benefit of any other stakeholders would be wrong. Hasnas states that "stakeholder theory," originally a theory of corporate management, has been manipulated by business ethicists to create a theory of corporate social responsibility. However, this theory is flawed, the result being that firms are managed in the interests of stakeholders other than the firms' owners. This is not only wrong, but is also inefficient. In addition, he argues that the main proponents of this theory are the very people who have benefited most from the increasing interest businesses are having to take in moral issues—that is, academics working in the field of business ethics.

DOING WELL BY DOING GOOD
The Economist

YES

To many people the very concepts of "business" and "ethics" sit uneasily together. Business ethics, to them, is an oxymoron—or, as an American journalist once put it, "a contradiction in terms, like jumbo shrimp." And yet, in America and other western countries, companies increasingly wonder what constitutes ethical corporate behavior, and how to get their employees to observe it....

The IMF is the International Monetary Fund. Why might people be protesting against the IMF?

Milton Friedman (1912–) is a U.S. economist famed for his free-market approach to managing a country's economy.

Prioritizing profits and shareholder interests

Protesters in Washington, D.C., were this week [April 16–22, 2000] railing against corporate immorality as well as the IMF. But plenty of people retort that companies should not be in the business of ethics at all—let alone worrying about social responsibility, morals, or the environment. If society wants companies to put any of these ahead of the pursuit of shareholder value, then governments should regulate them accordingly. Thirty years ago Milton Friedman … summed up this view by arguing that "there is one and only one social responsibility of business—to use its resources and engage in activities designed to increase its profits."

Even those who think companies do have wider responsibilities argue about the best way to pursue them. Ulrich Steger, … [of] the International Institute for Management Development in Lausanne, says that companies cannot possibly hope to pursue a single abstract set of ethical principles and should not try.... He says that companies' … first priority should be shareholders' long-term interests, but, within that constraint, they should seek to meet whatever social or environmental goals the public expects of them.

Can you think of an example in business in which "money and morality clash"? How might virtue "pay in the end"?

When money and morality clash, what should a company do? Most firms try to resolve this with the belief … that virtue will pay in the end. Yet they cannot always be right....

Don't lie, don't cheat, don't steal

In America, companies have a special incentive to pursue virtue—the desire to avoid legal penalties.... The first corporate-ethics office was created in 1985 by General Dynamics, which was being investigated by the government for pricing scams. Under pressure from the Defense

Department, a group of 60 or so defense companies then launched an initiative to set up guidelines and compliance programs. In 1991, federal sentencing rules extended the incentive to other industries—judges were empowered to reduce fines in cases involving companies that had rules in place to promote ethical behavior, and to increase them for those that did not.

What are the specific moral and ethical issues that defense companies have to face?

But the law is not the only motivator. Fear of embarrassment at the hands of NGOs [Non-governmental organizations] and the media has given business ethics an even bigger push. Companies have learned the hard way that they live in a CNN world, in which bad behavior in one country can be seized on by local campaigners and beamed on the evening television news to customers back home....

One victim was Shell, which in 1995 suffered two blows to its reputation—one from its attempted disposal of the Brent Spar oil rig in the North Sea, and the other over the company's failure to oppose the Nigerian government's execution of Ken Saro-Wiwa, a human-rights activist in a part of Nigeria where Shell had extensive operations. Since then, Shell has rewritten its business principles ... and worked harder to improve its relations with NGOs.

Remarkably, Shell's efforts had no clear legal or financial pressure behind them. Neither of the 1995 rows, says Robin Aram, the man in charge of Shell's policy development, did lasting damage to the company's share price or sales.... But, he adds, "we weren't confident that there would be no long-term impact, given the growing interest of the investment community in these softer issues." And he also concedes that there was "a sense of deep discomfort from our own people." People seem happier working for organizations they regard as ethical. In a booming jobs market, that can become a powerful incentive to do the right thing.

How might investors' growing interest in moral and ethical issues have a financial impact on companies such as Shell?

The quest for virtue

In America there is now a veritable ethics industry, complete with consultancies, conferences, journals, and "corporate conscience" awards. Accountancy firms ... offer to "audit" the ethical performance of companies. Corporate-ethics officers, who barely existed a decade ago, have become *de rigueur*, at least for big companies.... As many as one in five big firms has a full-time office devoted to the subject ... [and] for academic philosophers ... the business ethics boom has been a bonanza. They are employed by companies to run "ethics workshops" and are consulted on thorny moral questions....

An "audit" is normally a formal investigation of a firm's financial situation or accounts.

In developing a formal ethics policy, companies usually begin by trying to sum up their philosophy in a code.... Not surprisingly, codes are often too broad to capture the ethical issues that actually confront companies, which range from handling their own staff to big global questions of policy on the environment, bribery, and human rights.... Robert Solomon of the University of Texas says, "companies debate their values for many months, but they always turn out to have similar lists." There is usually something about integrity; something about respect for the individual; and something about honoring the customer.

Complicated issues

What code of practice would you suggest a firm adopt in these particular cases?

The ethical issues that actually create most problems in companies often seem rather mundane.... Such as ... when a company has to decide whether to sack an employee who is productive but naughty [or] "When an employee who you know is about to be let go is buying a new house, and you're honor-bound not to say anything," says Mr Solomon. "Or, what do you do when your boss lies to you? That's a big one."

Issues such as trust and human relations become harder to handle as companies intrude into the lives of their employees. A company with thousands of employees in South-East Asia has been firing employees who have AIDS, but giving them no explanation. It now wonders whether this is ethical. Several companies in America scan their employees' e-mail for unpleasant or disloyal material, or test them to see if they have been taking drugs. Is that right?...

Do you think companies have a right to check employees' e-mails or to carry out random drug tests?

Moral dilemmas of globalization

Some of the most publicized debates about corporate ethics have been driven by globalization.... One big problem is that ethical standards differ among countries.

Many companies first confronted the moral dilemmas of globalization when they had to decide whether to meet only local environmental standards, even if these were lower than ones back home. This debate came to public attention with the Bhopal disaster in 1984, when an explosion at a Union Carbide plant in India killed at least 8,000 people. Most large multinationals now have global minimum standards for health, safety, and the environment. These may, however, be hard to enforce. BP Amoco describes in a recent ... report a joint venture in inland China. "Concerns remain around the cultural ... differences in risk assessment and open reporting of safety incidents...."For instance, deference to older and more senior members of staff has occasionally inhibited open challenging of unsafe practices." BP Amoco thinks it better to stay in the venture and try to raise standards....

Rights and wrongs

Human rights are a newer and trickier problem. Shell has written a primer on the subject, in consultation with Amnesty International. It agonises over such issues as what companies should do if they have a large investment in a country where human rights deteriorate; and whether companies should operate in countries that forbid outsiders to scrutinize their record on human rights (yes, but only if the company takes no advantage of such secrecy and is a "force for good").

The force-for-good argument also crops up when companies are accused of underpaying workers in poor countries.... Stung by attacks on their behavior in the past, companies such as Shell and Nike have begun to see it as part of their corporate mission to raise standards not just within their company, but in the countries where they work....

How might a large corporation act as a "force for good" in a developing country in which working conditions are poor or in a country with a questionable or bad record on human rights?

The rewards of virtue?

Most academic studies of the association between responsible corporate ethics and profitability suggest that the two will often go together. Researchers have managed to show that more ethically sensitive sales staff perform better ... that share prices decline after reports of unethical conduct; and that companies that state an ethical commitment to stakeholders in their annual reports do better financially. But proving a causal link is well-nigh impossible....

And then there is the impact on employees. It may be true that they like working for ethically responsible companies. But, ... small firms, in particular, pay far less attention than bigger rivals to normalizing ethical issues and to worrying about their social responsibilities. Yet employment is growing in small companies and falling in big ones.

Reasons to worry

There may still be two good reasons for companies to worry about their ethical reputation. One is anticipation—bad behavior, once it stirs up a public fuss, may provoke legislation that companies will find more irksome than self-restraint. The other, more crucial, is trust. A company that is not trusted by its employees, partners, and customers will suffer.... Ultimately, though, companies may have to accept that virtue is sometimes its own reward. One of the eternal truths of morality has been that the bad do not always do badly and the good do not always do well.

Why might anticipation of bad behavior in a firm lead more people to take legal action against it? Why is trust so important?

THE SOCIAL RESPONSIBILITY OF CORPORATIONS
John Hasnas

The author commences his argument with a cynical point implying that the main beneficiaries from the recent adoption of a wider social responsibility by firms are academics specializing in the field.

NO

Are you looking for a promising new vocation? Tired of the humdrum routine of life as an investment banker, corporate attorney, or electrical engineer? Want to get in [to] a field with unlimited growth potential? Then you should consider a career as a business ethicist.

Wait a minute. A business ethicist? Aren't they the butt of all those jokes? You know, "I looked up the word oxymoron in the dictionary and it said 'see business ethics'"... Well, after years of being subjected to this derision, business ethicists are finally laughing all the way to the bank... Since 1990, there have been approximately 100 substantial corporate contracts for outside ethics consultants.... Ethicists can make from $25,000 to $150,000 performing ethical audits ... and from $1,500 to $4,500 a day running ethics training programs....

What accounts for this rash of corporate interest in ethics? Have hard-boiled, practical-minded executives suddenly seen the light? Has the Age of Aquarius finally dawned? Or is there a more mundane explanation? To suggest that the latter may be the case, let me tell you a story. I'll call it "A Brief History of the Social Responsibility of Corporations."

Before beginning, I should say a word about what this phrase means. To claim that corporations have social responsibilities is to claim that corporations have moral obligations to expend funds for socially beneficial purposes even when such expenditures have not been authorized by the stockholders.... Thus, ... I am not discussing either cases in which the stockholders have specifically authorized the expenditure of funds for social purposes, for example, non-profit corporations such as the Red Cross ... and for profit corporations in which the stockholders vote for "socially conscious investing...."

"Capital" in this context refers to finance. Why do stockholders advance money to business managers?

A story

Once upon a time, it was believed that corporations had no social responsibilities. This was because corporations were viewed as arrangements by which one group of people, the stockholders, advanced capital to another group, the corporate managers, to be used to realize certain specified ends. Under this view, the managers … were empowered to manage the money advanced by the stockholders, but were bound by their agency relationship to do so exclusively for the purposes delineated by their stockholder principals.…

Therefore, there could be, as Milton Friedman has expressed it, "one and only one social responsibility of business—to use its resources and engage in activities designed to increase its profits so long as it … engages in open and free competition, without deception or fraud." This view, known as the stockholder theory of corporate responsibility, was supported by a very simple moral argument. The stockholders advanced their money on the condition that it be used in accordance with their wishes. If corporate managers accepted the money on this condition and then proceeded to spend it to accomplish social goals not authorized by the stockholders, they would be spending other people's money without their consent, which is wrong.

What sort of "social goals" do you think the author is referring to here?

As you may imagine, this was not a very popular theory in academic circles. If corporations had no social responsibilities, what would there be for business ethics professors and consultants to do?… Fortunately, [a remedy] was at hand in the form of the "stakeholder theory."

Stakeholder theory

The stakeholder theory, as originally conceived, contended that a corporation's financial success could best be achieved by giving the interests of all stakeholders equal consideration and adopting corporate policies that produce the optimal balance among them.

As a management theory, the stakeholder approach implies no social responsibilities for corporations. It simply describes a method for improving corporate performance. However, … if an argument could be found that showed that corporate managers have a moral obligation to act in the interest of stakeholders other than the stockholders, even when this would not financially benefit the firm, then it would become a true theory of corporate social responsibility.…

When the author talks about "stakeholders," he is referring to all individuals who have some kind or "stake" or interest in the firm or corporation. This could mean not only stockholders, but also customers, employees, suppliers or partners, and the wider community.

A plot twist: staking a claim to autonomy

The argument that the stakeholder theory embodied the ethical obligations of managers was based upon Kant's principle of respect for persons. This fundamental ethical principle holds that every human being is entitled to be treated not merely as a means to the achievement of the ends of others, but as a being valuable in his or her own right.…

The stakeholder theorists applied this to ... business by claiming that corporations are bound to respect this principle as much as anyone else. Thus, corporations may not treat their stakeholders merely as means to corporate ends, but must recognize [them] as moral agents... But, because it is impossible to consult with all of a firm's stakeholders on every decision ... the firm's management has an obligation to "represent" the stakeholders' interests by giving each equal consideration.... As a result, corporate management has a fiduciary relationship not only to the stockholders, but to all the stakeholders, and may be required to sacrifice the stockholders' interests to those of other stakeholders.

In what circumstances might managers have to sacrifice stockholders' interest, i.e., profits, to the interests of customers or employees, say?

This argument ... not only derives corporate social obligations from the libertarian principle of respect for persons, but these obligations are so amorphous ... as to guarantee the need for countless academic articles to explain [them]. In fact, its only drawback is that it is clearly unsound.

There is nothing wrong with the claim that corporations are morally bound to respect the autonomy of their stakeholders, but this implies neither that stakeholders are entitled to a say in corporate decision-making nor that the corporation must be managed in their interest. The fact that

COMMENTARY: Federal sentencing guidelines

The federal sentencing guidelines were enacted in 1991 in the United States so as to give businesses and other organizations an incentive to monitor themselves in terms of ethical practices and responsibilities toward employees, customers, and the wider community. Under the guidelines any company that develops an effective corporate compliance program may receive a reduced fine, or may even avoid prosecution altogether, should any of its employees or other agents violate the law.

Such a compliance program must incorporate a number of factors in order for it to be deemed "effective" by the government. They include the establishment of standards and procedures to be followed by employees that are likely to reduce the likelihood of criminal conduct. These standards and procedures are to be communicated to employees and others through training programs, manuals, and so forth, and must be overseen by suitably high-level, trusted individuals within the company. The business must also institute suitable enforcement mechanisms, for example, reporting systems that allow employees to report, without fear of retribution, co-workers' or supervisors' criminal conduct. After detection of an offense adequate disciplinary procedures must be taken against the offending individual(s).

the stakeholders must agree to be "used" by the corporation implies only that no stakeholder may be forced to deal with the corporation without his or her consent....

Employees, suppliers, and customers negotiate for and autonomously accept wage and benefit packages, purchasing arrangements, and sales contracts, respectively. If managers were to break the agreement they have with the stockholders to maximize return on investment in order to provide one or more of these groups with benefits in excess of those they freely accepted, they would not be respecting the autonomy of these groups, but violating that of the stockholders....

"Maximizing return on investment" has the same meaning as maximizing profits.

A happy ending

For the last two decades, it has been ideologically unacceptable to argue that corporations could be ethically bound to "selfishly" pursue profit or that it is wrong to force those wealthy enough to purchase stock to expend funds to benefit downtrodden workers, local communities, or society in general. The stakeholder concept was so popular that in the late '70s and early '80s several corporations voluntarily amended their charters to permit managers to base their business decisions on their effects on groups other than the stockholders. This was followed by ... "constituency" statutes that permitted ... managers to consider the interests of employees, customers, suppliers, and communities in making business decisions....

The triumph of the stakeholder theory had a profound effect on the way corporations were viewed.... Corporations that met their obligations were described as having a good corporate character ...; those that did not, as socially negligent.... This had a major impact on the Federal Sentencing Guidelines for Corporations that were designed to revise and regularize the fines ... to corporations convicted of violating federal law. The Guidelines, which took effect in 1991, drastically increased these fines ... but allow for significant reductions for corporations that have ... an "effective" program to discourage illegal behavior by the firm's employees—that is, an ethics training program....

Now, when we consider that it is ethicists who supply these programs, we may be led to suspect that it is the adoption of the Federal Guidelines that is primarily responsible for the current influx of ethics consultants to BMW showrooms.... Unfortunately, it also suggests that the surge of corporate interest in ethics may not herald the Age of Aquarius after all, but is just one more example of businesses looking to their financial interest.

In conclusion John Hasnas argues that companies are not actually interested in ethics or morality as such, but in adopting ethical codes they are merely guarding their profits. Do you think this is true?

Summary

In the first article, presenting the argument in favor of more ethical behavior by companies, *The Economist* authors argue that greater moral and social responsibility by firms probably leads to greater consumer trust and confidence, and may well lead to an increase in investment in that particular firm or corporation. They also note it is in a company's interests to avoid the fines and legislation that might result from unethical behavior, and that people are more likely to want to work for companies that have an ethical code of practice. However, the authors end by concluding that a firm or business may have to accept that "virtue is sometimes its own reward."

In the second article John Hasnas argues a rather different viewpoint. His main points are based on Milton Friedman's "stockholder theory of corporate responsibility"—that businesses are responsible only to the owners of their stock. No other "stakeholders" should have a say in corporate decision-making, nor should management of a business be in the interests of groups other than the stockholders or shareholders. The author both precedes and concludes his argument by noting that the main beneficiaries of corporate social responsibility are business ethicists themselves.

FURTHER INFORMATION:

Books:

Boatright, John Raymond, *Ethics and the Conduct of Business*. Des Moines, IL: Prentice Hall, 1999.

Carroll, Archie B., *Business and Society: Ethics and Stakeholder Management*. Sun Prairie, WI: Southwestern College Publishing, 1996.

Seglin, Jeffrey L., and Norman R. Augustine, *The Good, the Bad, and Your Business: Choosing Right When Ethical Dilemmas Pull You Apart*. New York: John Wiley & Sons, 2000.

Solomon, Robert C., *A Better Way to Think about Business: How Personal Integrity Leads to Corporate Success*. Oxford, UK: Oxford University Press, 1999.

Useful websites:

www.economist.com
The Economist carries various articles on corporate policy, including social and ethical issues.
www.libertyhaven.com
Liberty Haven website contains articles broadly advocating a reduction in government intervention into business.
www.ussc.gov/general.htm
U.S. government site giving federal sentencing guidelines.

The following debates in the Pro/Con series may also be of interest:

In this volume:

Topic 2 Does capitalism inevitably lead to income inequality and environmental destruction?

Topic 9 Is globalization inevitable?

Topic 13 Should governments intervene to protect consumers?

In *Environment*:

Topic 10 Do corporations have a moral responsibility to nature?

SHOULD COMPANIES BE MORE ETHICAL IN THEIR DEALINGS?

YES: Firms do have responsibilities to "stakeholders" other than stockholders. Otherwise they face legal penalties and lose trust.

YES: Companies with an ethical code of practice are less likely to suffer legal penalties and will attract more investors

MORAL HIGH GROUND
Is it morally right for companies to safeguard the interests of customers, employees, and others?

CONTRADICTION
"Business" and "ethics" are contradictory terms. Can firms have an interest in "the greater good"?

NO: A company's only responsibility is to stockholders. Other groups enter into separate, autonomous contracts and arrangements with businesses

NO: If companies concern themselves with wider ethical and social principles, cash is diverted, and profits suffer as a result

SHOULD COMPANIES BE MORE ETHICAL IN THEIR DEALINGS?

KEY POINTS

YES: Firms need codes of practice to be able to address such issues as environmental standards and human rights records in the countries in which they operate

YES: If ethics, social responsibility, or environmental standards are to be put ahead of profits, governments should play a role in regulating

GLOBALIZATION
Does increasing globalization make ethical codes all the more important for companies?

REGULATION
If society wants firms to behave in a more ethical manner, should governments regulate accordingly?

NO: Companies operate overseas to increase returns to shareholders. Environmental standards, working conditions, etc., should be regulated by local governments.

NO: Voluntary codes and standards are often far more effective, particularly when motivated by the desire to avoid bad publicity

MULTINATIONAL CORPORATIONS AND THEIR ROLE IN WORLD ECONOMICS

A multinational or transnational corporation is defined as any business that owns or operates factories or production units in several different countries at the same time. The first true multinational was the U.S. sewing machine company Singer, which built its first overseas factory in Glasgow, Scotland, in 1867. Multinational corporations (MNCs) now include firms such as Shell, Nike, Nestlé, Pepsi, McDonald's, and the Body Shop.

Reasons for locating units abroad

Most such firms were originally founded in rich countries such as the United States, Switzerland, the United Kingdom, France, and Japan. As a successful firm expands, it enters international markets, trading to countries abroad. Then, as sales continue to increase, the firm may decide that it would be more efficient to actually locate subsidiaries abroad.

There are several reasons why a firm or corporation might decide to locate operating units overseas:

* Producing and selling in a major foreign market will reduce total transportation costs.
* The MNC will find it easier to maintain contact with customers in that country or region.
* The MNC may be able to gain access to raw materials and natural resources that are either not available or are more expensive in the home country.
* The MNC may wish to avoid certain import restrictions or taxes on imported goods.
* The MNC may be looking to set up operations in a country in which wages are lower, or perhaps where restrictions on working hours, health and safety regulations, and other employment legislation are more lax than at home.

In addition, governments abroad may provide subsidies to large firms or corporations—whether foreign or domestic-owned—to set up in particular localities where there is high unemployment. Such incentives may induce a firm to set up operations overseas.

Benefits ...

With increasing international focus on, and often criticism of, their activities, MNCs today go to great lengths to stress the benefits that they provide for host countries. Such benefits include providing new jobs, often in areas of high unemployment. In addition there are benefits in technology and knowledge transfer. MNCs often have more advanced technologies and different approaches to manufacturing certain products that can be imitated in the host country by local producers. So, for example, the highly successful production and management techniques of Japanese firms based in the United Kingdom have been copied by some British firms.

MNCs also contribute to exports in the host country, and it is often widely argued that consumers benefit where a new firm or subsidiary increases competition in a particular area. In such cases the MNC may have the effect of driving prices down and the quality of goods and services up, while there may also be a greater choice of products as local firms have to improve their products and services in order to compete with the foreign firm.

... and costs

The effects of MNCs on host countries are not always beneficial, however. In terms of competition the MNC may actually have an effect quite the reverse of that discussed above, forcing local producers out of business and thereby reducing competition and consumer choice.

Even where many local jobs are created, most of the profits made by a large MNC will eventually end up back in the country of origin. Some MNCs have also come under heavy criticism recently for their operations in the developing world. They are accused of exploiting local people by paying them low wages, providing poor working conditions, or using child labor.

MNCs also make such large profits that their annual turnover might dwarf the Gross Domestic Product (GDP) of some small developing countries. This and their potential to shift production around the world give them great bargaining power with local governments. For example, a large MNC may threaten to close down plants and shift production elsewhere to win concessions from a host government.

Some observers think multinationals should use their influence to improve the situation of workers in poor countries, rather than taking advantage of cheap labor and poor health and safety standards. Consumer action such as boycotts is becoming increasingly common where large corporations are perceived by the public to be exploiting their powerful positions and making large profits at the expense of local people.

The importance of MNCs in the global economy

Whether for good or ill the role of MNCs is likely to become increasingly important in the world economy. In the United States, for example, the proportion of manufacturing output produced by foreign firms increased from 8.8 percent in 1985 to 15.8 percent in 1996. In Turkey the labor force employed by MNCs is rising by 11.5 percent per year, compared to the 0.6 percent annual rise in its domestic labor force.

Topic 15
DOES ADVERTISING BENEFIT BOTH CONSUMERS AND PRODUCERS?

YES
"ADVERTISING"
THE FREEMAN, VOL. 22, NO. 9, SEPTEMBER 1972
ISRAEL M. KIRZNER

NO
"A HOLIDAY GREETING THE NETWORKS WON'T AIR: SHOPPERS ARE 'PIGS'"
THE WALL STREET JOURNAL, NOVEMBER 19, 1997
ROBERT BERNER

INTRODUCTION

Everyone today is familiar with different forms of advertising. It is one of the most common ways in which people get to find out about different goods and products. Advertising ranges from a card in a store window signaling childcare services to an Internet announcement of a record collection for sale to an image of an athlete on a six-story downtown billboard to billion-dollar TV, radio, and press campaigns aimed at promoting public awareness of a firm's brand name. It is an accepted part of business in all the world's developed nations, where it is the means for firms not only to provide information about their products but also to promote those products above their competitors'.

Classical theories of the free market emphasize the importance of providing information to the consumer about competing products and services to allow them to make sensible choices. Advertising, many firms feel, is the best way to do this. But advertising is also viewed with deep suspicion because its sole aim is to generate revenue for the advertiser. Many people believe that there is therefore little room in advertising for morality; advertisers, they point out, have every incentive to overstate the advantages of their product or service and to make it seem essential to potential purchasers. Some people believe that rather than simply informing the public about goods and services that they need, advertising sets out to convince people that they need things that in reality they do not. It does this by peddling images of lifestyles that seem happier and more successful than those of most consumers.

Since the publication in 1957 of the landmark book *The Hidden Persuaders* by Vance Packard, analysts and consumers have grown increasingly wary of the subtle techniques used by advertisers to convince consumers to buy goods.

In the modern sense advertising—the word has its roots in a Latin term meaning simply "to direct attention toward"—is closely allied with the mass media. It was already well established in the print media by the start of the 20th century, when the successive development of radio, the movies, television, and the Internet broadened advertisers' opportunities to reach the public. The first advertising agency, Volney Palmer, was established as early as 1841. Firms were quick to see the benefits of this new branch of business. They set up marketing departments whose purpose ranged from overseeing company sales strategy to packaging and advertising. As markets grew from the local to national to international and finally to global, advertising campaigns have become increasingly ambitious—and expensive—and, their supporters' claim, necessary.

Critics allege that during the same period that advertising has grown to be a multibillion dollar global business, the nature of advertising has changed. They point to the early days of advertising as a golden age of straightforward truthful advertisements that did little more than state what a product was and say where it could be bought. Such images contrast unfavorably, they argue, with the more sophisticated advertisements of today in which, for example, a car ad might include images of landslides and earthquakes but only one or two of the car itself, or where a sneaker ad uses a whole cast of sports stars but does not say anything at all about the sneakers themselves. Critics also argue that the industry uses seductive and often deceptive imagery to sell all kinds of goods. They further accuse the industry of helping make smoking, drinking, and abnormal body images, among other things, attractive to susceptible members of society, especially children and adolescents.

Product advertising may be seen as either beneficial or a hindrance to the producer and the consumer. The question is, can it ever be of benefit to both? In the first instance successful advertising conveys information about a product or service to the consumer and portrays it in a favorable light, normally in terms of price or efficiency, or both. If the product is both financially competitive and better than its competitors, advertising will benefit both the producer, who sells more goods, and the consumer, who pays a competitive rate for a good product. However, advertising may be a hindrance to competition if the campaign makes false claims about certain products and makes illusory distinctions about it and its competitors' "similar" products. This is known as negative advertising.

In the following articles Israel M. Kirzner argues that advertisers are being treated badly when they are accused of producing information that is offensive, fraudulent, and full of lies. He asserts that in actual fact, advertising in a free economy should add to consumer satisfaction. He states that it is an inarguable part of the free market economy. Robert Berner, by contrast, presents quite a different angle in his article about Kalle Lasn, an ex-advertising executive who now works to promote the anticonsumerist cause. In Lasn's view advertising sells an ever increasing array of goods to people who do not really need them, many of whom run up huge debts in order to keep up with consumerist culture. He argues advertising creates wants and encourages materialism.

ADVERTISING
Israel M. Kirzner

YES

Kirzner introduces his article by listing the most common criticisms that are made against advertising. These are the points he will go on to address.

Advertising has been badly treated by many who should know better. Let us examine some criticisms:
First, many advertising messages are said to be offensive.... Second, advertising, it is argued, is deceitful, fraudulent, full of lies.... Third, ... where advertising is not deceitful, it is at best persuasive. That is, it attempts ... not to fulfil the desires of man but to change his desires to fit that which has been produced.... A fourth criticism has been that ... advertising leads toward monopoly by building up a wall of good will, a protective wall of loyalty among consumers, which renders a particular product immune to outside competition.... Finally, ... advertising is condemned as wasteful. The consumer pays a price for a product, which covers a very large sum of money spent on advertising....

The free economy and how it functions

It is not my purpose here to defend each and every advertising message. I would rather discuss a free economy ... (and) show that in such a world, advertising would emerge with a positive role; that it would add to the efficiency with which consumer wants are satisfied; and that ... a large volume of the criticism would fade away were it understood what role advertising, in fact, has to play in a pure market economy.

Let me imagine a free market, in which there are no deceitful men at all. All the messages beamed to consumers ... would be the strict truth.... Further, let us imagine a pure market economy with government intervention kept to the absolute minimum.... Producers [produce] that which they believe can be sold to the consumers at the highest possible ... price. Entrepreneur producers, who detect where resources are currently being used in less than optimum fashion, take these resources and transfer them to other uses in the economy where they will serve consumer wants ... that are more urgently desired....

These are the conditions for "perfect competition," a model of industrial structure in which many small firms compete with one another to supply a single product. Economists often assume these conditions as a good starting point to illustrate the behavior of firms.

We will assume that there is freedom of entry into all industries.... All resource owners are free to sell their resources, whether labor, natural resources, capital goods ... to the highest bidder. In this way the agitation of the market gradually shuffles resources around until they begin to be used to produce those products [that] consumers value most highly. Consumers arrange their spending to buy the commodities they believe to be most urgently needed....

Open competition

In this model of the perfectly competitive economy, there would in fact be no competition ... in the everyday sense of the term. When we describe the laissez-faire economy as competitive, we mean an economy in which there is complete freedom of entry. If anyone believes that he can produce something that can serve consumers' wants more faithfully, he can try to do it. If anyone believes that the current producers are producing at a price which is too high, then he is free to try to produce and sell at a lower price. This is what competition means....

Although this model looks far removed from reality, some markets are more perfectly competitive than others. Can you think of any markets that are almost perfectly competitive?

Non-price competition

Now, economists and others understand generally that competition means price competition—offering to sell at a lower price than your competitors are asking, or offering to buy at a higher price than your competitors are bidding....

However, we must remember that there is another kind of competition, sometimes called "non-price competition."... Competition takes the form not only of producing the identical product [that] your competitors are producing and selling it at a lower price.... Competition means sometimes offering a better product, ... a product [that] is more in line with what the entrepreneur believes consumers [want to purchase]. It means producing a different model of a product, a different quality, putting it in a different package.... It means competing in many, many ways besides the price asked of the consumer....

Can you think of any other examples of ways in which producers compete with one another, other than by lowering the price of their product?

A false distinction

The late Professor Edward H. Chamberlin of Harvard popularized a distinction ... between "production costs" and "selling costs." In his book of almost forty years ago, *The Theory of Monopolistic Competition*, Chamberlin argued that there are two kinds of costs [that] manufacturers, producers, sellers, [and] suppliers incur. First, they incur the fabrication costs, the costs of producing what it is they want to sell. Second, they incur additional expenditures that do not produce the product, or change it or improve it, but merely get it sold. Advertising, of course, is the most obvious example which Chamberlin cited....

Nonprice competition is also sometimes referred to as "monopolistic competition."

Do you think Chamberlin's distinction between "production costs" and "selling costs" is a relevant one?

Ludwig von Mises (1881–1973) was a prominent economist in the Austrian school of economists.

The fallacy in the distinction between production costs and selling costs is fairly easy to notice.... We know that a product is not an objective quantity of steel or paper. A product is that which is perceived, understood, desired by a consumer. If there are two products otherwise similar to the outside eye which happen to be considered to be different by the consumer, then ... these are different products.

Ludwig von Mises gives the example of a restaurant. A man has a choice of two restaurants serving identical meals, identical food. But in one restaurant they haven't swept the floor.... The meals are the same. The food is the same. How shall we describe the money spent ... sweeping the floor? "Production costs" or "selling costs?" Does sweeping change the food? No. Surely, then, it could be argued that this is strictly a "selling cost." It is like advertising. The food remains the same but, because you have a man sweeping the floor, more people come to this restaurant than to that.

The author is suggesting that the costs of advertising are part of the whole package that is a product. As a consumer, would you be happy to pay 20 percent more, say, for a pair of jeans that has been heavily advertised?

But this is nonsense. What you buy when you enter a restaurant is not the food alone. What you buy is a meal, served in certain surroundings. If the surroundings are more desirable, it's a different meal, it's a different package. That which has been spent to change the package is as much production cost as the salary paid to the cook....

The provision of information

One of the standard defenses for advertising is that it provides a service which consumers value—the provision of information.... Advertising provides information, and this goes a long way to explain the role which advertising ... must play.... Information is produced; it is desired; it is a product; it is purchased jointly with the product itself; it is a part of the package; and it is something which consumers value.... It is something for which people are willing to pay....

What proportion of advertising is to provide information to consumers? And what proportion is to make consumers more aware of opportunities for buying products? Do you think these are both an important part of the package of costs of a product?

[Entrepreneurs] have not only to produce opportunities which are available to consumers; [they] have to make consumers aware of these opportunities.... An opportunity which is not known ... is simply not an opportunity. I am not fulfilling my entrepreneurial task unless I project to the consumer the awareness of the opportunity. How do I do that? I do that, not with a little sign on my door, but with a big neon sign; ... and better than that I chalk up the price; and better than that I make sure that the price is lower than the price at nearby [shops].... In other words, the final package consists not only of abstract academic information but in having the final product placed in front of the consumer in such a form that he cannot miss it....

The growth of advertising

Advertising has grown. Compare the volume of advertising today with the volume 100 years ago and it has grown tremendously. More! Consider the price of a commodity that you buy.... Find out what portion of that price can be attributed to advertising costs and it turns out that a much larger percentage of the final cost to the consumer can be attributed to advertising today than could have been attributed 50 years ago, 70 years ago, 100 years ago. Why?...

... [In] an affluent society there are many opportunities placed before consumers. The consumer enters a supermarket and if he is to make an intelligent decision he is going to have to spend several hours reading ... everything that's on the packages.... It's a tough job to be a consumer. And the multiplicity of opportunities makes it necessary for advertisers to project more provocative messages if they want to be heard.... The number of commodities is so great that in order for any one particular product to be brought to the attention of the consumer, a large volume of advertising is necessary.... Is it part of production costs? Very definitely, yes.... For an opportunity to be made available, it must be in a form which it is impossible to miss....

Do you think producers have a right to charge more for a product because they are competing against so many other products in the marketplace?

Take with a grain of salt

Of course, deceitful advertising is to be condemned.... But we live in a world where you have to be careful what you read, to whom you listen, whom to believe. And it's true of everything.... It is very easy to pick out the wrong messages to believe. Now, this doesn't in any way condone or justify deceitful messages. We have to recognize, however, while particular producers may have a short-run interest in projecting a message of doubtful veracity, that so long as there's freedom of competition the consumer has his choice of which product to buy [and] who to believe....

The author's final point is that people are free to believe advertisers or not, and so to buy a product or not. Is that the case with all consumers?

To blame advertising for the imperfections and weaknesses of mankind is unfair.... Advertising would be less deceitful if men were less deceitful. It would be more ethical, less offensive, if men were less offensive and more ethical. But advertising itself is an integral, inescapable aspect of the market economy.

... GREETING THE NETWORKS WON'T AIR
Robert Berner

NO

Picture the Scene—Katie Couric and Willard Scott all bundled up and cozy on Thanksgiving morning, watching the Cat in the Hat and Spider man float above Macy's department store.

Cut to a commercial—an animated pig superimposed on a map of North America smacks its lips and says: "The average North American consumes five times more than a Mexican, 10 times more than a Chinese person, and 30 times more than a person from India... Give it a rest. November 28 is Buy Nothing Day." Can't see it happening? Neither can the networks. That's what's driving Kalle Lasn crazy.

Do you find these statistics surprising? What kind of products do you "consume" that are not available to a person in India, for example?

Commercial trashing

For five years now, the former advertising executive turned anticonsumerism activist has been waging a grassroots campaign against Christmastime commercialism. His strategy—attack Christmas shopping one day at a time, beginning with the season kickoff on the day after Thanksgiving. Each year, Mr. Lasn calls for a 24-hour shopping moratorium on the Friday, which he has dubbed Buy Nothing Day. The commercial trashing commercialism is just his way of reaching the masses.

What do you think Kalle Lasn's objections might be to "Christmastime commercialism"?

Not ready for prime-time

But the Big Three networks aren't having any of it. "We don't want to take any advertising that's inimical to our legitimate business interests," says Richard Gitter, vice president of advertising standards at General Electric Co.'s NBC network, which refused to take the 30-second spot. Westinghouse Electric Corp.'s CBS, in a letter rejecting the commercial, went as far as to say that Buy Nothing Day is "in opposition to the current economic policy in the United States."

Never mind that few viewers would even see the commercial if it did air: Mr. Lasn's budget for the one network commercial is about $15,000, enough for only the worst of slots. Not surprisingly, the networks have also refused Mr. Lasn's repeated requests to run his 30-second spot encouraging viewers to participate in TV Turn-off Week. "I came from Estonia where you were not allowed to speak up

TV is largely sponsored by advertising—by firms and businesses that want to sell their products to consumers. Do you think it was right for the TV networks to refuse to show the Buy Nothing Day ad? Was it really against U.S. economic policy?

against the government," says the 55-year-old Mr. Lasn, whose family fled to the West in advance of the Russian takeover in 1944. "Here I was in North America, and suddenly I realised you can't speak up against the sponsor. There's something fundamentally undemocratic about our public airways."

Do you think Kalle Lasn is being censored because he wishes to speak out against advertising and commercialism?

A clear-cut case

After working in advertising in Tokyo in the late 1960s, Mr. Lasn moved to Canada and became a documentary filmmaker. It was in the 1980s that his activist streak got sparked while he was watching a local forestry company's commercial promoting clear-cutting as "forest management." Outraged, he put together his own TV advertisement documenting the downside of clear-cutting and the need to save old-growth trees. But local television stations "refused to sell us the air time even as they were running the other side's campaign," he says

Why do you think television stations were more sympathetic to the forestry company's promotion than to Mr. Lasn's more environmental stand?

Alternative advertising

In 1989, Mr. lasn founded the Media Foundation in Vancouver, British Columbia. The group—which he says had revenue of $500,000 last year and has five full-time employees—produces alternative advertising for student and environmental groups, including an anti-automobile commercial for Greenpeace. The foundation also publishes a quarterly magazine called *Adbusters* that sells for $5.75 a copy and, according to Mr. Lasn, has 40,000 subscribers. The magazine lambastes advertising's effect on popular culture and includes lampoons of famous ads. One parody of Camel cigarettes features a cartoon character called "Joe Chemo;" a jab at Calvin Klein's Obsession campaign shows a slender model seductively caressing a toilet, vomiting; and a "Big Mac Attack" ad displays a man on an operating table, hooked up to a heart monitor aglow with the Golden Arches.

What aspects of advertising are being protested against in these three parodies?

Supporters

Mr. Lasn counts among his supporters the Foundation for Deep Ecology, a San Francisco environmental group that says it has given him four $25,000 grants; the Centre for a New American Dream in Burlington, Vermont, which espouses eliminating debt and living simply in the tradition of Henry David Thoreau; and the like-minded Northwest Earth Institute in Portland, Oregon, which plans to hit the streets in Buy Nothing Day to issue "Christmas Gift Exemption" vouchers.

Henry David Thoreau (1817–62) was an American poet and essayist famed for his studies of nature and his simple way of life.

The biggest Buy-Nothing Day celebration is planned for Seattle. There, organisers will cut up their credit-cards outside

Santa Claus is suspended from the hands of a giant Buddha outside a shopping complex in New Delhi, India, in December 1997.

of downtown's West Lake Center mall. Entertainment will be provided by a group of elderly women called the Raging Grannies, who will perform to the tune of "Down by the Riverside" their song, "I Ain't Going to Run Up Debt No More." And Vicki Robin, author of the book *Your Money or Your Life*, will be dressed as a doctor, dispensing medical advice on the materialistic malady known as "affluenza."

Do you think people put too much emphasis on the importance of material goods in the West? Is this encouraged by advertising?

Space for debate

As for the snorting-pig commercial, at least some consumers will get to see it. For the third year in a row, Cable News Network Headline News has agreed to air the advertisement, and Mr. Lasn is paying $10,000 for a slot. "We should make our commercial space available to debate issues of our day," says Steven Haworth, a spokesman for the Time Warner incorporated network. Mr. Lasn is also asking local and cable-access stations to take the commercial.

That other networks refuse to broadcast the swinish swipe doesn't bother most constitutional-law experts, who point out that the networks aren't under any legal obligation to do so. "At least the networks make it clear who butters their bread," says Laurence Tribe, the Harvard Law School professor. But he adds: "The networks seem to have a short-sighted lack of wit."

Summary

The advertising industry earns billions of dollars each year, but who benefits as a result of this apart from advertisers themselves? Israel M. Kirzner argues that advertising also benefits producers—the firms and businesses that are promoting their products—and consumers, the people ads are aimed at in the first place. He argues that advertising provides information that is desired by consumers and also highlights purchasing opportunities that people may wish to take advantage of. Kirzner further argues that while it is easy to blame advertising for the "imperfections and weaknesses of mankind," that is unfair. In a free economy people are free to choose to believe an advertising message or not, to buy a product or not.

Conversely, Robert Berner writes about Kalle Lasn and his organization, the Media Foundation, who protest against Western consumerism. For Lasn advertising merely promotes materialism, selling more and more products and services to people who do not really need them and in many cases cannot afford them either. Various of Lasn's parodies and campaigns address other issues in advertising, such as the selling of products that are harmful to people's health and the promotion of unhealthy body images.

FURTHER INFORMATION:

Books:

Berger, Arthur Asa, *Ads, Fads, and Consumer Culture*. Lanham, MD: Rowman and Littlefield, 2000.

Frank, Thomas, *The Conquest of Cool: Business Culture, Counterculture, and the Rise of Hip Consumerism*. Chicago: University of Chicago Press, 1998.

Klein, Naomi, *No Logo: Taking Aim at the Brand Bullies*. New York: Picador USA, 2000.

Lasn, Kalle, *Culture Jam: How to Reverse America's Suicidal Consumer Binge—And Why We Must*. New York: Quill Publishing, 2000.

Ogilvy, David, *Ogilvy on Advertising*. Rancho Mirage, CA: Vintage Books, 1987.

Trout, Jack, and Steve Rivkin, *Differentiate or Die: Survival in Our Era of Killer Competition*. New York: John Wiley and Sons, 2000.

Useful websites:

www.libertyhaven.com
The Liberty Haven site publishes a wide range of articles on economic, political, and philosophical issues.
www.adbusters.org
News on the *Adbusters* magazine.

www.economist.com
Presents articles and news relating to economies and economics, including how firms compete with one another in the real world.

The following debates in the Pro/Con series may also be of interest:

In this volume
Topic 1 Is the free market the best form of economic organization?

Topic 13 Should governments intervene to protect consumers?

In *Media*:
Part 2: Advertising and the media

DOES ADVERTISING BENEFIT BOTH CONSUMERS AND PRODUCERS?

YES: Customers desire information about the products they are buying and are willing to pay for it

YES: In a free society people can make up their own minds whether or not a piece of advertising is truthful

INFORMATION
Does advertising provide impartial information that consumers wish to receive?

FREE TO CHOOSE
Aren't consumers free to choose what messages they believe and which products to buy?

NO: The information that advertising provides is not impartial—it is persuasive at best and in some cases is misleading or incorrect

NO: Many of the people that advertising is aimed at, for example, children and teenagers, are vulnerable to advertising gimmicks and persuasive messages

DOES ADVERTISING BENEFIT BOTH CONSUMERS AND PRODUCERS?
KEY POINTS

YES: Producers need to highlight the opportunities that are available to consumers in order to sell their products. Consumers need to know what is available to buy and where to buy it

YES: Advertising persuades people to buy far more products than they need. Over-consumption is unhealthy, lands many people in debt, and uses up valuable resources.

SIGNPOST
Does advertising provide an important signpost to consumers as to where they can buy the products they need?

CONSUMERISM
Does advertising promote materialism?

NO: If a consumer genuinely needs something, he or she can usually find it for themselves

NO: Advertising is simply one of the means by which firms compete with one another. This, along with the production of more goods and services, gives consumers a good deal, and promotes economic prosperity.

SPEAKING SKILLS

A good speaker knows the importance of presentation and delivery. Knowing one's subject is important, but knowing how to engage and speak to your audience is more so. The following guidance should help you develop good delivery and presentation skills. If you can use and adapt the advice below into different situations, you will find that it will help you in most facets of everyday life.

There are three types of main speech:
* Manuscript
* Memory
* Extemporaneous

We examine them in further detail below.

1. Manuscript

This type of speech has a prepared script, and the speaker needs notes. It is a formal type of delivery favored by politicians and people in the public eye, since it allows greater control over the exact wording of the speech. It is particularly useful when dealing with a sensitive subject, since it affords the speaker ultimate control. It is a good idea to practice the speech beforehand so that it flows more naturally. In fact, many speakers actually change or edit their speech while talking. Listen to President John F. Kennedy's inaugural speech, January 20, 1961 at: www.chicago-law.net/speeches/speech.html for a good example of this type of speech.

2. Memory

In this case a speech has been prepared that the speaker remembers rather than having to read it. Unless you have a brilliant memory and total recall, this is one of the most difficult types of speech to make. To get over a stilted and uneven approach, the speaker must remember the words fluently or have the ability to make off-the-cuff remarks in the event of forgetting the words. An excellent example of this type of speech can be found in the words of Martin Luther King, Jr.'s "I have a dream" address, more formally known as "Address at the March in Washington," August 28, 1963, which can be found at: www.chicago-law.net/speeches/speech.html.

3. Extemporaneous

This kind of speech calls for adaption and a certain amount of spontaneity. It is normally made at more personal occasions, such as weddings, anniversaries, or funerals. This does not mean that the speaker is completely unprepared, but rather that the speech draws on an outline or guideline notes. Talking "on the fly" can give the speech a dynamic feeling. A good and affecting example of this is Senator Edward Kennedy's eulogy for his brother Robert F. Kennedy, June 8, 1968. Go to www.chicago-net/speeches/speech to hear the entire speech.

GENERAL TIPS

The following factors will help you appear more confident and relaxed when making your speech.

1. Making your speech
a. Power: Remember that standing in front of an audience gives you a certain amount of credibility even before you begin to speak
b. Truth: Always be truthful, and do not lie, since that will give you the power to challenge an opponent even if you sometimes appear to be controversial
c. Emotion: Try to avoid excessive or inappropriate emotion unless the occasion calls for it
d. Clarity: Be clear and use simple, easy-to-understand language
e. Credibility: Use accepted sources and quotations to add credibility to your argument

2. Effective delivery
a. Know your subject to avoid nervousness or embarrassment
b. Be natural
c. Be lively
d. Use language and delivery to good effect
e. Judge your audience

3. Nonverbal communication
How you appear is as important as verbal communication because it can help stress or detract from a speech.
a. Appearance: Dress appropriately, since first impressions on your audience do make a difference
b. Attitude: Try not to appear overly confident since that may be misconstrued as arrogance
c. Posture: Do not lean, sway, or slouch
d. Arms: Avoid folding your arms, making excessive gestures, or clenching fists, although you can use your hands to add emphasis to important parts of your speech
e. Eye contact: Look at the audience as much as possible. Try to look at the audience as individuals rather than as a mass, and avoid looking above them or focusing on a distant object or window.
f. Voice and pitch: How you say things is as important as what you say. Try to develop techniques of engaging the audience, such as lowering your voice when you are making a serious point and pausing for dramatic effect. Try not to speak too quickly. Avoid monotones, since you will lose the interest of your audience.
g. Movement: Try to avoid excessive movement; it may make you appear agitated or nervous and thus less credible.

GLOSSARY

balance of payments a record of the value of a country's international trade, borrowing, and lending.

balanced budget a situation in which a government's planned expenditure equals its expected income. A budget deficit occurs if planned expenditure is greater than expected income, while a budget surplus results if government income is greater than expenditure.

black market an illegal part of the economy that is not subject to regulation or taxation and that often deals in high-priced, illegal, or scarce commodities.

boom and bust a phrase that describes a period of wild swings in economic activity between growth and contraction.

business cycle the periodic but irregular fluctuation in economic activity. Economists know that the business cycle exists, but they do not fully understand why. See also boom and bust.

capital the physical assets owned by a household, firm, or government, such as equipment, real estate, and machinery. Capital can also mean financial capital— money used to finance a business venture.

capitalism an economic system based on private ownership and enterprise and the free market. Capitalism has been the dominant economic system in the western world since around the 16th century.

central bank a public organization established to oversee and regulate a country's monetary and financial institutions.

commodity a primary product such as coffee, cotton, or copper. "Commodity" is also used to describe a good or service created by the process of production.

communism a political doctrine, based on the ideas of the philosopher Karl Marx, that seeks to establish social equality through central regulation of economic activity and

communal ownership. See also planned economy; socialism.

comparative advantage the advantage gained by a producer if he or she can produce a good or service relatively efficiently compared to other producers.

competition attracting or attempting to attract business from rival producers. See also perfect competition.

consumption the total amount of household use of goods and services over a period of time.

consumer good an economic good or commodity that is bought for use by a household rather than by industry, say.

corporation a firm or business that is owned by shareholders. See also stock; shares.

cost-benefit analysis the appraisal of a project or policy by comparing all its social and financial costs with its social and financial benefits.

deflation a downward movement in the general level of prices.

demand the desire for a particular good or service backed by the ability to pay for it.

depression a deep trough in the business cycle, usually marked by high prices and high unemployment. See also boom and bust.

devaluation a reduction in the official rate at which one currency is exchanged for another currency.

developing country a poor country that is undergoing a process of economic modernization through the development of an industrial and commercial base. Examples include India and Mexico.

dividends the amount of a corporation's profits that is distributed to shareholders.

e-commerce business that is carried out entirely or largely via the Internet.

economic efficiency in economics efficiency is often used as a measure of how well a system of resource allocation meets peoples' wants and needs. A system is efficient if no individual can be made better off without another individual being made worse off.

economic growth an increase in economic output per head of the population.

economies of scale factors that cause the average cost of producing a good to fall as output increases.

entrepreneurship the ability to perceive opportunities in the market and assemble factors of production to exploit those opportunities.

export a commodity from one country that is sold abroad.

externality a cost or benefit falling on a third party as the result of an economic activity that is not accounted for by those carrying out that activity.

factors of production an economy's productive resources—usually defined as land, labor, entrepreneurship, and capital.

fiscal policy the attempts a government makes to maintain economic balance by altering its spending on goods or services or its revenue-raising through taxation.

foreign exchange rate the rate at which one country's money is exchanged for another. The rate is often used as a measure of the relative strengths and weaknesses of different economies. *See also* devaluation.

free market a market in which supply and demand are not subject to regulation by the state (government).

free trade international trade that is not subject to restrictions or barriers.

full employment a situation in which everyone who is willing to work at the going rate is able to find employment, excluding those people who are switching from one job to another.

globalization the expansion worldwide of private corporations and of the culture of the countries they come from.

goods and services economic commodities; the basic units of economic activity.

gross domestic product (GDP) a method of measuring a nation's economic performance. GDP is the total value of the financial output within the borders of a particular country.

gross national product (GNP) GDP plus the income accruing to domestic residents from investments abroad, less the income earned in the domestic market by foreigners abroad.

import a commodity bought in from abroad.

inefficiency an economic situation or system in which an individual can be made better off without making any other individual worse off.

inflation an upward movement in the general level of prices.

intellectual property the creative work of inventors, artists, authors, musicians, and entrepreneurs.

interest the amount earned by savers or investors on their deposit or investment, or the amount paid by borrowers on their loan. The amount of interest is determined by the interest rate.

international debt money owed by one country's government to a government or bank in another country, or to an international financial institution such as the International Monetary Fund (IMF).

intervention government interference with market forces so as to achieve various economic ends—for example, wealth distribution or consumer protection.

investment capital formation, such as the building of a factory, that will lead to the production of goods and services for future consumption. Alternatively, expenditure on assets such as stocks, shares, and real estate from which it is hoped profits will be earned in the future.

Keynesianism an economic doctrine, based on the theories of J. M. Keynes, that advocates government intervention through fiscal policy to stabilize fluctuations in the economy.

laissez-faire a French term meaning "let it happen," originally used in classic economics to describe an economy with no government intervention.

land in economics a term that refers to real estate and all natural resources, such as oil, timber, and fish.

macroeconomics the name given to the study of the economy as a whole rather than the study of the detailed choices of individuals or firms. *See also* microeconomics.

the market an arrangement that facilitates the buying and selling of a good, service, or factor of production.

market failure imperfection in an economy that prevents the efficient production, consumption, or allocation of goods, services, and resources.

mercantilism an economic policy popular in Europe from the 16th to the 18th centuries that stressed the importance of exports to earn reserves of gold and silver and used high tariffs to prevent imports.

microeconomics the study of individual households and firms, the choices they make in individual markets, and the effects of taxes and government regulation. *See also* macroeconomics.

minimum wage a level of payment set by government legislation below which employers are forbidden to pay workers.

mixed economy a market economy in which there is both public and private ownership of the factors of production, and economic activity is carried out by both public and private enterprise.

monetarism an economic doctrine that regards the money in an economy (the money supply) as the main determinant of aggregate demand. Monetarists believe that attempts by government to increase output by stimulating demand will only result in inflation.

monetary policy the attempt to regulate inflation and economic activity by varying the money supply and interest rates.

money supply the amount of currency in an economy that can easily be exchanged for goods and services, usually including notes, coins, and bank deposits that can be transferred by writing checks.

monopoly a market in which there is only one supplier of a good or service for which there is no close substitute.

multinational corporation (MNC) an enterprise that operates in a number of different countries, and that has production facilities outside its home country.

nationalization the transfer of a privately owned enterprise to state ownership.

natural monopoly an industry in which technical factors (infrastructure requirements, say) prevent the efficient existence of more than one owner.

neocolonialism a relationship between a country and a former colony in which the business interests of the first continue to dominate the economy of the latter.

nonprice competition competing with other businesses by means other than lowering prices—for example, by advertising.

patent a legal document issued by the government that grants exclusive rights to the inventor of a product or service.

perfect competition an industrial structure in which many small firms compete to supply a single product. This model is often used as a starting point from which to analyze the behavior of firms.

planned economy an economy in which production and resource distribution are determined by a central authority, such as a government or planning agency.

poverty the situation facing people whose material needs are not satisfied. Poverty can be absolute (earnings below some specified minimum) or relative (the poorest 10 percent of a population, say).

price discrimination the selling of the same good or service to different buyers for different prices.

private sector that part of an economy in which activity is decided and the means of production owned by individuals or firms. *See also* public sector.

privatization principally the transfer of a government- (state-) owned enterprise to private control and ownership. Other forms of privatization may involve deregulation or subcontracting work to the private sector.

production a process whereby firms combine factors of production and existing products so as to make a final product.

productivity the ratio between the input of resources such as capital and labor and the resulting output of goods and services. Also known as "cost-yield relation."

profit the difference between a firm's total revenue and its total costs. Firms usually aim to maximize profits.

progressive taxation form of taxation in which an increasing proportion of income is taxed as income rises.

protectionism an economic doctrine that attempts to protect domestic producers by placing tariffs and quotas on imports.

public sector that part of an economy owned by a government or other public bodies, such as state administrations.

quota a limit on the quantity of a specific commodity that a country can import.

recession a severe contraction of economic activity marked by two successive quarters of falling GDP.

regressive taxation a form of taxation in which a decreasing proportion of income is taxed as income rises.

regulation the control or supervision of economic activities by government for reasons of health, safety, or fairness, say.

resources labor, land, capital, and entrepreneurship. Also called factors of production.

shares a fraction of the stock of a corporation. *See also* stock.

socialism an economic and political theory that advocates collective or government ownership and control of a society's resources. Within Marxist theory it is the transitional stage in a country's development from capitalism to communism. *See also* communism and planned economies.

stock the value of a corporation's assets in terms of the capital and funds it has available for investment at a particular point in time. *See also* shares.

subsidy a grant made by government to suppliers of goods and services.

supply the quantity of a good or service available for sale at a particular price.

sustainable development a form of economic growth that seeks to use renewable rather than finite resources and to minimize the permanent damage done to the environment by economic activity.

tariffs taxes placed on imports.

tax a compulsory charge placed on economic activity by governments. Taxes might be placed on wealth or income, on business profits as a sales tax on transactions, or as license fees on activities such as driving.

technology the set of methods by which different resources are combined to produce goods and services.

trade liberalization lifting restrictions on trade, for example, canceling tariffs.

underdeveloped country a country that has neither the capital nor the social organization necessary to grow or "develop." Many countries in sub-Saharan Africa are underdeveloped.

unemployment the condition of adult workers who do not have jobs and are looking for employment.

wealth the total assets of a household, firm, or country less its total liabilities.

welfare state a system of welfare provision by a government to keep its citizens healthy and free from poverty. Provisions typically include free healthcare, insurance against sickness or unemployment, old age pensions, disability benefits, subsidized housing, and free education.

Acknowledgments

Topic 1 Is the Free Market the Best Form of Economic Organization?

Yes: From "Free Enterprise—For All" by Robert Bearce, *The Freeman*, Vol. 34, No. 5, May 1984. Copyright © 1984 by The Foundation for Economic Education Inc. Used by permission.

No: From "The Economist's Blind Eye" by Wolfgang Sachs, *New Internationalist*, Issue 232, June 1992. Copyright © 1992 by Wolfgang Sachs.

Topic 2 Does Capitalism Inevitably Lead to Income Inequality and Environmental Destruction?

Yes: From "Red and Green: Eco-Socialism Comes of Age" by David Ransom, *New Internationalist*, Issue 307, November 1998. Copyright © 1998 by New Internationalist Publications Ltd. Used by permission.

No: From "The Virtue of Wealth" by Madsen Pirie in *The Economist, The World in 2001*. Copyright © 2000 by The Economist Newspaper and The Economist Group. Used by permission.

Topic 3 Does Privatization Always Benefit Consumers?

Yes: From "Privatization and American Business" by Lawrence W. Reed, *The Freeman*, Vol. 26, No. 10, October 1997. Copyright © 1997 by The Foundation for Economic Education Inc. Used by permission.

No: From "The Pirate Privateers" by Dani Sandberg, *New Internationalist*, Issue 259, September 1994. Copyright © 1994 by New Internationalist Publications Ltd. Used by permission.

Topic 4 Will IT and the Internet Create a "New Economy"?

Yes: From "The New Old Economy: Oil, Computers, and the Reinvention of the Earth" by Jonathan Rauch, *The Atlantic Monthly*, January 2001. Copyright © 2001 by Jonathan Rauch. Used by permission.

No: From "Is There Life in E-commerce"? by The Economist, *The Economist*, February 1, 2001. Copyright © 2001 by The Economist Newspaper and The Economist Group. Used by permission.

Topic 5 Does Government Intervention Do More Harm than Good?

Yes: From "Correction Please! The Free Market Works Fine, Except..." by Mark Skousen, *The Freeman*, Vol. 44, No. 9, September 1994. Copyright © 1994 by The Foundation for

Economic Education Inc. Used by permission.

No: From "The Vanity of Human Markets: Robert Kuttner Challenges the Prevailing Orthodoxy of Laissez-faire Economics" by Wen Stephenson and Robert Kuttner, *The Atlantic Monthly*, February 26, 1997. Copyright © 1997 by The Atlantic Monthly Company. Used by permission.

Topic 6 Should Welfare Be Abolished?

Yes: From "Does Welfare Diminish Poverty"? by Howard Baetjer Jr., *The Freeman*, Vol. 34, No. 4, April 1984. Copyright © 1984 by The Foundation for Economic Education Inc. Used by permission.

No: From "Out of Sight, Out of Mind" by The Economist, *The Economist*, May 18, 2000. Copyright © 2001 by The Economist Newspaper and the Economist Group. Used by permission.

Topic 7 Is the Minimum Wage Fair?

Yes: From "The Next Step: the New Minimum Wage Proposals and the Old Opposition" by Jared Bernstein and Chauna Brocht, Economic Policy Institute Brief, Issue 130b, March 8, 2000. Copyright © 2000 by the Economic Policy Institute. Used by permission.

No: From "Full employment—A Lesson From the Deserts of Saudi Arabia" by Keith Wade, *The Freeman*, Vol. 45, No. 2, February 1995. Copyright © 1995 by The Foundation for Economic Education Inc. Used by permission.

Topic 8 Should Wealth Redistribution Be Part of Government Policy?

Yes: From "Pulling Apart: A State-by-State Analysis of Income Trends" by Jared Bernstein, Elizabeth C. McNichol, Lawrence Mishel, and Robert Zahradnik, Economic Policy Institute Study, January 2001. Copyright © 2001 by the Economic Policy Institute. Used by permission.

No: From "Pulling Us Apart" by Charles W. Baird, *The Freeman*, Vol. 50, No. 5, May 2000. Copyright © 2000 The Foundation for Economic Education Inc. Used by permission.

Topic 9 Is Globalization Inevitable?

Yes: From "Forum on the Future: A Time Panel Agrees that the FTAA is the Best Bet for Regalvanizing the Hemisphere" by George Russell, *Time Magazine*, April 19, 2001. Copyright © 2001 by Time Inc. Reprinted by permission.

No: From "A Fete for the End of the End of History" by Naomi Klein, *The Nation*, March 19, 2001. Copyright © 2001 by The

Nation Company. Reprinted with permission from the March 19, 2001 issue of *The Nation*.

Topic 10 Are Protectionist Trade Policies Ever a Good Idea?

Yes: From "Why Economists Should Study Fairness" by Steven Suranovic, *Challenge*, Vol. 40, Issue 5, September/October 1997. Copyright © 1997 by M.E. Sharp Inc., Armonk, New York. Used by permission.

No: From "Unfair Protection" by The Economist, *The Economist*, November 5, 1998. Copyright © 1998 by The Economist Newspaper and The Economist Group. Used by permission.

Topic 11 Is the World Trade Organization Fair to Poor Countries?

Yes: From "Ten Common Misunderstandings About the WTO" by the World Trade Organization. Copyright © by the World Trade Organization. Used by permission.

No: From "Why Free Trade is Not Fair" by George P. Brockway, *New Leader*, Vol. 83, Issue 1, March/April 2000.

Topic 12 Should Rich Countries Cancel "Third World Debt"?

Yes: From "The Debt Burden on Impoverished Countries: an Overview" by Jubilee 2000/USA. Copyright © by www.j2000usa.org.

No: "Paying One's Debts" by Christie Davies, *National Review*, Vol. 42, Issue 24, page 43, December 1990. Used by permission.

Topic 13 Should Governments Intervene to Protect Consumers?

Yes: From "The Search for the Smoking Gun" by Jack Beatty, *The Atlantic Monthly*, February 7, 2001. Copyright © 2001 by Jack Beatty. Used by permission.

No: "Consumer Protection Through the Workings of the Free Market" by Jane Lanigan. Copyright © 2001 by Jane Lanigan. Used by permission.

Topic 14 Should Companies Be More Ethical in Their Dealings?

Yes: From "Doing Well by Doing Good" by The Economist, *The Economist*, April 20, 2000. Copyright © 2000 by The Economist Newspaper and The Economist Group. Used by permission.

No: From "The Social Responsibility of Corporations and How to Make it Work for You" by John Hasnas, in *The Freeman*, Vol. 44, No. 7, July 1994. Copyright © 1994 by The Foundation for Economic Education Inc. Used by permission.

Topic 15 Does Advertising Benefit Both Consumers and Producers?

Yes: From "Advertising" by Israel M. Kirzner, *The Freeman*, Vol. 22, No. 9, September 1972. Copyright © 1972 by The Foundation for Economic Education Inc. Used by permission.

No: "A Holiday Greeting the Networks Won't Air: Shoppers Are 'Pigs'" by Robert Berner, *The Wall Street Journal*, November 19, 1997. Copyright © by The Wall Street Journal. Used by permission.

Brown Partworks Limited has made every effort to contact and acknowledge the creators and copyright holders of all extracts reproduced in this volume. We apologize for any omissions. Any person who wishes to be credited in further volumes should contact Brown Partworks Limited in writing: Brown Partworks Limited, 8 Chapel Place, Rivington Street, London EC2A 3DQ, U.K.

Picture credits

Cover: Image Bank, Thierry Dosogne, **Associated Press:** Steve Miller 176; **Corbis:** Tim Bennett 76–77; Bettmann Archive 40, 60–61, 110, 168–169, 212–213; Macduff Everton 30; Kevin Fleming 138; Owen Franken 68; Michael S Yamashita 6–7, 196–197; **Hulton/Archive:** Keystone 34–35, 45, 210–211; **Hutchinson Library:** Jeremy Horner 98; **Image Bank:** Vicky Kasala 56; Frans Lemmens 17; **PA Photos:** European Press Agency 123, 164, 207

SET INDEX